Race in American Science Fiction

T0341971

INDIANA UNIVERSITY PRESS

Bloomington & Indianapolis

RACE
IN AMERICAN
SCIENCE FICTION

ISIAH LAVENDER III

This book is a publication of

Indiana University Press
601 North Morton Street
Bloomington, Indiana 47404-3797 USA

iupress.indiana.edu

Telephone orders   800-842-6796
Fax orders   812-855-7931
Orders by e-mail   iuporder@indiana.edu

♾ The paper used in this publication
meets the minimum requirements of
the American National Standard for
Information Sciences—Permanence
of Paper for Printed Library Materials,
ANSI Z39.48-1992.

Manufactured in the United States of
America

Library of Congress Cataloging-in-
Publication Data

Lavender, Isiah.
  Race in American science fiction /
Isiah Lavender III.
    p. cm.
  Includes bibliographical references
and index.
  ISBN 978-0-253-35553-9 (cloth : alk.
paper) — ISBN 978-0-253-22259-6
(pbk. : alk. paper) 1. Science fiction,
American—History and criticism.
2. Race in literature. I. Title.
  PS374.S35L37 2010
  813'.0876209355—dc22
                              2010015712

1 2 3 4 5 16 15 14 13 12 11

TO HEATHER, ALWAYS

I had my recurring dream last night. I guess I should have expected it. It comes to me when I struggle—when I twist on my own personal hook and try to pretend that nothing unusual is happening.

OCTAVIA E. BUTLER, *Parable of the Sower*

Who knows but that, on the lower frequencies, I speak for you?

RALPH ELLISON, *Invisible Man*

Contents

Contents

Acknowledgments

The completion of a decade-long project is a miraculous feat, and I could not have done it without God. Excitements and frustrations coupled with my own tenacity to see this book through to completion mean nothing without the support and influence of family, friends, colleagues, and institutions. I have missed a number of family functions to work on this book, and so I owe a debt of gratitude to my entire family for allowing me the space to think, write, think some more, rewrite, and still think some more.

Unbeknownst to me at the time, the kernel of this book was formed at the University of Iowa in Bluford Adams's class on race and ethnicity in twentieth-century American literature. Brooks Landon, my mentor and friend, may have had the biggest influence on this manuscript by reading various drafts and critiquing bluntly throughout the years as well as sending me to the Afrofuturism lecture series at Stanford University during the spring of 2004. Likewise, I have to thank Rob Latham for candid conversations about race in science fiction. Additionally, Margaret Bass, Doris Witt, Venise Berry, and Horace Porter had a hand in shaping the early stages of this project while I was at Iowa. I would also like to thank Vickie Dingman, Gayle Sand, Diana Bryant, and Joseph Henry for their unwavering support during my graduate years at Iowa; they helped me in a variety of ways, from making travel plans to getting the photocopier to work. My movie-going partners Nigel Gomez, Brian Bialkowski, Jennifer Brown, and Jon Garfinkel were also essential to this book considering the many bad films they sat through at my behest and the many valuable books they recommended.

A number of significant contributors to my success have been uncovered at the University of Central Arkansas. I have to thank Bonnie Selting, Dwayne Coleman, and Paulette Bane for reading and commenting on my manuscript; Terry Kearns for making it possible to land the job at UCA even with science fiction as my specialty; Wayne and Ellen Stengel for shuttling me to a variety of films in Little Rock, some good, some bad; Wendy Castro for listening to my struggles with the manuscript; David O'Hara for listening to my struggles with the manuscript while running; Chuck Bane for listening to my struggles with the manuscript at a variety of movie theaters; Philip Anderson for writing support letters in my attempts to find funding for this project; my department chair, Jay Ruud, for his belief in my right to pursue this avenue of research; Raymond Frontain, Sara Shumaker, and Peter Mehl for their knowledge of the academic publishing game; Maurice Lee for signing off on travel requests; and Barbara Stanley and Tina Kennedy for helping me with those pesky photocopiers. I also have to thank my students who allowed me to make intuitive leaps between texts, history, culture, and real life.

Likewise, I also have to thank Grace Dillon, DeWitt Kilgore, Lisa Yaszek, Mark Bould, Sherryl Vint, Joan Gordon, Farah Mendlesohn, Robin Reid, Nalo Hopkinson, Brian Attebery, Graham Murphy, Mike Levy, Patricia Melzer, Andrea Hairston, Veronica Hollinger, Elizabeth Hoim, David Higgins, Megan Bygness, Richard Landon, James Landau, Darja Malcolm-Clarke, and so many more for meaningful conversations about science fiction at ICFA and SFRA conferences over the years. John Lowe and Angeletta Gourdine also shaped who I am in terms of my thinking on race. The spiritual guidance of Pastor Darren DeLaune of New Life Church in Conway, Arkansas, has also been of consequence to this project.

In addition to thanking the University of Central Arkansas for supporting my research with a summer stipend in 2005 and various travel grants in my time at UCA, I must acknowledge that a small part of chapter 6 first appeared as "Technicity: AI and Cyborg Ethnicity in *The Matrix*" in volume 45.4 of *Extrapolation*. Likewise, an earlier version of chapter 5 first appeared in volume 34.2 of *Science Fiction Studies* as

"Ethnoscapes: Environment and Language in Ishmael Reed's *Mumbo Jumbo*, Colson Whitehead's *The Intuitionist*, and Samuel R. Delany's *Babel-17*." A small bit of my introduction first appeared as "Critical Race Theory" in *The Routledge Companion to Science Fiction* and has since been revised. Finally, I am especially appreciative of Indiana University Press, Jane Behnken and Susanna Sturgis in particular, for recognizing the potential of this manuscript and taking a chance on it.

I simply cannot thank my wife, Heather, enough for all of her love, support, prayer, and sacrifice. I must also thank my sons—I. Kingsley Lavender and Frazier Noah Lavender—for keeping me focused. Likewise, I would like to express my appreciation to my sister Melissa for hiding books when we were children, thus arousing my curiosity to find out why. Finally, I wish to thank my deceased parents for their efforts to instill a lifetime love of reading.

Race in American Science Fiction

Introduction   Mapping the Blackground

Recently, I decided to gain a better appreciation of our country's struggle with racism by visiting Central High School, a National Historic Site in Little Rock, Arkansas.[1] I wanted to better understand the histories of our desegregation efforts by seeing for myself one place where the civil rights movement triumphed during the month of September 1957. When nine black students attempted to integrate the leading white high school in the state, they were denied entry, and the attention of our nation, not to mention the world, was riveted through television on the ensuing battle between the state and federal government in an effort to end segregation and associated notions of racial purity, white supremacy, and violent oppression. This battle actually originated in the North during the antebellum era when the U.S. Supreme Court resolved to preserve school segregation in Boston, Massachusetts, with the 1849 decision *Roberts v. The City of Boston.* Of course, the Supreme Court's 1896 *Plessy v. Ferguson* decision is even more infamous and telling since it established the "separate but equal" doctrine which the country used to validate racism particularly in the South.

With the entire world watching, the Little Rock Nine—Minnijean Brown, Elizabeth Eckford, Ernest Green, Thelma Mothershed, Melba Pattilo, Gloria Ray, Terrence Roberts, Jefferson Thomas, and Carlotta Walls—needed an escort by the federalized Arkansas National Guard to even approach the school. They were truly brave that month during the "Little Rock Crisis" facing such an unreasoning hatred that is difficult to imagine. As Daisy L. Gatson Bates, the Arkansas president

1

of the National Association for the Advancement of Colored People, famously declared, "Any time it takes eleven thousand five hundred soldiers to assure nine Negro children their constitutional rights in a democratic society, I can't be happy."

The science fictional conceit of time travel helps me to imagine the events of September 4, 1957. At the command of Governor Orval Faubus, the Arkansas National Guard barred the nine students from entering the school. If I simply close my eyes, time travel permits me to set foot on Park Street, to see the beautiful architecture of the high school itself, and to witness an angry white mob literally nipping at the heels of those nine black children—spitting, shouting, making rude gestures, and, above all else, violently hating. I can hear the foul vitriol spewing from the collective mob psyche—"Kill those NIGGERS!" or something along those lines. I can imagine fear causing my blood to race through my veins, pound in my ears, as I walk with those nine courageous youth.

All of a sudden, the deep bass booming from the trunk of a tricked-out white Cadillac Escalade, stopped at the intersection of Park Street and Daisy L. Gatson Bates Drive, snaps me back into the present. I think to myself how things have changed in the fifty-three intervening years, and I begin to notice the deteriorated urban neighborhood surrounding the school. White flight coupled with the "lost year"—Little Rock closed its schools to both white and black students during the 1958/59 school year—provided another wrinkle in the battle for civil rights.[2] The remains of segregation resonate powerfully across time and place. My surreal experience is the stuff of science fiction (sf). This rumination caused me to think "what if" . . .

* * *

What if the lead character of a 2009 network television show, a young and beautiful white woman, were involved in a "platonic" relationship with an older black male character, a visible other? This exact scenario occurred when Joss Whedon's science fiction series *Dollhouse* debuted on the Fox Broadcasting Company on February 13, 2009. Whedon consciously pushes the racial envelope by featuring a mixed partnership between Echo (Eliza Dushku), an "active," and her "handler," Boyd

Langton (Harry Lennix). The basic premise of the show is that wealthy, powerful, and connected people can hire members of the illegal and secretive Dollhouse, actives/dolls with imprinted memories, to create a variety of personas for any kind of engagement ranging from sex to assassination. Actives are escorted to and from their engagements by the handlers. After the assignment, the doll's entire memory of the job is wiped clean. For example, the original episode, "Ghost," features Echo first as a party girl and second as a hostage negotiator.

As the show progresses, Echo's fragmented memories begin to return as she struggles for self-awareness and the recovery of her true identity. Langton protects her from danger outside and within the Dollhouse, and she sometimes protects him as well. In the second episode, "The Target," Boyd is injured by Echo's date, a zealous hunter who tracks human prey through the wilderness. A companionable intimacy necessarily develops between Echo and Boyd because trust is essential to the success of each engagement. Even in its remotest sense, for a black man "handling" a white woman was a lynching offense in America's immediate past. Whedon's decision to feature this mixed pairing for much of the season nearly got the show cancelled in its first season. This, in my estimation, was because of an inherent yet unconscious audience discomfort caused by the perceived taboo of miscegenation or race mixing.

This pairing is a dangerous retelling of racial stereotypes regarding white women, black men, and sex, and it unintentionally echoes Richard Wright's searing classic *Native Son* (1940), where the alienated black youth Bigger Thomas is hired to chauffer the wealthy Daltons around Chicago and ends up accidentally smothering the young white socialite Mary Dalton to death in her own bed, dismembering her corpse, and running for his life from a lynch mob in the middle of winter. Of course, Bigger is caught, tried for rape and murder, and sentenced to death. Even hinting at a possible mixed relationship, as Whedon does, evokes the powerful racial myth of the black male rapist. This very real unease among the show's audience prompted a new creative direction, where Whedon installs former FBI agent Paul Ballard (Tahmoh Penikett) as Echo's new handler in the season finale, "Omega," after Agent Ballard ends his search for "Caroline," i.e., Echo, by discovering the Dollhouse's location. Though I admire

Whedon's attempts to portray equality on television, I believe that the viewing audience's deeply embedded belief structures are essentially racist when it comes to an interracial dynamic between men and women. Unfortunately, Whedon gives in to audience pressure during the show's second and final season, when Boyd Langton is revealed as the nefarious head and founder of the Rossum Corporation,[3] essentially the creator of the Dollhouse ("Getting Closer"). In the penultimate episode, "The Hollow Men,"[4] Langton turns on Echo and nearly kills her before having his own memories remotely wiped by Topher Brink (Fran Kranz), scientist and designer of Dollhouse technologies. Langton is imprinted as an innocent, strapped into an explosive belt, and instructed to blow up the company's computer mainframe in an attempt to save the world from the evils of mind control technologies. More or less, the show's primary black character is lynched for his earlier racial transgressions—forcing a white woman into prostitution. In my opinion, science fiction has an unwarranted reputation for being "progressive" in matters of race and racism.

***

Further reflection urged me to thinking "what if" . . . What if an American scientist devised a whitening process for the country's black population, and all blacks became white? Would its race problem be solved? George Schuyler, a controversial black journalist and author, considers such a scenario during the Harlem Renaissance in his 1931 novel *Black No More* (hereafter *BNM*) by playing "on the perception that some African Americans 'wish to be white'" (Kuenz, 173). Schuyler's character, Dr. Junius Crookman, is a black scientist who has conducted research on rare skin diseases such as "vitiligo" in Germany, and who declares that he has invented a three-day process "to turn darkies white" (Schuyler, *BNM*, 24) through "electrical nutrition and glandular control" over hair and other facial features such as lips and eye color (27).[5] Set in the Jim Crow era, Crookman's discovery creates a rush among America's black citizens who desire to leave the oppressed black race behind by paying the requisite fee to his start-up company Black-No-More, Incorporated.[6]

Max Disher, the ostensible hero of the novel and an accomplished hustler, is the first among millions to undergo the process in the near-future Harlem. In three days' time, there is "no more jim crow" for him: "As a white man he could go anywhere, be anything he wanted to be, do most anything he wanted to do, be a free man at last" (26). As the story unfolds, Max infiltrates white southern society by changing his name to Matthew Fisher, marrying a blond debutante, and passing himself off as a race scientist to the head of the Knights of Nordica, a white supremacist organization modeled on the Ku Klux Klan. In his first speech to the organization, Matthew/Max promotes notions of white supremacy and racial paranoia. He is "a hit simply by spouting Negrophobic clichés he has heard all his life from whites" (Reilly, 108). Along with Reverend Givens, an apparently white supremacist, Matthew/Max creates social and political unrest in the name of greed by capitalizing on southern white paranoia as the black population vanishes and chaos ensues: mulatto babies are born everywhere; white workers go on strike; businesses fail; and a heated presidential race based on a racial purity platform ends with a horrifying lynching scene.

This graphic and brutal lynching occurs when the Democratic vice presidential candidate and his statistician, Snobbcraft and Buggerie, flee from the uproar generated when the press outs them as Negroes. Their plane crashes near Happy Hills, Mississippi, during a revival where the pastor, Reverend McPhule, is praying for Negroes to lynch. Snobbcraft and Buggerie appear in blackface, claim to be white men at the first mention of lynching, and are later proven to be black by the late-arriving newspaper. They are subsequently stripped, beaten, castrated, disfigured, freed, shot, captured, and burned at the stake as well as having their skeletal remains picked over for souvenirs. The Happy Hill episode is clearly reminiscent of the countless acts of violence against blacks that took place in the United States, especially in light of the Red Summer of 1919 following World War I. It is doubly ironic in that the archetypal white racists Snobbcraft and Buggerie are lynched as despised "niggers" by a virtuous religious group extremely conscious of color. As critic Michael Peplow states, "The Happy Hill scene, ultimately, is a microcosm of what would happen in and to America if a 'mad' scientist tried to rob her of her oppressed minority" (257).

Eventually, most American citizens end up a happy shade of brown either through skin products, tanning, or birth. In a matter of seven years, Crookman's inexpensive treatment dismantles racial hierarchies that took countless generations of social, economic, and psychic investment to produce and maintain. Crookman enacts the ultimate integration dream by changing blacks into whites.[7] With this novel, Schuyler dares to answer the unspoken white desire for blacks to vanish, leaving behind a seemingly white world.

The power of Schuyler's satire rests entirely upon America's obsession with race. In the preface to his novel, Schuyler makes this point plain: "With America's constant reiteration of the superiority of whiteness, the avid search on the part of the black masses for some key to chromatic perfection is easily understood" (13). BNM is a powerful critique of the racial hierarchy of American society and our preoccupation with skin color and concepts of racial purity and white supremacy. Schuyler scathingly and humorously takes aim at social distinctions based on skin color, and through this strategy he makes an explicit science fictional account of race and racism in American culture. In fact, the novel's lengthy subtitle, *An Account of the Strange and Wonderful Workings of Science in the Land of the Free, AD 1933–1940*, suggests a strong conviction about the arbitrary—even worthless—nature of race from a scientific standpoint.[8] Likewise, the novel's dedication reveals Schuyler's thinking on the irrational fear of color and its inherent foolishness: "This book is dedicated to all Caucasians in the great republic who can trace their ancestry back ten generations and confidently assert that there are no Black leaves, twigs, limbs or branches on their family trees" (unnumbered page). Schuyler deliberately foregrounds race and racism in American culture through sf. In this context, he expresses the irrational and unscientific functioning of race and racism in the past, present, and, perhaps, future of the U.S.

As a black writer of sf during the pulp era, Schuyler is important because he is a part of the genre's blackground, a term created here to define the embedded perceptions of race and racism—intended or not—in Western sf writing and criticism. "Blackground" brings race and racism to the foreground of science fiction as it relates to the critical discussion of the black/white binary. Through this term, I question racialized structures and, perhaps more importantly, American culture in the genre. Indeed, thinking about the blackground of sf in new ways makes discernible a range of race meanings. I trace the development of scientific racism through literary, cultural, and scientific discourses and how this shapes sf. I link social concepts such as miscegenation and passing for white with a variety of classic sf motifs—aliens, androids, cyborgs, and so on—and effectively create a viable dialectic to examine the pervasiveness of race in sf. Likewise, I utilize meta–slavery narratives, alternate histories, extrapolations of the Jim Crow era, and contagion narratives as more conventional maps of sf. I also conceptualize blackground as a way to illustrate new models for race-reading in sf that employ established critical categories such as ethnoscapes and technicities. To begin mapping this blackground, as such, I propose a new definition of a critical idea already in existence—the other—by combining a sense of it with personhood (identity) and neighborhood (environment) to produce a notion of "otherhood."

All this is not to say that no other racial or ethnic binaries exist because they do; for example, fear of the "yellow peril" presents a host of Asian stereotypes, *and* the frontier mythology of the American West, populated with a horde of noble savages, is often demonstrated in space opera. Also, some depictions of race and racism are a subtle part of a text's background, such as Ursula K. Le Guin's *The Left Hand of Darkness* (1969), while other portrayals of race and racism like *Black No More* overtly foreground the entire plot. Clearly, then, conversations on race and racism in sf have always existed, but only recently have these conversations emerged into the foreground of its criticism where scholars and critics seem to approach race and racism in similar manners. In this book, however, I am primarily interested in sf's treatment of the black/white binary rather than in the other dimensions of the American obsession with color or a generalized critique of the intersections between race and racism. Attempts have already been made to do such work with varying degrees of success and with other racial binaries in mind as well. Yet I believe that there is not only plenty more space available for this kind of work but also an urgent need.

Science fiction often talks about race by not talking about race, makes real aliens, has hidden race dialogues. Even though it is a literature that talks a lot about underclasses or oppressed classes, it does so from a privileged if somewhat generic white space. If science fiction is about social change, let us talk about how this change comes about from an "other" space, a black space. This is absolutely one of the joys of sf and other speculative writings. Science fiction actually *does* think about the fact that things could be different and to not utilize that potential in it, I think, is limiting, if not downright disturbing. There is something to learn from investigating the black/white binary, and this book, with its explorations of cultural memories rooted in the thinking of otherhood, is further proof of this potential.

While otherhood is not exactly a new term, its meaning for sf is innovative because it attempts to change how racial difference is viewed by exposing the history and practice of discrimination operating inside and outside the genre simultaneously while also studying ways writers have used sf to expose and combat racism. "Just as it has been recognized as 'feminist friendly,' [sf] is uniquely suited for the critical study of race" because its "depiction of aliens, artificial persons, and supermen in subordinate positions, as well as its imagination of exotic landscapes and alternate histories," permits us to change and look in different ways at "our cultural memory of past events" (Lavender, "Ethnoscapes," 188). For instance, alien "others" stand in for racial "others" and vice versa. These archetypes are seemingly transposable. It would seem, then, that continual encounters and struggles with the "other" are the hallmark of true Western experience. In my estimation there is nowhere better than sf to examine the fear and excitement generated through alien encounters with race and racism. As a part of the blackground of science fiction, otherhood itself maps this dark territory.

Otherhood begins with thinking about race along the black/white binary. With this type of thinking, we can locate the historical consciousness embedded in sf in imagined events juxtaposed with real events in the space-time continuum. In this manner, I study the specific overlaps of history and imagination with proper seriousness as they relate to human experience. These relationships express meanings of otherhood that map racial discourse in sf and that can represent a variety of differences in relation to science, technology, and culture. Otherhood is capable of creating a cultural fluidity, a flexibility of insight, between historical reference and imagination of the future of race. With concepts of otherhood, we can examine degrees of black marginalization in sf (i.e., blackground).

Otherhood mapping is a descriptive representation of various science fictions or parts of various science fictions. For every element of one racial set, there is a unique element of another set available for mapping. To demonstrate, a human face could be described as being from dark brown to pink in color, but an alien face could be something else altogether, such as green and scaled with bug-eyed, iridescent pupils and no nose, or a robot face could be brightly polished silver and humanoid. These maps establish some of the features and details of race and make possible exploration and analysis to locate racism in sf.

To illustrate this point, the term "skin job" is used by the character Bryant in Ridley Scott's film *Blade Runner* (1982) as a racial slur in reference to the fugitive replicants, synthetic humans or androids. Bryant states: "Don't be an asshole, Deckard. I've got four skin-jobs walking the streets." In the theatrical voiceover version of the film the racist connotation is made even more explicit when the bounty hunter Deckard states: "Skin-jobs. That's what Bryant called Replicants. In history books he's the kind of cop who used to call black men niggers." As film scholar Adilifu Nama rightly suggests, "The presence of black people in *Blade Runner* is squarely located in the past—that is, the 'history books' that Deckard's narration suggests—and the visual absence of black people in *Blade Runner* further reinforces the idea that 'blackness' itself is historical and no longer exists" (57). Nevertheless, the term "skin job" powerfully reminds viewers of this very absence. In a conventional sense, "skin" means the soft or flexible external covering of a body, but it could also mean the outer surface of a machine that differs from the interior parts. Referring to the skin of a machine in the context of the film is racist because the "synthetic" humans irritate "real" human sensibilities by getting under the *skin* of the "real" humans, so to speak, to the point of hatred.

"Skin job" is used for the same purpose in the new television rendition of *Battlestar Galactica*, in the February 24, 2006, episode, "Downloaded." Samuel Anders, the leader of the human resistance on the Cylon-occupied colonial world, refers to the clone models as "skin jobs" shortly before detonating a bomb under one of the Cylon dwellings. Anders declares: "That skin job with Starbuck—'Sharon' they called her—she said that when they download, they remembered everything. Right up until the end. These skin jobs are going to remember being blown into tiny little pieces." Ironically, Anders is himself a Cylon, as revealed in the final episode of season 3, "Crossroads, Part 2." "Skin job" exemplifies "otherhood" and exists in the blackground of sf when fictional settings are used to define racism, a human hatred of a *technological* difference: a difference created by man based on mechanical expressions of humanity as opposed to the biological differences between the races based on skin color. "Skin job" is a representation that compares the element of "skin" in one set of racial signs familiar to us to elements in a different set of signs, such as artificial persons or perhaps posthumans, in a defamiliarized yet racist way.

Depictions of such signs marked out in the details provide a layout of the blackground for us, and otherhood helps us to locate racial issues in a specific text; in the body of work by one writer in relation to other writers; in other eras of time; and in other mediums and traditions of sf such as film, television, comics, and music, as well as various themes and icons of the genre. Likewise, otherhood establishes the mapping of a single racial/ethnic element, or set of elements, and its potential distortions. Indeed, otherhood aids in perceiving the shapes and textures of meaning in sf and determines how, why, and to what extent they are bound together in an always shifting racial formation. (From another point of view the racial structures of sf may be static.) That said, my book will map a few ambiguous places in the blackground of sf as a step toward encouraging further explorations of race and racism in the genre.

The relationship between race and sf has been largely overlooked by scholars with the exception of an odd essay here or there not related to sf written by either Samuel Delany or Octavia Butler. The fictional writings of Delany and Butler, prominent black writers of sf whose work often foregrounds racial issues, suggest that race and racism *are* only discussed in the contexts of those writers. Even though sf seems to be uniquely suited to the critical study of race with its depiction of aliens, artificial persons, cyborgs, psi-powered beings, and exotic landscapes, sf critics pay scant attention to the relationship itself. The excitement and fear generated through these encounters with the "other" make clear matters of racial and ethnic contact, where prejudices, discrimination, hatred, and stereotypes, as well as empathy, tolerance, patience, and acceptance, take place because of difference. Sf will become "a powerful literature of change" when it reaches the "point where writing from or about a racial minority is neither subversive nor unusual" (Leonard, "Race," 262). When cultural studies and critical race theories are applied to science fiction, knowledge analogous to afrofuturism is produced in the blackground of sf.

Although this conversation on race and racism in sf criticism has slowly become apparent in the past twenty-five years, afrofuturism has greatly amplified the discussion. To frame the history of this dialogue, the first special issue dedicated to race in sf occurs in 1984 with *Black American Literature Forum*, while the substantive debate on afrofuturism begins in 1993 when Mark Dery defines the term in a collection of interviews with Samuel Delany, Tricia Rose, and Greg Tate published in the *South Atlantic Quarterly*. Alondra Nelson next uses the term in 2002 "to challenge the notion of a future without race" when she guest-edits a special issue of *Social Text* featuring articles on afrofuturism (Lavender, "Critical Race Theory," 190). And the most recent rendition of this debate on afrofuturism appears in a 2007 special issue of *Science Fiction Studies* guest-edited by Mark Bould and Rone Shavers, where Bould charges that "sf avoids confronting the structures of racism and its own complicity in them" (Bould, "The Ships," 180). Consequently, afrofuturism illuminates the blackground of sf and its history with concerns of race and technology.

Along with afrofuturism, an increasing amount of scholarship has been published on racial issues in science fiction and technoculture in the past decade or so. Elisabeth Leonard's groundbreaking anthology, *Into Darkness Peering: Race and Color in the Fantastic* (1997), is the first text of consequence to undertake a discussion of race in the fantastic. In fact, the subject has been continually gaining popularity and respect with the publication of critical works such as De Witt Kilgore's influential *Astrofuturism: Science, Race, and Visions of Utopia in Space* (2003), which posits spaceflight as a possible solution to race issues in America, and Adilifu Nama's convincing *Black Space: Imagining Race in Science Fiction Film* (2008), the first full-length study of how race and racism function in sf film.[9] Additionally, scholarship addressing the intersections of race and technology has enhanced the study of sf.[10] For example, Lisa Nakamura's *Cybertypes: Race, Ethnicity, and Identity on the Internet* (2002) addresses issues of race and racism on the World Wide Web. Likewise, Martin Kevorkian's *Color Monitors: The Black Face of Technology in America* (2006) compellingly argues that the black male body has been unconsciously raced as a natural machine in popular culture. All of this scholarship represents the various relationships between sf and race where cultural experiences and technological progressions illuminate sf's blackground.

Outside the traditional bind of the black/white binary, different iterations of the color line clearly manifest at the intersections of race and racism in sf. Unfortunately, sf has mirrored rather than defied racial stereotypes throughout much of its history. For instance, the myth of the noble savage is the dominant conception of North America's indigenous people; these Native Americans have an innate natural simplicity and virtue uncorrupted by European civilization. Put another way, American Indians have been romanticized as "wild" men possessing a fierce sense of savage honor and wisdom—undeniably, a blatant example of racism. This myth coupled with the "indefinitely receding frontier" of space exploration, populated with endangered alien stand-ins for Native Americans and Latinos, is able to keep the idea of the American West forever alive (McGregor, 247). As Christine Morris explains, "In space opera there is this same intellectual dichotomy between the idyll and the life of the savage, and in space opera as in horse opera, Indians are a natural target" (303). Yet this myth continues to endure in the popular imagination. For Mary Weinkauf, "The existence of the American Indian in science fiction is a reminder of a tendency to exploit and even annihilate those who stand in the way of progress, a recurring theme from Wells to Le Guin," but she later adds this caveat: "Science-fiction writers use Native Americans as a symbolic warning that progress is dangerous to tradition and as a plea to appreciate different lifestyles" (319).

Andre Norton's thoughtful treatment of the noble savage stereotype in *The Beast Master* (1959) is an illustration of how space opera can expose a kind of racism in sf, where Native Americans continue to face genocidal tendencies on other planets. The novel's "Navajo" protagonist Hosteen Storm considers such things as identity, ancestry, prejudice, and cultural destruction in his dealings with the Norbies, a race native to the planet Arzor (11). Such digressions exploring other color binaries in sf underscore the importance of developing the critical tools necessary for investigating racial formations in a meaningful way.

Just as Native Americans are stereotyped as noble savages, Asian Americans are targets for discrimination in sf as well. Critical analyses such as Patrick Sharp's *Savage Perils: Racial Frontiers and Nuclear Apocalypse in American Culture* (2007) also show that rampant paranoia concerning vast Asian hordes invading America existed in the late nineteeth and early twentieth centuries. White authors of the time used the popular concept of social Darwinism to concoct racist ideas with Asians embodying a perceived threat to Western living standards. This cultural anxiety is historically known as the "yellow peril" and is impossible to disassociate from our conceptions of the Orient in science fiction. The nineteenth-century influx of East Asian laborers willing to work for very low wages resulted in "the Chinese Exclusion Act of 1882," which "stopped the legal immigration of all Chinese except teachers, students, merchants, diplomats, and tourists," according to William Wu (2–3).

The growing sense of American nationalism is supported by sf writers who imagined future wars with Asian powers for control of the world. For example, M. P. Shiel's *The Yellow Danger* (1898) and Edward Pendray's *The Earth-Tube* (1929) are the best among the earlier stories while Scott's film *Blade Runner* and William Gibson's groundbreaking novel *Neuromancer* (1984) reinvent the supremacy of the Orient. Istvan Csicsery-Ronay believes that fear of the yellow peril is "a model that easily expanded into Social Darwinian fantasies of race wars" (221–22). Some sf writers present battles in which the West opposes the rise of a superior Asian culture with preemptive strikes. Others show Asians as scientifically superior and merciless, a dreadful combination, and reason enough for annihilation. Yet Edward James detects a "general change in racial attitudes concerning [sf's] treatment of the 'yellow races'" in the cyberpunk subgenre through its depiction of multinational conglomerates based in the Orient that run the world by controlling the development of technology (28).

Whereas American Indians and Orientals provide exotic images, Africa creates a sense of primitivism as the Dark Continent in the sf imagination as it appears in the work of writers like Edgar Rice Burroughs, Michael Crichton, A. M. Lightner, Paul McCauley, and

Mack Reynolds.[11] Perhaps the best example of primitivism in sf is Mike Resnick's short story "Kirinyaga" (1988), in which a group of East African émigrés from Kenya has come to establish their Kikuyu tribal utopia on an isolated, artificial habitat modeled after the African savannahs. Shunning all things Western, trouble arrives when Koriba, the ancient village "witch doctor," decides to uphold the custom of killing a child born feet first to avoid a tribal curse (716). Maintenance, an off-world monitoring agency, chooses to intervene despite the black colonists' claims of autonomy. Such unwarranted interference reproduces postcolonial history where resistance proves futile. With their culture destroyed once already, the Kikuyu are trapped in a colonial system forcing them to experience otherness yet again.

Black fantasy writer Charles Saunders has even called "outer space. . . . as segregated as a South African Toilet" in regard to the lack of involvement by African Americans in speculative genres (J. Bell, "Interview," 91). Because of this troublesome depiction of black identity, Saunders feels that "the onus is on" black people to tell the stories they want to read instead of having "people like Mike Resnick . . . tell them for us" ("Why Blacks Should Read," 404). In response to Saunders's plea for blacks to use Africa as an influence in their speculative writing, black writers such as Steven Barnes, David Anthony Durham, Carole McDonnell, Nnedi Okorafor-Mbachu, Nisi Shawl, and Gregory L. Walker have recently answered the challenge.[12] We also have Saunders's own revised and reissued *Imaro* series as well as Caribbean influence in the work of Bill Campbell, Tobias S. Buckell, and Nalo Hopkinson.[13] Consequently, explicit explorations of sf's blackground by writers of color with colored characters in raced worlds are on the rise as an alternative to a kind of universal white space.

If nothing else, otherhood is about the portrayal of race by any speculative writer in sf regardless of his or her background. It is meant to question racial patterns that have been both familiar and unfamiliar in sf's blackground. For me, otherhood is why a writer like Tobias Buckell stands out. Despite his white origins in the Caribbean, Buckell is racially conscious and projects this awareness in his multiracial worlds featuring the black mercenary Pepper. Otherhood in relation to how it's dealt with in sf's blackground (what this book terms the black/white binary) questions our fears of difference, our hesitancy to explore other models of reality that challenge our beliefs, rules, security, and ultimately, our identity. To this end, I have structured my chapters around traditional ways of reading this binary, such as extrapolations of slavery, segregation, and contagion narratives, as well as specific concepts largely of my own invention like ethnoscapes and technicities. Such an arrangement may reveal hitherto undiscovered aspects of sf, and provide a broader context for reexamining the genre.

In chapter 1, I look at the state of science fiction race criticism and view the development and practice of racism in the science fiction community. Beginning with the wellsprings of sf theory, mainly Darko Suvin and Samuel R. Delany, I position otherhood within it as a new mode of race reading. Then I consider the importance and utility of emerging theories for race-reading in science fiction, such as afrofuturism, before considering a tradition surrounding social Darwinism in Western culture that continues to influence and shape science fiction. I follow this point by critiquing the widely perceived authority of science discourse, a perception driven by approval of the ideal of pure research. I explain how this perceived authority can serve to generate prejudice and racism in sf. It is one of the cultural tasks of science fiction to draw attention to and to challenge racist attitudes in part by interrogating science discourse. While my discussion centers on various types of criticism, I use texts by Octavia E. Butler, H. G. Wells, and others to reflect how otherhood works in general as a mode of reading the blackground of science fiction.

With chapter 2, I examine and apply the national experience of slavery to sf texts by first considering the dehumanization process as told in slave narratives; its continuing ramifications as neo–slave narratives; and its ultimate expression as science fiction "meta-slavery" with its time travel motifs, alternate histories, alien contacts, and future visions. In this way, I am able to get at notions of disempowerment, unconscious reflections of racism, and also direct confrontations of racist attitudes displayed in the genre. Many science fiction writers work out complicated feelings toward the "peculiar institution" by creating representations of the historical events of slavery, charging their retellings of the past with their own rationality and truth, making them vivid and unflinching accounts of evil in their attempt to come to some kind of closure with fabulist impulses. In light of these purposes, this chapter revolves around the analysis of texts by Isaac Asimov, Butler, Steven Barnes, David Brin, and Delany.

Chapter 3 considers extrapolations of the Jim Crow era in American history. Though our national memory tends to remember issues of segregation as they were played out in landmark U.S. Supreme Court cases in the areas of education and public transportation, the separatism tales of science fiction offer many views of segregation, some that uphold blatant structures of racism, others that deconstruct them, and still others that provide optimistic and pessimistic solutions to problems of the color line. Our reality is deliberately distanced by writers creating the social, political, and cultural possibilities of race in other places and times. This extrapolative style of thinking about race is intriguing for science fiction because the entire course of historic world events can be reimagined and changed by writers, and in this chapter I make close connections between the writers who distance us and concepts of otherhood as it relates to blackground. And so my discussion in this chapter focuses on texts by Ray Bradbury, Evie Shockley, Schuyler, Walter Mosley, and Derrick Bell.

Chapter 4 investigates ailments of race linked to the notion of contagion as a race metaphor in science fiction. This chapter explores the idea of the one-drop rule and miscegenation. Sf narratives built around the threat or devastation of some form of contagion frequently manifest racial fears and assumptions. Whether the product of nature or technology, accident or design, contagion narratives depict change so swift and so drastic that it can underscore or undermine a wide range of cultural assumptions, including those about race. In every case, however, these narratives derive their power from fear of the ready and rapid transmission of a harmful disease or idea from person to person. And this fear shares many characteristics with the fear of race mixing. Consequently, many sf contagion narratives manifest protocols of racial discrimination and sometimes challenge racist assumptions. Discussion centers on texts by Greg Bear, Butler, John W. Campbell Jr., Tananarive Due, Walter Miller, and Mosley.

With chapter 5, I posit a novel way to think about the various environments that sf provides as well as a new way to think about science fiction characterization. An ethnoscape provides a symbolic transfer of meaning between racial/ethnic politics and the shifting world of the sf text, resolving the contradictions of homogeneity and exposing the ways that sf unthinkingly reproduces white privilege. The writer constructs a socio-spatial environment in which to tell a story, but the reader can reconfigure those arrangements, draw out the assumptions and implications of the text to perceive its ethnoscape. Even if the fictional socio-spatial environment is constructed so as to foreground issues of race, it will nonetheless contain tensions, contradictions, and connotations beyond the author's control and in which the reader can discern the text's ethnoscape. The ethnoscape foregrounds the human landscapes of race and ethnicity as constituted by sf's historical, social, scientific, and technological engagement with the present. This chapter features analysis of works by William Gibson, Robert A. Heinlein, Ursula K. Le Guin, Delany, Ishmael Reed, and Colson Whitehead.

In chapter 6, I consider technologically derived ethnicity, "technicity," as one pervasive manifestation of these new race paradigms in science fiction. I define technicity as the integration of various technologies with humanity to produce new racial forms such as AI (artificial intelligence), cyborgs, artificial people, and posthumans. Technicity is a reimagining of how race is affected by technology, a way of imagining how individuals might newly conceive identity within increasingly technological worlds. Key works by Nalo Hopkinson, Harlan Ellison, Gibson, Philip K. Dick, and Frederik Pohl are investigated.

My conclusion asks if science fiction has changed enough to incorporate readings of race and racism within its curious history and production; to withstand illuminating its blackground. The task of engaging this social past, a past kept alive by cultural memory, becomes difficult because of political correctness and how it colors present views of history. Otherhood is a particular way of thinking about race relationships in science fiction which have previously suffered from incomplete and trivial reflections. It highlights the interwoven relationships between science fiction and race where cultural experiences, social knowledges, singular visions, technological progressions, and mixed realities are rigorously questioned by looking at historical and futurological worlds. In this respect, science fiction can help us better understand what directions to take in struggling against racism and striving for equality. Consequently, I challenge the sf community to live up to its "progressive" label. To accomplish this task, I offer two impressions. First, I present my thoughts on the science fictional paradigm shift America experienced with the election of its "first" African American president. Second, I discuss Robert Heinlein's unforgettable novel *The Moon Is a Harsh Mistress* (1966) to illustrate the interconnections between each chapter in this book. With this in mind, subsequent cultural anxiety has been echoed through a science fiction aesthetic in film, literature, and reality.

Although otherness, alienation, and difference are motifs frequently explored in the genre, sf has been largely "color-blind," depicting racial discrimination as a relic of the past and race as a biological fiction. This book will investigate the "racing" (engaging, acknowledging, discovering, and/or elucidating race and racism) of sf in the context of a "blackness" informed by cultural studies, postmodernism, and America itself. Put another way, the science fictioning of race is increasingly drawn from postcolonialism, from the popular imagination, and from works emphasizing biological factors. Yet there remains a danger of letting such a discussion fade into the background as efforts are made to draw attention away from such connections through the academic perceptions of the sf status quo. Contrary to critical opinion, this literature does *not* shed light on ideas of racial otherness in terms of the black/white binary just because it *does* break down oppositions with its prevalence of cloning, hybrids, cyborgs, and so on. Our attention needs to be focused on why this omission occurs when considering the futurist imagination dealing with entrenched problems.

For what I am trying to accomplish, a sexy term such as afrofuturism seems too restrictive in scope even though it has been successful at drawing attention to race in sf. Despite the clunkiness of the term "blackground" (and that it is not meant to be a tacky pun), I have not been able to find a better one. I use "blackground" as an interpretive/critical effect and trust it to challenge the perpetuation of racism in sf. There may be no proper way of racing sf, but "blackground" is *meant* to instigate significant change in how we approach race and racism in the genre. After all, American sf has participated in the discourse of science and the politics of race during its nascent years, and it continues to do so. This participation has obscured a really simple fact: African Americans have been forced to confront a sense of "blackness" grounded in the stuff of science fiction that has taken root in American culture.

The exact ways in which my book is, if not unique, then different from all of the others now emerging are difficult to quantify. Although I am not the first scholar to advocate the race-reading of science fiction, my interrogation goes far beyond the usual recognition of the importance of race in sf due to the contribution of black writers such as Delany, Butler, and Hopkinson. I am careful to include much earlier sf, some of which was inescapably, if not overtly, racist. My subject is the odd construction of race in a literature that has both reflected and constructed concepts of otherness informed by and distorted by science, oversimplified science, pseudo-science, incorrect science, and out-and-out fantasy. This book is my attempt to design another critical method to encourage and direct attention to long-overlooked racial aspects of science fiction.

Nonetheless, I have two additional answers to what makes my book distinct—one short and one long. The short answer is that this book is unique mainly in that it brings together for the first time race criticism and sf agendas to see the kinds of reciprocal relationships these two discourses have with each other, each at times informing and at times challenging the other. Simply put, my view is that science fiction is a form that engages race in complex and profound ways.

The long answer involves intuition. My hunch is that race, more particularly "blackness," is always in the background of this historically "white" genre, and I hope to be forgiven my repeated sin of awkward coinage—"blackground," "otherhood," "meta-slavery," "ethnoscape," and "technicity"—for what it reveals. These terms describe how sf's estranged landscapes and powerful technologies extrapolate and model new racial formations in addition to old ones, thus providing a compelling anatomy of a previously neglected dimension of the genre. Therein lies the key: my study is distinctive precisely because it offers readers a critical vocabulary for understanding the role of race in what is commonly assumed to be a deracinated popular genre. Appropriately enough, I put key concepts from critical race studies, literary theory, and science fiction studies together in what I hope are exciting new ways.

I also believe this approach makes my work comprehensible within the tradition of black studies even as it locks me into the classic black/white racial binary. Given that that binary is a dominant feature of American culture, this lends "blackground" some critical traction and analytical power. However, I am fully aware that blackground does pose a historical/social limit for the more general claims that I make about race in sf. So my use of "otherhood" is a way around the specificities of blackground. It allows me to suggest that the racial binary is merely the foundation for race as a preoccupation of science fiction. This move gives us a way of thinking about how the genre plays with race, making of it something other than a simple reflection of historic and current social conditions. The implication is that sf, as a medium of social extrapolation, produces all kinds of "others." In this respect, my study is a framing and expression of the idea that American sf is characterized by an investment in the proliferation of racial difference, that racial alterity is a fundamental part of sf's narrative and social strategies. I recognize, however, that new differences provide fertile ground for new racisms. Thus the political and economic hierarchy empowered by the black/white binary remains in place while the binary itself evaporates when it is no longer based on biological markers. To this end, I have been influenced by Stuart Hall's concept of "cultural racism" (339).

This gut feeling of mine leads me to think my exploration of the reciprocal relationship between "racing science fiction" and "science fictioning race" brings to light and analyzes the numerous ways in which sf is far from being the "postracial genre" its writers and critics have long assumed it to be. Science fiction is actually transmitting assumptions of racism even in stories that are ostensibly envisioning a future where race has become irrelevant. To this end, I attempt to harness the signature language of modernity—science fiction—to explore and better understand the American heritage of race and racism related to black experiences with displacement, dispossession, and alienation filtered through more familiar racist structures such as slavery, Jim Crow, or offensive language.

1   Racing Science fiction

Science fiction produces alien and divergent neighborhoods, with strange and dissimilar signs, shifting identities, and distorted realities of existence. For example, Octavia Butler's *Parable of the Sower* (1993) is a dystopian novel set in the not too distant future around the city of Los Angeles, where downward spiraling middle-class people live in interracial walled communities for protection against the decaying and regressing social order of twenty-first-century America. This sf narrative takes the form of an autobiographical journal relating Lauren Olamina's intimate experiences of the world as her community crumbles around her. She begins a new religion, Earthseed, where "God is change," as she flees north through the ensuing anarchy and violence with her multiracial band of survivors, encountering various situations, ranging from gunfights and cannibalism to escaped slaves and wildfire (*Sower*, 3). Ultimately, the destiny of Earthseed is to take root among the stars (*Sower*, 199). Butler's story is of great consequence to readers because she explores the psychological and spiritual repercussions of racism on a disintegrating country that illustrate the importance of examining attitudes, assumptions, and feelings by which society has conditioned everyone.

   Lauren is afflicted with hyperempathy syndrome, a congenital disease passed to her from her mother, an abuser of a drug called "Paracetco, the smart pill" (*Sower*, 11). Hyperempathy syndrome is a delusional ailment, which causes Lauren to experience the pain and pleasure of others around her. This illness creates in her a profound sense of compassion, allowing her to fight the sense of hopelessness and indifference surrounding her. It grants her the wisdom to lead people. In this light Lauren learns to value community and all it offers—solidarity, activism, and self-reliance. She and her followers must learn, teach, adapt, and grow. As Butler writes: "Embrace diversity. Or be destroyed" (*Sower*, 181). And so by embracing all that her community is, Lauren adapts, in the Darwinian sense, in order to survive.

Butler and other sf writers like her use sf to move us outside of our normal comprehension and allow us to see how race operates culturally. This kind of writing takes us beyond the scope of our ordinary experiences and forces us to mediate between what we already know about race and what we can learn about it by reading sf. The means to accomplish this kind of mediation relates to concepts of otherhood. And in terms of the black/white binary, sf authors would do well to examine settings, signs, and characters, even themselves, based on how otherhood fits science fiction. Butler does understand these relations, and her Parable books present a bleak, nightmarish view of a possible future in alarming detail—where there is unchecked violence and crime; the rapid spread of drugs like pyro, which induces people to start fires; gangs, drug addicts, and homeless people dominating the streets; greedy multinational corporations buying up pieces of the country; federal deregulation of minimum wages, which allows (debt) slavery to make a comeback; escalating energy, food, and water prices; spreading hunger; a corrupt, lazy, and ineffectual police force; simple diseases such as measles and cholera raging out of control; an exponentially increasing birth rate; global warming; a growing gap between the rich and poor; declining educational systems; polygamy; the failure of moral teachings from various religions, most especially Christianity; the decay of modern communication technologies such as television and dependence on older technologies such as public radio for world news; dismantling of the space program; rusting cars, guns and fire—literally social chaos caused by a convergence of social, environmental, and economic crises. As Peter Stillman describes it, "The United States is no longer the storied land of freedom and plenty" (18). In other words, twenty-first-century American life is a living hell.

Though Butler's second novel is complicated by dual narrators, Lauren and her resentful daughter, Larkin/Asha Vere, *Parable of the*

Talents (1998) continues the story of Lauren and her fledgling Earth-seed religion, where "change is the one unavoidable, irresistible, on-going reality of the universe" (75). The U.S. is dominated by lawless-ness, violence, slavery, and religious fanaticism, among other things. Lauren's missing brother, Marcus, is back from the dead and rescued from slavery. Later, the first Earthseed community, Acorn, is destroyed; Lauren and her followers are enslaved with electronic "slave collars" by brutal extremists known as the Church of Christian America (*Talents*, 189); her husband dies in the reeducation camp that Acorn becomes; and her baby daughter is kidnapped and conditioned. Yet somehow Lauren manages to survive and spread the teachings of Earthseed. As the story comes to its end, Lauren is revered as a deity, but she is estranged from her now grown daughter as well as from her brother, a prominent minister in Christian America and an opponent of Earth-seed. Lauren dies before the first Earthseed ship rockets into space, but her ashes are sent with the crew to seed the stars. The second Parable novel is possibly greater in consequence than the first because Butler makes visible the strength and perseverance necessary to unlearn racist patterns and resist oppression. Here is a writer attempting to come to terms with the hurts suffered as a result of racism.

With its depictions of slavery, concentration camps, and religious zealotry, *Parable of the Talents* addresses issues of racism and persecu-tion far more directly than its predecessor. The "potential" of Earth-seed to overcome differences such as race or class or sexual preference is a part of the struggle for survival (*Talents*, 361). The promise of human diversity is knotted with the "apocalyptic potential" of "the current racial formation of American society" (Phillips, 306). Butler embeds her critique of racism in the background of the text in such a way that the ability to reason, create technology, and use scientific advances is the only plausible means to potentially survive and progress beyond the evolutionary dead end of discrimination. As described by Patrick Sharp, "The key to Darwin's vision of evolution was technology: [Darwin] argued that humans had been naturally selected for their ability to invent and use technology" (4). Capitalizing on this senti-ment, Butler's writing estranges reality in such a way that addresses concerns about our lack of preparedness for change as a society and as individuals. As Lauren declares, "If we're to be anything other than smooth dinosaurs who evolve, specialize, and die, we need the stars" (*Talents*, 179). Leaving Earth is the only solution to the coming race war that Lauren is able to envision. The Parable books are politically poignant because many people are afraid to look at reality; instead, they close their eyes and hope it will go away or become better. It is in sf writing such as Butler's that we see a need for the necessary critical tools to interrogate a genre permeated by racial assumptions.

Butler's Parable books are important to science fictional race discourse in many ways. First, she offers an incisive critique of race and class in postmodern culture by creating the walled community of Robledo, which happens to be an interracial mix of blacks, whites, Asians, and Latinos struggling to survive together in the midst of social, economic, and environmental crises. Butler's use of diversity shows us that embracing human differences would eliminate many of the difficulties that we face today because it would dismantle the problem of the color line as society restructures itself. Second, Butler promotes the importance of building a community through thinking, teaching, and activism, where diverse groups of people work together to solve current social problems created by distrust, prejudice, hate, and greed in conjunction with separatism. As Madhu Dubey acknowledges, "The process of finding unity in diversity is necessarily risky and difficult, requiring the ability to interpret unfamiliar cultural codes and the alert balancing of suspicion and trust typical of urban social interactions" ("Folk," 113). Third, through questioning dominant social paradigms and dismissing them, Butler undermines racial coding in sf with a black woman protagonist without explicitly talking about race. Her work is an effective counter model against racist images presented in the works of white writers, and lends itself nicely to investigating the obvious tensions between these competing representations.

What may be thought of as "black" science fiction has been written by many people of diverse backgrounds—black, white, and other. Of course, factors from race and class to geography and the media help determine how these people write their own kind of black sf. However, addressing this "blackness" in sf is central to changing how we read, define, and critique the genre itself. It is essential to build a dialogue with existing theories of sf, racial science, and popular culture in order to create new ideas about how to apply sf studies to race.

Acknowledging and dealing with race in sf may have a significant cultural effect for the twenty-first century because it can prepare us for the looming social changes that may descend upon us as America ceases to be dominated by the white majority, such as those imagined in Butler's Parable novels. We will be in strange territory with such alarming changes, and sf has already charted a few new paths through that territory. These paths present both opportunities and challenges for society to establish new values. In this regard, sf criticism is essential for stimulating appreciation of diversity. Many sf critics, as well as scholars outside the field, coincidentally suggest spaces in which race can be explored in the genre. Brian Aldiss and David Wingrove's *Trillion Year Spree: The History of Science Fiction* (1986) and Brooks Landon's *Science Fiction after 1900: From the Steam Man to the Stars* (1997) are very important to the premises (and promises) of seeing sf criticism through the unique concepts of blackground and otherhood. These authors begin to fill in the historical gaps in our knowledge of sf and its various movements, and by ignoring race in their work, they let us see the vast need to address race and all of its complexities in sf. In fact, these texts further buttress my belief that an underdeveloped, and perhaps checked, tradition of resistance to the sf genre exists. Representations of race in many of the various themes, motifs, metaphors, and icons of the sf tradition are being resisted. Race and racism in sf has hardly been discussed by scholars or fans in any meaningful way. A cultural critic could turn the tradition on its head by offering an overview of sf similar in scope to Aldiss and Wingrove and Landon that discusses racial codes. There are many other sf works that function in much the same way, hinting at racial spaces open to question in science fiction. In other words, room exists in sf to query racial spaces.

For instance, Mark Rose's *Alien Encounters: Anatomy of Science Fiction* (1981) establishes a framework for the sf genre by defining its controlling paradigm as the alien encounter. He states, "We can observe the way the concern with the human in relation to the non-human projects itself through four logically related categories," which he identifies as "space, time, machine, and monster" (32).[1] Rose begins here to devise a valuable model that can be used to uncover problematic representations of race as "alien" others. External encounters with aliens symbolize the internal conflicts of a humanity marked, or perhaps scarred, by racial experience, our continual state of difference. Aldiss mentions that "the essential American obsession" in science fiction "is with the Alien—and thus perhaps with self-identity" (Aldiss and Wingrove, 119). To amend his statement: the American obsession with race is often superimposed onto science fiction aliens. Somewhat ironically, Sharon DeGraw welcomes "an extraterrestrial Other" as a "replacement for terrestrial othering focused on ethnicity, race, nationality, or gender" (16). In this respect, Istvan Csicsery-Ronay Jr.'s commentary on aliens is more pointed in terms of race. He notes that sf constructs "alien-human difference as analogous to terrestrial racial difference," permitting "much the same imaginary sleight-of-hand as the concept of race" (228). The sheer volume of criticism pertaining to the alien dictates that I expand and enrich my exploration of race and racism by touching on the subject of other beings.

Other scholars use the cyborg as a metaphor to complicate notions of identity, such as race that exists on the edge of the human-machine boundary, or to speculate on the idea of a posthumanity: human-artificial hybrids that are disturbingly other. Envisioning exactly how the cyborg occupies a new race position becomes possible when thinking about future projections of human racial history. In the same way, posthumanism changes how we think about our physical being by raising new questions of what is innately or naturally human. Scott Bukatman's *Terminal Identity: The Visual Subject in Postmodern Science Fiction* (1993) looks at the intersection of man and machine as a posthuman subjectivity. Donna J. Haraway's classic essay, "A Cyborg Manifesto" (1991), also provides a blueprint for investigating new manifestations of race ideology, the cyborg imaginary. Likewise, N. Katherine Hayles's *How We Became Posthuman: Virtual Bodies in Cybernetics, Literature, and Informatics* (1999) relates how posthumanism challenges human subjectivity through the increasingly complicated technological development of man machines such as the cyborg or artificial intelligence. "The fact remains that technology is rapidly making the concept of the 'natural' human obsolete," as Sherryl Vint describes it in her book *Bodies of Tomorrow: Technology, Subjectivity, Science Fiction* (7). Tension will manifest between humanity and its mechanical progeny along the lines of race and racism, a "new" racism based on "old" ways of thinking about difference. For instance, Philip K. Dick's novel *Do Androids*

Dream of Electric Sheep (1968) complicates what it means to be human in regard to race in one important way: androids pass for human. The severity of discrimination against biological androids, manufactured human beings in the text, is clearly a human fear that manifests racism based on a paranoid belief that machines could replace men.

My own thinking diverges here from that of posthumanist scholars in that I consider these new beings as new races. For example, would constructed humans or informational systems be privileged over their human counterparts? Is individual consciousness essential for machine races? How would this machine identity evolve? How would humanity interact with these other beings? How should race exist if the human body cannot be distinguished from a computer simulation or a cybernetic being? Certainly, sf criticism inspires a hotbed of ontological questions in regard to race and racism.

Aldiss, Landon, Rose, Bukatman, Haraway, Hayles, and Vint suggest spaces where race-reading can be mapped as well as analyzed; they call to mind the deep, dark spaces in criticism defined here as blackground. However, these readings do not go far enough to provide a combination of spatial and social locations ideal for exploring ideas of race. In dealing with the shortage of race criticism, blackground becomes invaluable in seeking to fill in the logical gaps and spaces left by other scholars. Because sf helps us think about the continually changing present through the dual lenses of defamiliarization and extrapolation, it also helps us to think about alternate tomorrows as well as to question images of these tomorrows, distortions of the various historical presents and realities.

We begin at the intersection of Darko Suvin and Samuel R. Delany. Suvin's *Metamorphoses of Science Fiction* (1979) outlines the intellectual gravity and verve necessary for investigating the various textual codes of sf, and Delany's *The Jewel-Hinged Jaw* (1977; hereafter *JHJ*) pinpoints the language of sf as a word-by-word, sentence-by-sentence revisionary reading process that produces innovative meanings unique to sf. Suvin supplies a rigorous definition of sf aimed at the content of the genre, and Delany provides a style-conscious definition designed to unveil the distinctive means of expression in sf. Placed together, the trenchant perceptions of these two stars provide a blueprint for deciphering the content and style of sf as the genre presents alternate referential worlds.

As a result, science fiction has cultivated and encouraged new ways of reading because of the many valuable attempts at defining it. In the tradition of Suvin's and Delany's theories, I am attempting to articulate otherhood in relation to the blackground brought forth in this book as my own mode of reading that offers a new way of interpreting race and racism in sf. I feel that investigating the state of race criticism in terms of how otherhoods work on blackgrounds will illuminate the development and practice of racism in the sf community. Both Suvin and Delany serve as a foundation for this thinking.

Perhaps the most renowned and influential sf theorist, Suvin defines "science fiction as the *literature of cognitive estrangement*" (4; italics in original). Suvin's celebrated definition of sf is one of the wellsprings of the genre because it brings a measure of respectability to the study of this "popular" genre in the academic world. His definition also remains a continual source of information over thirty years later. It provides sf with a sense of importance to scholars working in other fields—but why?

In his effort to garner high regard for sf, Suvin emphasizes literary theory in his definition by constructing carefully arranged binary oppositions between everyday forms of fiction and sf and establishing a framework of estrangement. Normal "mainstream" fiction operates through a recognizable framework of naturalism or realism that provides an accurate representation of humanity and culture. The world of the text is similar to our own world; it is concerned about the facts and rejects the visionary component of sf. However, sf functions through estrangement, that is, by presenting something familiar in a way strange enough to make it unfamiliar.

Estrangement ironically separates the known from the unknown, creating a sense of the alien about a familiar object or concept. In other words, the ordinary world is defamiliarized; it is presented in a way that is exceedingly, and perhaps eerily, different from our own experience. In Suvin's usage, estrangement is a response to genuine originality. For Suvin, "The attitude of estrangement . . . has grown into the *formal framework* of the genre" (7; italics in original). Nonetheless, Suvin realizes that estrangement alone is not enough to distinguish sf from other genres because estrangement is also produced in fantasy, horror, gothic fiction, fairy tales, myth, and so on. Cognition comes into play here by making a distinction between sf and everything else in literature.

Cognition literally means the act of knowing based on elements of perception. This knowing can be further reduced to empirical factual knowledge, and in turn empirical knowledge is gained through applying scientific methods of recognition, formulation of a problem, and collecting data through experimentation and observation to form and test hypothetical solutions to the problem. For example, Francis Crick and James Watson discovered the double helix structure of DNA in 1953, and this breakthrough has made many medical advances possible. Cognition, then, becomes a procedure of analyzing and understanding the alternative reality of sf texts that is generated through estrangement.

Hence, cognitive estrangement expresses an alternative invented make-believe world, but develops this world with a scientific severity adhering to the natural rules of the universe. Often, the "cognitive estrangement" paradigm allows for a conceptual breakthrough where one model is replaced by another, thus providing the idealized reader with a changed or altered perception of the world according to the rules of science or perhaps the conventions of modern culture.[2] A change in perspective causes the reader to realize new ideas or interpret the world differently. Thus, this reader is able to see beyond old theories and wrap his/her mind around new ones. The perspective shift seems to be a dialectical movement of perception. Certainly, the idealized reader can arrive at a new understanding of politics, social environments, materialistic desire, technological marvels, and perhaps even race through "cognitive estrangement."

In contrast, there is Samuel R. Delany, a black gay writer and critic of science fiction. One of Delany's monumental contributions to the study of science fiction is the notion of "subjunctivity," a concept that looks closely at the style of writing in sf. He describes subjunctivity as "the tension on the thread of meaning that runs between (to borrow Saussure's term for the 'word') sound-image and sound-image" (*JHJ*, 31). The concept of subjunctivity does three things. First, it splits apart content and style by focusing on style. Second, it differentiates between kinds of fiction. And third, it establishes degrees of subjunctivity within sf itself.

In subjunctivity, content functions as the topic treated in a written work; content represents the work's events, physical detail, and information. The analysis of this underlying content is performed through classification, tabulation, and evaluation of its key symbols in order to ascertain its meaning. This manner of interpretation in criticism is fine for naturalist fiction, but not for sf. "Put in opposition to 'style,' there is no such thing as 'content,'" according to Delany (*JHJ*, 21). Content focuses on information presented by words placed together in a specific arrangement. Information separated from the content of the words generates the meaning of the text. Delany does not mean that content is not important, rather that the form of the content, the way it appears on the written page, is subject to style. Juxtaposed with style, content becomes unstable because "even the literal meanings of various sentences and phrases are all read differently in science fiction from the way they are read in mundane fiction" (Delany, *Starboard Wine*, 49). Sf requires a unique mode of reading because of the rift between content and style. Language that can be easily understood in mundane fiction may signify something entirely different and unrelated in sf. Science fiction's "style," says Delany, separates it from all other forms of fiction because of the capacity of science fictional metaphors.

Because of style, subjunctivity also separates sf from other genres by emphasizing the interaction between the reader and the text. Subjunctivity permits Delany to explore variations of images built and modified through words to capture the sense of wonder generated through science fictional phrases. Considering various kinds of writing, subjunctivity definitively positions sf between news, naturalistic or realistic fiction, and fantasy. For example, one kind of subjunctivity, fantasy, is linked with *events that could not have happened*. And the sf kind of subjunctivity connotes *events that have not happened*, such as time travel. Certainly, "*events that have not happened* are very different from the fictional events that *could have happened*, or the fantastic events that *could not have happened*," as indicated by Delany (*JHJ*, 32; italics in original). The highly stylized language(s) of science fiction used to describe events that have not happened can obscure racialist meaning in any text because the images created by sf authors often mask the presence of race and racism. This is exactly why otherhood is needed to break through the façade of a white-oriented genre, meaning that the potentialities of human progress require change and science fiction can lead the way.

The third way in which subjunctivity functions at the level of sf is to determine degrees within the genre itself because fundamental differences exist between the kinds of *events that have not happened*. First, events depicted in sf *might happen:* they have the potential to take place. Stories that might occur are extrapolative and usually follow along the lines of technological development. Second, there are *events that will not happen*. These stories entail fantastic elements woven into science, such as hollow-earth tales. Third, some sf stories function as warnings of technological, environmental, or societal disaster. They symbolize *events that have not happened yet*. Fourth, Delany identifies the parallel-world story as a degree of sf subjunctivity symbolic of *"events that have not happened in the past,"* such as "Philip K. Dick's *The Man in the High Castle"* (*JHJ*, 32; italics in original). Subjunctivity as a concept, then, offers critics and fans alike a comprehensive understanding of how style affects sf through distortions of language representing the present. Science fictional language distortions embedded in style introduce unusual opportunities to explore race and racism within the genre.

The obvious merits in defining ways of reading sf as Suvin and Delany do are the creation of a poetics for understanding the literature produced by sf, from the very bad through the very fine, and the relationship between readers and texts. Otherhood is a mode of reading sf separate from Suvin's cognitive estrangement and Delany's subjunctivity. I believe racist attitudes are masked via cognitive estrangement (science) or changed via subjunctivity (ifness), but they are revealed and examined via otherhood (race approach). Race and racism are obscured by these otherwise fascinating modes of reading (less so in Delany's critical work as this subject is not central to his scholarship, though racial issues are certainly part of his fiction).

Otherhood's rhetoric draws attention to race and racism as they are constituted by sf's historical, social, scientific, and technological engagement with the present. In my view, race essentially indicates the presence of diverse ethnic groups in alternative worlds as well as outlines the details of characters; but it should not reduce the deeds or impact of racialized characters as it often does in early-twentieth-century sf. However modest, otherhood answers the challenge presented by the rise of cultural studies by providing a future-oriented examination of humanity. Otherhood as a mode of sf reading evolves from traditional thinking about race to radical race thinking.

Traditional thinking about race presumably begins with the body of literature composing the blackground of sf—from the recovery of older sf focused on race in general to the continuing explosion of new race-centered fiction focused on the black/white binary. Important new anthologies featuring speculative themes by people of color have recently appeared.[3] A case in point is Sheree Thomas's Dark Matter series. With the publication of *Dark Matter: A Century of Speculative Fiction from the African Diaspora* (2000) and its follow-up, *Dark Matter: Reading the Bones* (2004), Thomas has created a definitive collection of stories and essays representative of a rich, yet untapped tradition of speculative writing. More importantly, her provocative title "Dark Matter" suggests a metaphor for discussing the speculative fictions of black writers. Dark matter is literally invisible space debris whose existence has been deduced because of its gravitational effect on other visible bodies. Black-authored sf is like dark matter because these works are seemingly invisible to readers, yet have an indisputable pull on the genre.

As a testament to this undeniable pull, white critics and black writers offer various speculations on the location of blacks, both writers and readers, in sf in the twentieth century. Bearing in mind that this speculation is only plausible guesswork, a lively exchange takes place in the back pages of the literary journal *Science Fiction Studies* (in the Books in Review and Notes & Correspondence sections) between Kathleen Spencer, Fred Lerner, and Graham Stone across volumes 14, 15, and 16, from 1987 through 1989. The gist of the debate concerns the small number of black writers of sf throughout the twentieth century, especially in the early years of the pulps. After recognizing the modern efforts of Delany, Butler, and Steven Barnes, Spencer concedes all will agree that the number of black writers is "strikingly low . . . so low as to need explanation" (Spencer and Stone, 247). She closes this exchange by speculating about why many blacks apparently do not participate in sf: editorial discrimination, concealed identity, "unequal access to education and to jobs," leading to silence among black writers (248). More recently, in *The Subject of Race in American Science Fiction* (2007), sf scholar Sharon DeGraw posits that "a discussion of race has been, and in some cases continues to be, viewed as antithetical to the science fiction genre. A glaring indication of this distinct separation is found in the lack of an entry for 'Race' in the contemporary *Encyclopedia of Science Fiction*" (103). So blackground relates not only to how sf critics view the works of sf authors and the subject matter of the books, but also to the scarcity of black-authored sf.

To date, I believe only one black sf writer of the 1930s, George Schuyler, more noted as a satirist and journalist, has been unearthed. Using the pseudonym Samuel I. Brooks, Schuyler published in the *Pittsburgh Courier* a weekly pulp-style sf adventure (featuring the black mad doctor Belsidus in his conquest of Africa and later the Western world) that was collected as *Black Empire* (1991) by Robert A. Hill and R. Kent Rasmussen. Amidst the questions concerning the lack of black sf writers, an unasked yet profound question surfaces: what does sf offer its black readership and its black authors? What does the genre say to African Americans?

Of course, various answers to the question above have been supplied by major and emerging black science fiction writers over the years. Only Spencer nods in the direction of Samuel R. Delany's deft criticism during the debate. In fact, two of Delany's many critical collections—*The Jewel-Hinged Jaw* (1977) and *Starboard Wine* (1984)—precede the debate. However, Delany is not alone in giving his answer relating to the impact of sf on black people. Octavia Butler, arguably the most famous black sf writer; Walter Mosley, the celebrated black detective novelist who has recently moved into sf; and Nalo Hopkinson, an emerging talent, each articulate informed responses to the question: what does the genre offer its black participants? The black critical reply is not necessarily any more valid than the white critical response, but clearly the black sf community has a better grasp on the reality of the racial situation because of its members' lived experiences as an oppressed people.

For example, Delany has offered many opinions in the past thirty years on what sf offers African American readers. He wonders, "Just exactly how does the situation of [Asimov's] robots in these stories [*I, Robot*] differ from the reality of the racial situation of [his] world?"

(*Starboard Wine*, 29); he also ponders "what the 'improved racial situation' was actually going to look like" as presented in *Starboard Wine*: "Oh yes, *equality* was a word I knew; but what would it look like, feel like, smell like?" (31) In effect, this kind of ruminating has made Delany a far more perceptive observer of the present world and its racial situation by allowing him to question the various images depicted in sf.[4] Delany has much to say on the issue of what sf potentially means for blacks, as do other sf writers and critics, such as Octavia Butler.

Butler responds to the question of the African American relationship to sf frequently and in a variety of ways. In an early interview published in *Black Scholar* (April 1986), Butler relates a conversation that she had with a white editor: "He said that he didn't think that blacks should be included in science fiction stories because they changed the character of the stories . . . you could use an alien instead and get rid of all this messiness and all those people that we don't want to deal with" (Beal, 18). In her own essay "Positive Obsession" (1995), she reveals what she thinks is good about sf with a series of rhetorical questions:

> But still I'm asked, what good is science fiction to Black people? What good is any form of literature to Black people? What good is science fiction's thinking about the present, the future, and the past? What good is its tendency to warn or to consider alternative ways of thinking and doing? What good is its examination of the possible effects of science and technology, or social organization and political direction? At its best, science fiction stimulates imagination and creativity. It gets reader and writer off the beaten track, off the narrow footpath of what 'everyone' is saying, doing, thinking—whoever 'everyone' happens to be this year. And what good is all this to black people? (134–35)

Sf offers black people a chance to think about the future of race relations as they are impacted by science and technology and to rethink painful moments in racial history such as slavery in uncommon ways. In this respect, Butler demonstrates how the questioner's insensitive "air" reflects a perceived imbalance in social power at the expense of African Americans as other, meaning lesser. She is committed to the struggle against racism, not to mention other problems like sexism, by raising awareness through her writing.

Another author foregrounding otherhood in relation to blacks is Walter Mosley. He has recently crossed into sf with novels like *Blue*

Light (1998), *Futureland* (2001), *47* (2005), and *The Wave* (2006). Mosley states: "Science fiction promises a future full of possibility, alternative lives, and even regret . . . through science fiction you can have a . . . a black world, or simply have a say in the way things are. This power to imagine is the first step in changing the world" ("Black to the Future," 405–406). He makes a bold prediction in direct response to the issue of black participation in the field: "Within the next five years I predict there will be an explosion of science fiction from the black community" (407).

Additionally, Nalo Hopkinson, one of the most celebrated of a new generation of black sf writers, reiterates the dark matter metaphor in a 1999 interview. Hopkinson thinks that "there's an invisible readership of people of color. You rarely see them at cons, so it becomes easy to think they aren't there" (Rutledge, "Speaking in Tongues," 590). As a black reader of sf, I have to agree with Hopkinson. She firmly believes that "if black people can imagine our futures, imagine—among other things—cultures in which we aren't alienated, then we can begin to see our own way clear to creating them" (592). As Hopkinson suggests, the implication that black Americans tend to avoid sf is insincere at best. Even if the issues of race are seemingly relegated to the sidelines with visions of a raceless future, race remains a part of sf by its very absence.

Sf is a literature of possibility, and as such it certainly demands a mode of reading critical to race and racism in order to go along with increasing black participation in the field. And a body of race criticism focused on sf has begun to emerge in response to this demand, this dark matter, advancing various theories, ideas, and directions for race-reading. The triangulated intersections of mainstream literature and criticism with African American culture and sf provide fascinating points to take up the study of race in the genre.

Critics in the 1970s, among them Eric Rabkin and Robert Scholes, regularly assumed, however, that sf had resolved the various problems of racism in a future America with the notion of a unified humanity where race fades away. Rabkin and Scholes claimed that "the presence of unhuman races, aliens, and robots, certainly makes the differences between human races seem appropriately trivial, and one of the achievements of science fiction has been its emphasis on just this feature of human existence" (188).

This assumption is contradicted and overturned, however, by critics of the new millennium close to thirty years later. In 2003 black sf scholar De Witt Kilgore states:

> Within this logic, the problem of racism can be erased if its victims forgive its perpetrators and if we all forget the history of racialization and the richness of cultural variation. The problem with this solution is that it enshrines white masculinity, unmarked or troubled by culture, race, and gender, as the norm to which all "difference" must assimilate. (231)

In agreeing with Kilgore four years later, British sf scholar Mark Bould adds:

> Whatever their intentions, sf's color-blind future was concocted by whites and excluded people of color as full subjects; and because of the particularities of US history, the most obvious omission was that significant proportion of the population descended from the survivors of the West-African genocide, the Middle Passage, and slavery. ("The Ships," 177)

Bould states later in the essay, "Sf avoids confronting the structures of racism and its own complicity in them" (180). Both Kilgore and Bould are touching upon issues of power that were oversimplified by an older generation of critics. The earlier distortion, or perhaps evasion, by members of sf's critical circles on issues of race touches on the question of whether or not science fiction is the open, progressive community that it likes to think it is. Kilgore and Bould are emblematic of the shift to radical race thinking in the genre as they begin to make significant inroads.

As demonstrated by Kilgore's and Bould's incisive commentary, a body of race criticism in sf has emerged as various theories, ideas, and directions for reading race have been articulated, if not accepted, in recent years. These models include afrofuturism, Kilgore's own astrofuturism, and black militant near-future fiction. Not only are black theories of sf being developed, but a documentary film, *The Last Angel of History* (1996), and the Afrofuturism and Carl Brandon Society websites also consider the role of sf in black culture.[5] The fact that these web pages exist is significant for all minorities who might not have access to this communication technology for a variety of reasons. As Alicia Hines, Alondra Nelson, and Thuy Tu report, "The 'digital divide' has become popular shorthand for the myriad social and cultural factors that shape *access* to technological resources" (1). Another revealing area has been the huge amount of critical attention focused on the work of the two best known black sf writers, Samuel R. Delany and Octavia E. Butler. Critiques and analyses of their work must be considered mainstays in sf. However, the body of criticism on these two writers is simply too large to engage with here in a cohesive fashion.

To better understand the work being done on race and racism in sf, we have to consider the cultural politics involved in the construction of a racialized sf criticism focused on race, power, and technology. By tradition, black voices have been rejected and black experiences have been left out of criticism. This is what makes the first attempt to codify a black system of thought so important. In this respect, the best-known theory of black coded readings of race in sf, afrofuturism, has been around since 1993, nearly twenty years. Mark Dery coined the term, stating, "Speculative fiction that treats African-American themes and addresses African-American concerns in the context of twentieth century technoculture—and, more generally, African-American sig-nification that appropriates images of technology and a prosthetically enhanced future—might, for want of a better term, be called 'Afro-futurism'" (736). He goes on to say: "The notion of Afrofuturism gives rise to a troubling antinomy: Can a community whose past has been deliberately rubbed out, and whose energies have subsequently been consumed by the search for legible traces of its history, imagine possible futures?" (736). Afrofuturism considers the ways in which technology is said to be changing black culture and its potential.

Afrofuturists feel that sf unceasingly symbolizes events that have shaped black culture, such as the legacy of slavery and the forced abduction and relocation of Africans to a strange land governed by strange white beings. In other words, the African American histori-cal and cultural condition is inherently the stuff of sf. Slavery as the foundation of the U.S. depended on the "systematic, conscientious, and massive destruction of African cultural remnants," according to Delany (Dery, 746). As such, the afrofuturists claim that black arts, especially music, resonated with a sense of alienation with the mix-ing of technology and sound (synthesizers, turntables, scratching, and sampling) while at the same time referencing the displacement of slavery. Artists such as Sun Ra, George Clinton, and OutKast quickly come to mind.[6] But afrofuturism has expanded to claim all black cultural production—music, dance, painting, theater—and in particular literature. This is to say that nearly all black writing is sf because of black peoples' perceived and experienced dislocation in the Western world dating back to the transatlantic slave trade. Herein lies the flaw of afrofuturism. Afrofuturism is its own aesthetic register that "merely" borrows from the sf tradition by adopting some science fictional motifs such as the alien encounter or time travel to explore black life—past, present, and future—as well as how technology impacts black people. Afrofuturism is separate and distinct from sf, not synonymous with it.

Not surprisingly, a novel such as Ralph Ellison's *Invisible Man* (1952) may be considered as afrofuturist with its themes of profound alienation, erasure of a black future, and dystopia. The unnamed narrator struggles to fit in anywhere—college, Liberty Paint factory, or the Brotherhood—as he seeks his future when forced to migrate from the Jim Crow South. When he recollects the events that landed him beneath the streets of New York stealing electricity in the first place, the protagonist realizes he has no future in a whitewashed world and continues to hibernate indefinitely. *Invisible Man* is afrofuturist, but is *Invisible Man* science fiction?

My answer is no. Though there does appear to be something speculative about the novel, particularly when considering the hospital scene after the explosion at the paint factory or Rinehart's shape-shifting ability or the narrator's time in his underground hideout itself, some kind of recognized science fictional textual apparatus is necessary for a work or works to be called sf. As afrofuturist scholar Lisa Yaszek points out in regard to Ellison's novel, there was no name "for a literature predicated upon both realist and speculative modes of storytelling" until the emergence of afrofuturism (41). Over thirty years earlier, John Pfeiffer made a similar observation regarding sf and African American literature in *Extrapolation:* "Both literatures [sf and African American] could supply or reflect the altered content and perspective that social transformation requires. Science fiction sometimes does; Black American writing almost always has" (35).

Essentially, both critics feel that both sf and African American literature are future oriented in that they depict radical social change. This thinking comes apart, however, when we consider its totalizing ideological construction from a sociohistorical perspective. Both sf and African American literature are the consequence of cultural memory: they are related to the rise of industry and slavery, respectively—two key factors in the history of the United States. However, the argument that all blacks are primarily alienated from themselves and their collective past is simply not true for present generations. For better or worse, African Americans and other colored people have an existence in America.

In *Astrofuturism: Science, Race, and Visions of Utopia* (2003), De Witt Kilgore presents an approach to race and sf that is altogether different from that of afrofuturism. His theory focuses on the hard and popular sciences, race, and utopian visions, something he calls astrofuturism. More to the point, Kilgore's theory argues that spaceflight will free us from the cultural myopia of racism as technology expands the human horizon, shaping all of us into something better, perhaps something posthuman. The idea of astrofuturism is significant because in Kilgore's reckoning black people and other minorities are not absent from these possible visions of the future. In fact, for Kilgore the imperative of spaceflight "demands a progressive, evolutionist account of physical reality and social history; correspondingly, the political hopes fostered by astrofuturism are classically liberal in orientation" (3). Moreover, he believes the optimism engendered by the twentieth-century space race might "free [humanity] from the powerful hierarchies of our world" (238). The narrow focus of astrofuturism benefits sf race studies because it promotes freedom and equality, offers technological hope for a multicultural world, and even celebrates the social transformation of humankind—but that is the problem. Astrofuturism excludes other sf motifs that might be pertinent to race studies, such as alternate history, dystopia, time travel narratives, aliens, supermen, artificial people, and lost-race tales. As valuable as they are, afrofuturism and astrofuturism are only a part of the blackground; neither should be thought of as the one governing idea for the study of race and racism in terms of the black/white binary in sf. These theories have established the right to explore discernable links among blacks, technology, and the future, yet they, like otherhood, are only other ways of reading, interpreting, and questioning the deeply rooted perceptions of race and racism in the genre.

Another relevant idea in sf is the notion of a race revolution. Kali Tal does not think of her term "black militant near-future fiction" as a theory, but as "one subgenre of African American science fiction," where "African Americans join in violent revolution against the system of white supremacy" (66). There are more than a few such novels in black literature with a "take down *the man*" theme, or as Tal terms it, "kill-the-white-folks futurist fiction," enough that this theme could be offered as a model for black sf (67). But does this theme alone make a novel sf? The premise is clearly linked to the science fictional idea of presenting an alternate world where violent black revolutions in America could happen, a change in the relationship of power as such.[7] Then again, Tal carefully indicates, "black militant near-future fiction is a genre that lends itself to the expression of that absurdity" because such extreme examples of revenge could never happen (88).

A good example of this black militant near-future fiction is Sam Greenlee's novel *The Spook Who Sat by the Door* (1969). The plot involves a senator running for reelection who accuses the CIA of segregation in order to garner the Negro vote. Because the senator plays his "race card," Dan Freeman is selected for CIA training only to become a token black agent, special assistant to the CIA director. Freeman retires from this role after five years and trains a Chicago gang, the King Cobras and others like them, in CIA tactics and black history to foment revolution while posing as a social worker. However, the story itself is difficult to recognize as belonging to sf because it has been excluded from critical circles in sf through canon formation; the sf canon only had room for the brilliance of Samuel Delany at that point in American sf history. Perhaps, the discomfiture of the white literary establishment has kept this book buried in relative obscurity, and Tal's thinking represents a worthwhile rescue.

Either way, *The Spook Who Sat by the Door* is a political measure of the 1960s black sentiment toward white America, and its sf veneer does little to mask a Black Power ideology "promising rupture and new realities" (Bould, "Come," 221). It offers new world conspiracies of the invisible black malcontent with an agenda to free the black poor through revolution. In fact, the novel can claim to be sf only in that it is a political fantasy set in a world disturbingly like our own. It is an acute critique of the fragility of the color line. Certainly, there have been plenty of white politicians who have hired blacks to sit and do absolutely nothing but provide colored window dressing, but this novel helps readers recognize empty symbols within sf and society.

To read Black Power sf such as *The Spook Who Sat by the Door* in conjunction with Tal's notion of a black militant near-future fiction is a good idea, if a somewhat limited one. Tal's notion provides a new direction to conduct research that reaches far back in time to include Martin Delany's nineteenth-century insurrection novel *Blake, or the Huts of America*. In other words, black militant near-future fiction provides a new way of thinking about social developments in U.S. history. However, the idea is limited because if pushed too far it will only exacerbate stereotypes of angry black men. For better or worse, black militant near-future fiction, along with afrofuturism and astrofuturism, is a part of science fiction because it fills a particular niche in the study of race and racism in the genre. In other words, each of these theories makes it possible to more accurately assess the checkered heritage of race in sf by building an environment focused on changing people's thoughts in a radical way.

Unquestionably, a rich vein of ideas for sf is the science of biology, which has been mined time and again by writers seeking to craft stories of evolution, aliens, and exotic landscapes. Biology can offer a master sf narrative of sorts because it creates alien cultures that reflect either positively or negatively on humanity. Strategically, sf writers use the extraterrestrial emblem against which to compare and contrast the racial situation by offering social commentary on these alien models of humanity. This connection has been historically accomplished through social Darwinism. Science fiction, then, reflects current social problems set against a fictive history beyond our experience of historical reality—the bugs of Robert Heinlein's *Starship Troopers* (1959) readily come to mind.

It is important to remember that the "science" of race has been developed more or less exclusively by white men of various European extractions in an effort to prove their own racial superiority. Undoubtedly, racial science and pseudo-sciences have had some bearing on sf from influential editors, such as Hugo Gernsback and John Campbell, and esteemed writers, among them Isaac Asimov and H. G. Wells, as well as on critics and fans. From the start of social Darwinism, the impact of scientific racism on sf can be traced to the present. This impact includes examining how the social codes and representations of race have changed over time in American sf.

In sf, social Darwinism is certainly a master narrative when considering the subject of race. Social Darwinism creates binary systems that divide humanity, and we as a species cannot seem to cross such divisions as inferior/superior, self/other, us/them, or, in particular, the black/white binary. Seemingly, an absolute border must always be established between the culturally constructed races of the world. This separation is radical in the sense that it has always led to violence against, and destruction of, those who are considered different. While the roots of racism stretch well beyond the advent of social Darwinism in 1859, a tradition of speculation around this idea in Western culture has influenced and shaped sf as both have changed throughout time.

Scientific racism disguised as social Darwinism has harmed both American culture and sf because through extrapolation it traces human evolution to the posthuman and beyond. Consequently, we need to map out the historical framework of intersections between scientific racism, culture, and sf. Therefore, my interest lies in exploring the friction between scientific racism and the demands of history relating to racialized sf. To do this, I have to question what produces the racist patterns in sf by explaining social Darwinism and its relationship with American culture and history as well as with literary production. At the center of this tangled web of relationships is the notion of race-thinking and its various incarnations as social Darwinism, biological determinism, eugenics, genomics, degeneration theory, and so on.

Possibly the single most important intellectual event of the nineteenth century was the publication of Charles Darwin's *The Origin of Species* (1859), in which he expressed his ideas on biological change as a theory of evolution. Of course, the idea of evolution had been around long before Darwin, but none of the competing theories were able to capture the popular imagination because they were not so well expressed. A brief review of Darwin's evolutionary theory offers four essential factors to remember. First, the element of variability suggests that divergence in the characteristics of an organism from the species norm takes place over time. Second, the characteristic of heredity implies that the sum of the qualities and potentialities genetically derived from one's ancestors would be passed onward through the genes. Third, the quality of excessive fertility means that organisms with beneficial hereditary variations stay alive longer to produce more offspring for the species. And fourth, the aspect of selection entails a natural process that results in the survival and reproductive success of those individuals or organisms who best adjust to their environment. This ability to adjust leads to the perpetuation of genetic qualities suited to that particular environment. This natural selection is by chance rather than by divine planning, and the most fit eventually produce new species.

In its radical challenge to accepted notions of man's creation and character, Darwin's theory painstakingly demonstrates that man is a product of nature as well as subject to nature's whims. In truth, he shattered the existing theological opinions pertaining to man's beginning. As a result, Darwin's theory of natural selection is synonymous with the entire concept of evolution, and Darwin himself has become legendary. "The key to solving social problems" had been found because Darwin's skill with language convinced the educated masses that the science of biology had "uncovered the mystery of life and deciphered the enigma of evolution" (Barkan, 137).

Darwin's biological theory of evolution also became a social theory of evolution. His theory crossed the boundary between science and culture when it transformed into "social Darwinism." It is important to note that social Darwinism is based on an erroneous and inappropriate extension of Darwinian theory to the evolution of societies, rather than species. As such, social Darwinism has nothing to do with biology—and little to do with Darwin himself—although it has often been used in support of racist arguments. Even if social Darwinism has been thoroughly discredited in the modern scientific community,[8] it is still very potent in the popular imaginary of recent sf television shows if the Sci Fi Channel's reimagining of *Battlestar Galactica* (2003) or the USA Network's *The 4400* (2004) are accurate indications.[9] To a large extent then, Darwinian theory is a driving engine of racialist sf because of the scientific entanglements of racial history within the genre. Though Darwin was against racism, his theory "provided a new rationale within which nearly all the old convictions about race superiority and inferiority could find a place" (Gossett, 145).

Indeed, the phenomenon of social Darwinism elevated race as an issue for science as scholars and scientists scrambled to justify the superiority of white culture and to rationalize "that black and white races had evolved as separate species" (Smedley, 237). "Survival of the fittest" is one notion that gained the necessary cachet to justify racism. The English sociologist Herbert Spencer coined this expression, the most popular phrase generally attributed to evolutionary theory, in 1851, eight years before Darwin published *The Origin of Species*.[10] Darwinian principles could be used to support almost anything if the situation was sustained by the notion of the "survival of the fittest." Racism, "justified" as a "scientific" response, became rampant as ideas concerning evolution that were mistakenly attributed to Darwin came into vogue. A moment of otherhood happens because of the transference of real social messages onto sf as people explore relationships of race, racism, and power.

Nowhere is this idea more apparent than in H. G. Wells's quintessential time travel narrative, *The Time Machine* (1895). The future world that Wells envisions is unquestionably racialized as he extrapolates from Darwin's evolutionary ideas, though traditional critical opinion emphasizes the class allegory projected in the novel where class struggle brings about human degeneration. Nonetheless, Neil Barron indicates:

> So much attention has been given the Eloi and Morlocks during that passing moment—the year 802,701—that too many critics read the novel solely as a statement of the inevitable fate of Western industrial society—the evolution of humanity into two distinct species. This Marxian projection is but one of the dichotomies of the period that the Eloi and Morlocks may suggest. (21–22)

One of these other dichotomies is race. *The Time Machine* is a nameless man's account of the development of mankind, if not all life on Earth, as he journeys into the remote future with a machine that he himself builds and from which he witnesses the end of the world. In the year 802,701, the Time Traveller observes that humanity has divided into two distinct species, the passive and bucolic Eloi and the brutish Morlocks; ultimately both species die out.[11] In other words, Wells opens the way for a Darwinian reading of the future, where humanity devolves into two contrary ends of evolutionary possibility. In an inventive complication of existing racial stereotypes, Wells establishes the darker childlike and vacuous Eloi as the food supply of the white, inhuman, almost alien Morlocks. Both races evoke memories of slavery—the Eloi are mindless, docile primitives and the Morlocks are "ape-like" savages (45). The physical difference between the two races is startling when considered in conjunction with how they both accentuate contrary myths concerning blacks. On the one hand, the Eloi are sympathetic figures because of their placid temperament and are fondly regarded by the Time Traveller. And on the other hand, the Morlocks are portrayed as callous monsters whom the Time Traveller has no hesitation about indiscriminately killing. Placed together the divided vision of evolution provided by Wells signals the triumph of nature over humanity—the utter regression of culture. Wells takes his grim Darwinian extrapolation even further into the future, ending with the flopping tentacled "thing" about "the size of a football . . . hopping fitfully about" on the beach (106).

From a historical perspective on science, scientist Stephen Jay Gould informs us of how Darwin's theory forced mid-nineteenth-century scientists to change their racist thinking. Using Louis Agassiz, "the greatest biologist of mid-nineteenth-century America," as a primary example, Gould describes Agassiz's original position, "that God had created blacks and whites as separate species. The defenders of slavery took much comfort from this assertion, for biblical proscriptions of charity and equality did not have to extend across a species boundary" (243). However, Agassiz abandons this theological stand by constructing scientific claims supporting racism. He turns to the practice of phrenology to display the base nature of blacks compared to whites. Damien Broderick points out, "Agassiz, in any event, did not measure skulls and brains in a value-neutral laboratory, a social vacuum, and *discover* Negro inferiority" (68). Instead, Agassiz was driven by the racist culture in which he lived to fabricate his racist findings.

In Wells's novel, the Time Traveller's arrogance, much like Agassiz's, is clearly marked by his conviction that the race of men in this future time period is inferior and savage, if not inhuman. The Time Traveller makes a racial link himself by comparing his time among the Eloi with a Negro's hypothetical visit to late-nineteenth-century

London "fresh from Central Africa" (41).[12] He ponders: "Think how narrow the gap between a Negro and a white man of our own times, and how wide the interval between myself and these of the Golden Age!" (41). In this analogous comparison of the Negro's abilities to the white man's and the Eloi's abilities to his own, the Time Traveller's sense of racial superiority is overwhelming as he mocks what is left of humanity by calling this distant future the "Golden Age." Wells's use of evolution in a far future environment to ridicule society is a vivid display of how racial dynamics are created by mere surroundings and chance circumstances. And in relation to my point, Wells demonstrates in this particular book sf's historic inability to see race and racism.[13]

Although historians of science and others may differ in their opinions about the impact of *The Origin of Species*, only now are the many inferences of social Darwinism concerning race beginning to be known. I say this because social Darwinism has the remarkable ability to seemingly reincarnate or reinvent itself in various guises as time passes. It has an enduring appeal for two such reasons: race-thinking and Darwin's facility with language to express his theory. As Linda Bergmann notes, Darwin "succeeds because he engages the mind and respects and addresses the emotions provoked by such a new way of seeing the world. That most readers have acquiesced is a measure of his achievement" (94–95). His style of argument gained immediate influence for his conclusions, whereby recognition of natural selection as the vital mechanism in biological change had revolutionary implications for the biological and social sciences. His use of language cleared the way for social Darwinism by creating a conflict between science and culture in regard to race. So then, "what we call 'race,'" according to Joseph Graves, "is the invention not of nature but of our social institutions and practices," and "the social nature of racial categories is significant because social practice can be altered far more readily than can genetic constitution" (2). Race and racism in this light are social conventions governed by the illusion of science's incorruptibility put to ill use by fostering hatred and discrimination.

The operation of natural selection, its variability, is the very thing that makes Darwinian reasoning indispensable to race theory. Thus, science, heavily influenced by Darwin in the twentieth century, provides the foundation for an ideology of race encompassing the world.

In other words, science is now responsible for articulating the correct truth about race as well as for providing scientific evidence to support this dubious truth. The general principles of natural selection were co-opted and adapted to reflect the struggle between different races, leading to nature's development and production of superior races.[14] Significantly, the notion of race in the United States signals a fixed and inflexible boundary between white and black based on the belief that hereditary differences are permanent. As a result, rigid cultural beliefs concerning race govern American society and grant status and privilege to some groups and not to others, since physical differences cannot be transcended. The scientific basis provided by the theory of natural selection has been critical in making existing physical and social differences seem inviolable, thus legitimating racism as a system that changes over time. Of course, the intolerant nature of racism is intellectually, if not emotionally, connected to all xenophobic attitudes whether or not they are ethnocentric, supernatural, or geographic in origin.

At the end of the nineteenth century, social Darwinism was fully disguised as scientific racism, and racial ideas travel across the Atlantic between Europe and the United States to maintain racial hierarchies. Scientists indulged in pseudo-sciences such as phrenology, craniometry (which dealt with the size, shape, and proportions of skulls among human races), and degeneration (a theory of human retrogression revealed through deteriorating mental and physical abilities in individuals) to justify racism by conflating facts and opinion. The use of pseudo-science to validate racist beliefs as an extension of social Darwinism is truly malicious because it involves the selective collection of data as well as manipulation of this data to support certain assumptions or arguments. Pseudo-science represents superficial and insincere scientific research. True scientific research disregards religion, offers structured doubt to garner a theoretical knowledge of the natural world as its marvels are explained, and adheres to the principle of science for the sake of science. Social Darwinism's ability to reshape itself is what makes it a dangerously powerful agent of scientific racism.

A striking example of scientific racism in the twentieth century is the notion of eugenics, the pseudo-science that deals with the improvement (as by control of human mating) of hereditary qualities of race and breed. The eugenics movement was chiefly "interested in attempting to prove that geniuses tend to come from superior human stock, and that feeblemindedness, criminality, and pauperism are also strongly influenced by hereditary factors," according to Thomas Gossett (155). "Overtly combining science and politics," Sharon DeGraw asserts, "eugenics connected scientific theories with social reform" (7). Francis Galton, a cousin of Charles Darwin, began the eugenics movement in England and advocated a policy of selective breeding to eliminate detrimental weaknesses such as alcoholism, prostitution, drug addiction, and an assortment of other social diseases. He introduced the word "eugenics" as well as the biological motto "'nature and nurture,' which precipitated so much controversy over the relative importance of heredity and environment" (Gossett, 155).

Certainly, it seems as though there are two distinct eugenic notions arising from the early twentieth century. One approach might be considered positive. It entails a planned improvement of the human species by creating a racial stock of superior individuals and then regulating their reproduction to create a pure race of "super" humans. The positive strategy is at the root of the "Aryan Myth"—a hypothetical ethnic type descended from early speakers of Indo-European languages, or Nordic. Nancy Kress's Hugo and Nebula Award–winning novella *Beggars in Spain* (1991) is a good example of the optimistic intent of eugenics. In the story, set in the twenty-first century, Kress extrapolates from eugenic notions by having scientists genetically modify selected children to never sleep. The "Sleepless" display greater intelligence, psychological balance, ideal fitness, and near immortality. However, the optimism of the text takes a turn for the worse as the story's protagonist, Leisha Camden, and the other Sleepless encounter America's racist response to their remarkable difference, their "evolutionary fit[ness]" (173). Eugenic stories are an important part of racing science fiction because many people—writers, readers, and scholars—are intrigued by the idea of creating a master race of human beings, homo superior as it were.

The second approach is negative in the extreme because it advocates the destruction of inferior races as well as the elimination of inherited defective traits (a precursor to some of the twenty-first century's ideas about genetic engineering). Political acceptance of the eugenic movement across Europe and in the United States is what allowed the Holocaust to happen as Nazi Germany abused the "Aryan Myth" in order to spur its military toward the near genocide of all Jewish peoples. Philip K. Dick's alternate history novel *The Man in the High Castle* (1962) is an excellent illustration of the negative consequences of eugenic beliefs. In this novel the Axis powers have won World War II. Presumably, after exterminating the Jewish race, the Nazis turned their attention to black people by using nuclear weapons as the *"the Final Solution of the African Problem"* (25). In planning their conquest of the world, Nazi Germany is plotting against their Japanese allies with "Operation Dandelion . . . an enormous nuclear attack on the Home Islands [of Japan] without advanced warning of any kind" (188).

A second, and equally remarkable, example of scientific racism has been the historical abuse of genetics throughout the twentieth century. Coupled with Darwin's theory of natural selection, Gregor Mendel's research, which involved variation, mutation, and heredity in pea plants and was published in a little-known journal in 1866, though not formally recognized until 1900, became a cornerstone of biology, and subsequently of scientific racism as well. The fledgling science of genetics provided a gratifying explanation for natural selec-tion—heredity is almost invariable, but favorable changes in genetic structures remain intact and provide a chance for newer adaptations. Scientists desired to improve human potential and eliminate harm-ful traits by artificial selection rather than leave it to the natural course of evolution. The scientific revolution in biology truly began in 1953 when Crick and Watson figured out the structure of the DNA molecule.

While twenty-first-century applications of genetic testing are yet to be fully developed, it is not difficult to imagine the dawn of genetic discrimination in sf terms. The Andrew Niccol film *Gattaca* (1997) quickly comes to mind, in which a natural-born and inferior man liv-ing in a sterile genetically improved world feigns the identity of a supe-rior one to achieve his ambition of space travel. Law scholar Frank Wu reckons, "The human genome project threatens to give us knowledge for which we are not ready. All of us have hidden weaknesses, some incurable and even fatal. We will meet in genetic testing the most aggressive form of rational discrimination" (212). There is little room for doubt that the meaning of racial difference is changing because of the impact of genetics. As sf scholar Sherryl Vint notes, "Both science fiction and discourses on genetics are concerned with marking the boundaries of humanity" (*Bodies of Tomorrow*, 56). The possibilities for remaking mankind are frightening and exciting at the same time as science increases its understanding of the human genome through mapping and studying the entire structure. The tremendous potential of genetic science to discredit racism (and even the notion of race itself) as completely inconsistent with the biological reality of human existence is a noteworthy dream. Although we certainly like to think that scientific progress pushes prejudice and discrimination to the side, science fiction suggests otherwise.

I have discussed specific examples of how scientific racism historically poses as social Darwinism, which in turn masquerades as honest scientific inquiry with sf examples such as *The Time Machine, Beggars in Spain, The Man in the High Castle,* and *Gattaca.* Still, the question remains: how does social Darwinism relate to sf? I will briefly argue that sf has achieved several related objectives in its management of scientific theories. First, it has made scientific speculation popular, meaning that it has made various scientific theories understandable to many people without substantial knowledge of science. Second, sf functions as an unconscious barometer of public attitudes. This function is particularly beneficial in understanding the assumptions of our society before, now, and later, in technocultural terms, because sf's vision concerns the cultural and philosophical consequences of technological advancement and scientific progress. Third, sf increases our knowledge of the human condition, meaning that it enriches our understanding of Western society's violent past. Fourth, evolutionary ideas abound—from Darwin to cyborg theory—and have a lasting influence on the genre. Indeed, ideas such as man evolving into a superior race of beings or battling for survival with competing species are conventions of sf. As Brian Aldiss puts it, "Evolutionary speculation has become, and remains, one of the staples of science fiction. It lends secular perspective to the human drama. The glacier-like grandeur of natural selection and adaptation colours our thought" (94). It should come as no surprise when I state that social Darwinism is one of the master narratives that govern racial thinking within sf.

In twenty-first-century America, some hold that science is inherently superior to other academic disciplines because it is driven by a public perception of pure and impartial research attempting to find the truth of existence through the accumulation of facts, data, and information. Science should be easily understood, have an everyday application, or make common sense—an American credo of sorts—yet it does not for the most part, because it is often too obscure and too technical for the public to grasp. Perhaps it is the cryptic nature of the information provided by science that gives it authority over people. We can certainly imply that we feel secure in the belief that scientific knowledge will improve our lives. As social scientist Christopher Toumey declares, "Science does not really deserve such awe, nor do most scientists believe such things about it. But many nonscientists do. Thus, to invoke the symbols of science is to make policies sound, commodities desirable, and behavior legitimate. By definition, these things are meritorious when they have the appearance of being scientific" (6). From a humanities standpoint, scientific knowledge seems to be the wrong mode of questioning a racialized sf in terms of authority.

The authority of science and its perception of superiority is a fallacy built on social and political prejudice. Gould is absolutely right when he states we must recognize "our belief in the inherent superiority of pure research for what it is—namely social prejudice—then we might forge among scientists the union between theory and practice that a world teetering dangerously near the brink so desperately needs" (213). We forget that scientists are human beings after all, subject to the same passions as ordinary people. When I think of all the harm that science has done concerning race, I must concede Gould's point. Public respect for science is affirmed on the mere appearance of scientific authority. This authority is tapped into quite easily by television, music videos, films, and other manifestations of pop culture, especially sf, by invoking something as simple as a test tube. I maintain that sf borrows from this global view to mask awareness of race and racism. The important question that needs answering remains: why does sf do this? I am left wondering if science fiction writers still continue to frame ideas of race through invoking the cultural influence of science.

Clearly, then, sf is problematic because it has resisted race-reading. It has displayed racist attitudes and presented "solutions" for the race problem by imagining postrace worlds, albeit imperfectly. Race is a continually elastic conception where physical differences are no longer essential to its operation as displayed in sf. The difference between reactionary and progressive sf may be whether it views race and racial difference as "biological" and therefore real. For me, one of the functions of sf is to draw attention to and challenge racist and ethnocentric attitudes, in part by interrogating science. Both science and literature are linked by how they express information using rhetorical means. However, science is measured objectively while literature is analyzed subjectively. Still, the link between science and literature is more important than what splits them apart.

In understanding sf, it is important to be mindful of how generic conventions utilize scientific language. Such conventions—DNA, particle physics, radiation—must be invoked to generate the illusion of reality that sf needs in order to be convincing. Thus, sf is granted a sense of cultural authority. Scientific language in sf stories is used to create the story, not by engaging our subjective experience, "but to operate a narrative fiction. Frequently, the rhetoric of science is a sop to reason, allowing the reader to indulge in a fantasy which may be entirely irrational," according to sf critic John Huntington (*Rationalizing Genius*, 79).

Sf assumes a rhetoric of change by always questioning the cultural moment. It occupies a privileged position from which it is capable of attuning its readership to the intersections of scientific theory, technological development, and social conventions. These intersections are significant because they put human interests such as race on display, making it essential that we question the social implications of these imagined worlds. I think sf subverts cultural, historical, and even technological boundaries where we encounter social problems such as racism generated by the misuse of science, among other things. Unlike science, sf also allows us to reflect on real life where we can transform the social values presented in texts into something more beneficial by assessing our feelings on race matters. This approach to sf, I feel, is something new.

Certainly, discrepancies exist between claims of what sf critics believe they as critics are doing in regard to race and what is actually being done. Sf as a cultural production, however, supports racism as a system (and perhaps postracial moments too) in its near and far-flung histories and visions of the future. The concept of otherhood addresses the problem of systemic racism in sf and the underlying reasons for neglecting to get rid of it. As a matter of convenience, many sf scholars have presumed that racial distinctions will become insignificant when represented in the possibilities of science fiction. In other words, providing racialized characters becomes irrelevant to a future that transcends race. I find this supposed vanishing of African Americans, Asian Americans, Latinos, Native Americans, and white ethnics exceedingly odd—astonishing, really. However, it seems unlikely that collective cultural attitudes on the subject of race will be overlooked in sf because they are so deeply rooted. After all, sf writers depict futures of conquest, power-mongering, hegemony, greed, and the like. Race and racism are no less a constant than human greed or the desire for dominance.

The greatest problem of the twentieth century, the color line, as first articulated by W. E. B. DuBois, has yet to be explored convincingly in sf. The science fictional expression of otherhood, like the DuBoisian double consciousness, only more so, is the objective of this study.[15] National concerns such as immigration, reverse discrimination, affirmative action, cultural diversity, the mixed-race movement, racial profiling, and terrorism test our developing society daily. These issues are also depicted in sf. We can foreground issues of the color line in sf and possibly transcend them by deliberately remaining aware of how race is buried in the genre. To this end, the next chapter will necessarily focus on depictions of slavery in science fiction as both the logical and unavoidable starting point in this particular discussion of race and racism.

2

Meta-slavery

Read as a labor-based technology, race has been used to code black human beings in the New World as natural machines essential for the cultivation of the physical landscape and capable of producing wealth. From this standpoint, Ben Williams realizes that "the mechanical metaphors" used for blacks "embody a history that began with slavery" (169). Forcibly uprooted from Africa, alienated by the middle passage, dehumanized in the Americas, and controlled by strange white men, is there any wonder that the slavery experience has been interpreted as the very substance of sf for blacks? Describing his own experience with slavery in *The Interesting Narrative of the Life of Olaudah Equiano* (1789), Olaudah Equiano writes, "If ten thousand worlds had been my own, I would have freely parted with them all to have exchanged my condition with that of the meanest slave in my own country" (33). Evoking the sf theme of other worlds as long ago as 1789, Equiano speaks of trading ten thousand other worlds to be free of the inequities of slavery. In fact, this passage displays how Equiano compares his time as a slave in his own country, present-day Nigeria, to his initial experience of the European slave trade in the hold of a slave ship headed for the West Indies. Fittingly, the historical legacies of slavery and colonization, which have shaped black cultures in the Americas, are easily taken up within sf motifs to explore the dynamics of power and race.

Slavery is not science fictional. It is, however, a "peculiar institution" that can be made even more peculiar when imagined in terms of technological forms of bondage or captivity. Sf constructions of slavery

tend either to recontextualize captivity narratives in terms of new technologies or to employ technology to relocate in time the observation
or experience of bondage as a cultural norm. Either approach uses
technology or science to distance and defamiliarize the institution and
practice of slavery, resulting in constructions of slavery as neo–slave
narratives or *meta-slavery narratives*. As the epitome of racism, then,
slavery is the inevitable starting point of any exploration of a race in
science fiction.

With this in mind, Samuel R. Delany's celebrated *Stars in My
Pocket like Grains of Sand* (1984), set in the far future on a distant
planet, Rhyonon, opens with the line "'Of course' . . . 'you will be a
slave'" (3). The lead character, Korga, voluntarily undergoes Radical
Anxiety Termination at nineteen years of age, rendering him incapable
of independent thought while ridding him of his anger, antisocial disposition, drug addiction, and sexual deviance (3). This "gamma ray la-
ser" technology painlessly strips Korga of his identity, and he is sold into
a life of corporate slavery by the RAT Institute, where he is chronically
underfed and overworked, dressed in ill-fitting clothes while routinely
beaten and cursed at by his supervisors before being allowed to rest in
a filth-encrusted cage (6).[1] This is his life for twenty-two years, except
for a few days when he is illegally sold to a nameless rich woman and
later recaptured. Only corporations can legally possess slaves on this
particular planet.[2]

During his brief time as a fugitive slave, the previously illiterate
Rat Korga is given a black sensory glove by the rich woman that restores and even improves his mind, and he takes full advantage of
this by reading voraciously. Gaining the ability to read is a powerful
moment in the text because Delany consciously mirrors "the classic
slave-narrative scenario in which learning to read is an illicit act of
discovery" (Dubey, *Signs*, 239). However, Rat Korga's glove is yanked
off upon his recapture, allowing the RAT procedure to reestablish its
grip, and his mind is cast back into darkness.

The prologue ends suddenly as the inhabitants of the planet apparently blow themselves up in what is known as "Cultural Fugue"—a
nuclear holocaust caused by socioeconomic failure and conflicting
political systems, resulting in planetary extinction (70). Rat Korga,
who was working in an underground refrigerated storage vault at the

moment of the explosion, is the only survivor to be dug out of the smoking ruins of Rhyonon. The remainder of the novel explores the romance between the former slave Rat Korga and the industrial diplomat Marq Dyeth, ambassador to alien worlds, on the planet Velm. Their bond threatens to destabilize another planet that is polarized by two political factions, the Family and the Sygn, a destabilization that could end in Cultural Fugue.

In *Stars in My Pocket like Grains of Sand*, Delany deliberately distances our cultural memory of slavery by providing a reappraisal of the peculiar institution's legacy through the future. The success of his story hinges upon alien cultures echoing the sociohistorical structures of the United States of America. Slavery in the text results in civil war and the destruction of Rhyonon. Delany uses "cultural fugue" to critique the destructive power of American slavery and to force reconsideration of the tenuous nature of racial tolerance in America today. Although he does not engage with race directly, Delany does suggest that sf has the ability to free the United States from the psychological legacy left by slavery.

Undoubtedly, American slavery survives in our cultural imagination, in our records, even in our sf. Terry Bisson's provocative *Fire on the Mountain* (1988), for example, describes an alternative history where John Brown's raid, with the assistance of Harriet Tubman, succeeds at Harpers Ferry. The resulting changes include a socialist black republic in the Deep South that shapes much of the world's politics. Bisson's novel demonstrates that slavery is very thoughtfully studied by the author, giving us a feel for its social environment, its common activities and values, as we progressively compile as much of its tradition as possible. Yet some aspects of the slave experience will always remain outside of this constructed history because the manner in which history is written is largely flawed. I say "flawed" because individual authors bring their various prejudices to bear on historical records and translate happenings through specific agendas. In other words, they influence our understanding of slavery by carefully shaping and manipulating our knowledge. This influence, positive or negative, affects how different races perceive historical slavery and each race's position in relation to it. Racism, then, becomes specific to these social experiences recorded in history, charging "black" and "white" subjectivities in different ways, and fixing identities in racial categories that have proven nearly impossible to transcend.

A case in point, William Styron's Pulitzer Prize–winning *The Confessions of Nat Turner* (1967), offers a fictionalized account of the brutal and violent 1831 Southampton, Virginia, slave revolt led by the infamous Nat Turner, in which fifty-nine white people died. Black objections to the novel concern the possible misrepresentation of history and the appropriation by white writers of the iconic image that Turner symbolizes for many black Americans. Undeniably, some people will feel that Styron's race undermines the artistic value of his novel as a social document because he has little personal association with slavery as a white man in America. Styron is a white man from the South using a black historical figure to talk about slavery. His reinterpretation of the past through his neo–slave narrative clearly diminishes the blacks' sense of ownership of this history. But even more, his interpretation sees only white men as historical subjects, and as a white American male he is fundamentally incapable of seeing beyond that fact. In defense of Styron, I believe that people on both sides of the color line have to deal with the consequences of slavery. "Although slavery has ended," Sherryl Vint comments, "its traumatic and continued effects on Americans, both black and white, have not been dealt with" ("Only," 242).

One way of dealing with these consequences, as demonstrated by Styron, is the neo–slave narrative. African American literary scholar Bernard Bell coined the term "neoslave narrative" in his book *The Afro-American Novel and Its Tradition* (1989) by labeling Margaret Walker's novel *Jubilee* (1966) the "first major neoslave narrative: residually oral, modern narratives of escape from bondage to freedom" (289).[3] Bell uses "neoslave narrative" to describe the writing of contemporary black writers, "fabulators" who "combine elements of fable, legend, and slave narrative to protest racism and justify the deeds, struggles, migrations, and spirit of black people" (285). By returning to fictional representations of the antebellum South, contemporary writers use the historical era of slavery to critique the status of race relations and engage in cultural politics. Writers accomplish this task by informing their fiction with the firmly bound characteristics of the slave narrative established by escaped slaves such as Frederick Douglass and

Harriet Jacobs. At present, "neo–slave narratives" are widely read and have become an important tool in revising history, literature, and the promise of freedom.[4] Black authors use this revised slave narrative form to comment on current racial politics in the United States by imitating its structure, revising its conventions, and demonstrating an unbroken cultural connection of African American experience. Neo–slave narratives are a repository of cultural memory as they witness and testify to the dehumanization process and our negligent attempts to forget. Importantly, the neo–slave narrative confirms the abiding worth of the slave narrative as a reflection on oppression and freedom, yet these fictional accounts are steadfastly framed by the conventions of the slave narrative. Thus, sf is a perfect medium for such excursions into the past as well as the future.

From this point of view, the careful interplay of science fiction and contemporary thought on racial memories makes apparent a pattern of how significant relationships relate to the traumatic experiences of humanity. With sf's motifs of time travel, alternate history, alien contact, and future visions, meta-slavery narratives capitalize on the freedom sf provides from the restraints of race and racism. For instance, Cherene Sherrard's short story "The Quality of Sand" (2004) tells of Delphine, an Afro-Caribbean woman who roams the Atlantic as a pirate captain disrupting slave trafficking. She and her crew become the "scourge of the triangle trade" by sinking slavers and rescuing their human cargo (12). This story, and others like it, encompasses the proper realm of sf meta-slavery tales. Meta-slavery cannot be understood without a historical understanding of slavery and its literature, because meta-slavery takes slavery's conventions, such as violence, human chattel, and identity, as its subjects and goes beyond them by changing our understanding of them.

Connections between the historical reality of slavery and its narrative arc—slave narratives, neo–slave narratives, and meta-slavery tales—have to be made in order to recognize how sf motifs contribute to the dialogue on race. These connections take us clear of what we "think" we know about history and cultural memory. I acknowledge that a genre label such as "sf" must necessarily be permeable because it may overlap with other genres such as fantasy, magical realism, westerns, and in some cases fictional autobiography. To successfully negotiate this territory, we need to be triangulated among mainstream criticism, African American literature and culture, and sf itself when slavery is the issue at hand.

Mainstream as well as African American literature usually bases itself on character development and relationships between characters to reflect human reality as it occurs in the familiar world. But sf is as much about the environment, the constructed world, as it is about character. In truth, sf is more about the environment, the characters' relationships with the environment, and what these interactions can tell us about the possible futures and alternate pasts of humanity in the present. Hence, the extrapolative element changes our empirical world in either slight or significant ways; the setting is often somewhere else in space and time, like a comet, a spaceship, or even an antebellum plantation. Likewise, we cannot assume anything about the world of the sf text because its rules are most likely different from those in our experience of narrative realism—that is to say, we have to first recognize and understand the innate conditions of the sf text before we can grasp the story itself. For instance, the Sleepless in Kress's *Beggars in Spain* face all the jealousy, fear, hatred, prejudice, violence, oppression, and discrimination generated by the historical legacy of slavery in America.[5] Thus, Kress's future vision is able to take full advantage of the racial past because of the defamiliarized environment.

Because science fiction in general and meta-slavery in particular allow us to think about slavery in an artificial time continuum, we can see both the flaws in the telling of racial history and the most extreme outcomes of racism and oppression that have resulted in the "peculiar institution" of American slavery. We break away from the "actual" historical continuum when we read sf, going forward and backward in time, experiencing alternative realities and an unfamiliar humanity, leaving us free to change our history, our society, and ourselves in our examination of its process. Science fiction also gives us the chance to envision less virulent forms of bondage in addition to imagining the best possible alternative—a world without slavery. It gives us imagined possibilities to choose change for the better.

Indeed, in sf new things can be said about the intersection of otherhood and the literary challenge of reading and understanding. Such a thoughtful intersection offers transformative approaches to the study of race, because slavery can be situated beyond its historical conventions with one of otherhood's critical expressions, *meta-slavery*. The prefix *meta* calls attention to the distancing and analytical dimensions that sf provides in shedding light on representations of *slavery*. These dimensions, in turn, enable writers to transcend the narrative arc between historical and literary accounts of captivity and take us into a space where the interplay of past, present, and future allows readers to experience slavery and examine the painful social divisions it has created in our culture. Meta-slavery narratives help us realize how and why racisms rip and tear the fabric of society. Out of thousands of robot stories in science fiction, grandmaster Isaac Asimov's use and governance of robots seems the perfect place to begin a discussion of slavery and technology.

With his influential collection *I, Robot* (1950), Asimov describes the ascent of robots in relation to humanity. *I, Robot* is a collection of nine interrelated stories spanning roughly sixty years in robot history, from 1998 to 2059; the stories are linked by an interview with Dr. Susan Calvin, the world's first and best "Robopsychologist" at "U.S. Robots and Mechanical Men Inc." (vii–viii). As the interview progresses, Dr. Calvin relates many of her problematic encounters as well as those of her colleagues, Powell and Donovan, with robot/human evolution. From the beginnings of robotics in "Robbie" to the provocative conclusion with "The Evitable Conflict," Asimov influences our perceptions of intelligent machines by giving us glimpses into a possible future world of science and technology. The problem with this world is that slavery has been reinvented for humanity's mechanical offspring with three laws.

Central to Asimov's future are the famous three "laws" of robotics: First, "a robot may not injure a human being, or, through inaction, allow a human being to come to harm"; second, "a robot must obey the orders given it by human beings except where such orders would conflict with the First Law"; and third, "a robot must protect its own existence as long as such protection does not conflict with the First or Second Laws" (44–45). These laws ensure that humanity remains in charge, perhaps an unthinking construction of what might be called meta-slavery, wherein technology, i.e., enslaved robots, presents conditions that distance us from historical human slavery but promote interrogations of its essential characteristics. Asimov's laws regulate robot behavior toward humanity by placing conditions upon robot actions. More specifically, while Asimov's three laws are intended to ensure the safety and superiority of humans, they actually ensure the technological bondage and inferiority of robots.

In essence, the three laws require robots to protect humans from harm, to follow the commands of humans to the letter unless this conflicts with the first law, and to practice self-preservation if, and only if, the self-saving act does not interfere with the first two laws. Arguably then, Asimov is refashioning the slave codes that subjugated blacks while he serves a progressive philosophy based on the assumption that technological consciousness can be denied free will because it is inherently inferior. The concept of free will is obviously key because it is a repetition of the antebellum period in American history, a human sense that African slaves did not possess wills and were therefore not human. Asimov's relatively simple laws dictate that mechanized beings shall always be subordinate to humanity because men are afraid of their own creations; that the relationship between man and machine must be that of master and slave because robots are rivals that will surpass human capabilities. Therefore, humans must protect themselves by creating a limiting consciousness for robots in the form of a positronic brain. Such benign edicts are the basis of Asimov's seemingly inadvertent endorsement of racism as an acceptable starting point for relationships between conscious, intelligent entities. Ultimately, the robots of the stories take command of the Earth in a quiet uprising led by the "passing" robot Stephen Byerly. Robots can better protect humanity as a whole by managing the world's resources.

It is questionable whether Asimov saw the racial implications in his stories—that the difference between humanity and the robots mirrors, mechanically, the difference between white masters and black slaves. I am suggesting, however, that in science fiction robots represent technological descendants of humanity, thus becoming a logical step in our transformation to posthumanity. I contend, then, that these implications must be examined. If, for example, Asimov is indirectly suggesting that the practice of slavery is required for the betterment of humanity at the expense of artificial persons, he is apparently unconscious of the racist innuendo. Other scholars pick up on the underlying robot as slave connotation, and a formerly "hidden" race dialogue emerges. Consequently, I think it would be useful to investigate a few critical responses to Asimov's celebrated laws.

Polish sf writer and critic Stanislaw Lem critiques Asimov's three laws in his essay "Robots in Science Fiction" (1971). Lem justly claims that Asimov's "laws of robotics . . . give a wholly false picture of the real possibilities" by inverting "the old paradigm: where in myths the homunculi were villains, with demoniac features" (314). Lem goes on to make a parallel between man-robot relationships and that of "'the good white man' and the 'good-natured black servant'" (314). He states, "Asimov has thought of the robot as the 'positive hero' of science fiction, as having been doomed to eternal goodness by engineers" (314). Because Asimov's three laws are modeled on the stereotyped relationships that Lem has identified, particularly that of the master and slave, he finds it impossible to forgive Asimov for creating the robot laws that condemn them to be harmless to man as well as dumb, since a robot could not change its programming and subsequently evolve. Lem himself believes that the human attempt to play God by creating an artificial man, i.e., a robot, is an illogical one because it would not make sense for humans to build robots if these automatons were higher beings. In terms of sf, Lem considers the relatives of robots, cyborgs and computers, as having better value for the genre because they have an unlimited potential for stories whereas robots do not have infinite promise as mirror images of us.

Asimov himself proudly admits in his essay collection *Asimov on Science Fiction* (1981), "Robots can be the new servants—patient, uncomplaining, incapable of revolt. In human shape they can make use of the full range of technological tools devised for human beings and, when intelligent enough, can be friends as well as servants" (88–89). Asimov's robots resonate with the antebellum South's myth of a happy darkie—a primitive, childlike worker without a soul, incapable of much thought—cared for by the benevolent and wise master. This resonance is hard to ignore. As Edward James has observed in his own critique of Asimov, "The Three Laws restrain robots, just as the slave-owner expected (or hoped) that his black slaves would be restrained by custom, fear and conditioning to obey his every order" (40). Clearly, then, an otherhood reading allows us to consider the historical roots of *I, Robot*'s cultural bigotry.

The intersection of slavery, history, and sf suggests that these kinds of stories have a place in American cultural memory. Thus, meta-slavery tales are a kind of living history of slavery as told in sf. I believe that the meta-slavery metaphor is a particularly effective way to produce meaning from science fictional accounts of slavery, enabling us to achieve an artificial yet telling relation to the social structures in which slavery occurred. To conceive of meta-slavery in this way is to undermine the dominant, controlling, and authoritative myths of history such as social Darwinism. Meta-slavery changes, alters, and transforms our perceptions of slavery by its artificial yet "telling" nature. Perhaps the ultimate dream science fiction holds out for African Americans is the prospect for freedom of social transformation through science and technology; and this prospect demands a mental release from the legacy and turmoil left behind by American slavery.

Recognizing this need for release in addition to other insufficient underrepresentations is critical to identifying science fiction's historical impact on race relationships. More appropriately, sf literature must attend to the outright violence of the Jim Crow era along with attempts to scale back gains made by the mid-twentieth-century civil rights movement. When sf literature does not address these issues, it obscures the necessity of seeing race through an essential lens of otherhood, that is, along both *neo-slave* and *meta-slavery* narrative lines. Sf writer Octavia Butler is one who uses time travel, aliens, and genetic engineering in her work to interrogate slavery's historical paradigms.

Against the backdrop of Asimov's ambiguous trace of racialized paradigms, various works of Octavia Butler—*Kindred* (1979), "Bloodchild" (1984), and the Xenogenesis trilogy (originally published in the 1980s, collected and published as *Lilith's Brood* in 2000)—display how the temporal undercurrent of conversation on race relations takes place in sf. Butler's work might be considered as a rebuke to Asimov because of its explicit, visceral, and above all intelligent remembrance of slavery.[6]

Very few sf stories can be remotely classified as belonging to both the neo–slave narratives and the meta-slavery tales. *Kindred* is the only novel that comes readily to mind. I think it is necessary to distinguish between the roots of meta-slavery tales and neo–slave narratives because not many sf narratives can be or should be associated with the principles of neo-slavery. These principles reflect the complicated relationships between masters and slaves, particularly among the enslaved, as we witness courage and shame, love and hate, and the resulting anxieties meticulously depicted by modern writers in such a way as to encourage cultural awareness of this painful era in U.S. history. While certain attributes are shared with neo–slave narratives, meta-slavery tales go beyond this paradigm because they are not limited by the preexisting patterns of the slave narrative itself as most neo–slave narratives are. Also, the neo–slave narrative tradition is limited from a definitional standpoint in ways that sf is not. I believe the resources that sf can bring to bear on black experiences are simply greater than realistic modes of writing. Meta-slavery is the contact point between different types of reading protocols in relation to sf and the sociohistorical past of slavery.

In contrast to Asimov's work, a novel such as Octavia Butler's *Kindred* is very difficult to place because it does qualify as a fictional "rememory"[7] of slavery as well as being science fictional. Rememory brings the past into the present, forcing us to account for the experience of slavery and the problems slavery has caused for people living today. Rememory is a way of sharing the past experiences of others; it establishes a relationship between then and now. Thus, Butler takes us through time, making intimate contact with the historical reality of slavery. Put another way, "incorporating time travel, one of the common tropes of science fiction," allows Butler to establish "the movement between past and present as the central event of her novel" (Spaulding, 43). Though *Kindred* was considered a fantasy by Butler herself and as historical fiction—a neo–slave narrative—by most other academics, the aforementioned effect is achieved and made possible through science fiction alone.[8] Sandra Govan notes: "Butler's works do something else not generally asked of good historical fiction. They reach an entirely different audience, an established science fiction readership which, taken as a whole, is more accustomed to future histories and alien spaces than it is to authentic African and African American landscapes" (95). Put simply, *Kindred* surpasses the neo-slave-narrative paradigm by challenging our historical understanding of slavery and renewing it painfully. We lay claim to this silent past through her main character's struggle for identity and freedom because Butler chooses to utilize time travel and its inherent disorientation, alien contact, and displacement as her source of revelation.

Kindred is a postmodern slave narrative that uses the scientific fantasy of time traveling to change our conception of American history and position us to experience the horrible realities of slavery. Dana, a black woman living in 1976 San Francisco with her white husband, Kevin, tells the story as a first-person account of slavery. The couple is celebrating Dana's twenty-sixth birthday when she is impossibly and suddenly pulled back across time and space to early-nineteenth-century Maryland into the heart of the antebellum South—slavery. Rufus Weylin, the only white son of a plantation owner, is drowning in a river, and Dana saves him before she is scared back across time to her own present by an angry white man holding a rifle to her face. Yet she will return again and again to the plantation after this initial summons to save Rufus, consequently experiencing life as a slave as each trip lasts longer, becomes more intense and perilous. Dana's interaction with human beings from a different era is akin to alien contact because she is not truly familiar with their customs or beliefs despite her historical knowledge of slavery. In safeguarding Rufus, Dana will make certain that he reaches adulthood and has a girl child with his misappropriated slave Alice. This child will be the beginning of Dana's family line.

With this novel, Butler asks a pertinent question: "How can anybody endure being a slave?" Butler's answer is that Dana must survive her visits to the past to ensure her very existence in the future. While Butler's response may seem a simple one, there are three points of contention that complicate it: the tangled relationships of Dana, Alice, and Rufus; the intertextual moments between *Kindred* and actual slave narratives; and finally the time travel motif itself. Through the perspective of otherhood, all three of these factors together grant an authentic feel to Butler's text that makes it something more than a neo–slave narrative.

Conflict arises from the tragic love triangle of Dana, Alice, and Rufus. Dana and Alice are inextricably chained together by time, blood, and history just as they are tied together as "one woman" in Rufus's irrational mind: "'You were one woman' . . . 'You and her. One woman. Two halves of a whole'" (257). Because of this absurdity, Rufus coerces Dana into helping him rape Alice because of his unrequited and destructive love: "Go to her. Send her to me. I'll have her whether you help or not. All I want you to do is fix it so I don't have to beat her. You're no friend of hers if you won't do that much!" (164). Learning to do as she must, Dana fosters the subjugation and rape of her friend and matrilineal forebear, Alice, by Rufus. Dana reflects on the surreal nature of having willingly aided in the victimization of Alice, who "was like a sister," by Rufus, who "was like a younger brother" because "it was so hard to watch him hurting her—to know that he had to go on hurting her if my [Dana's] family was to exist at all" (180). The situation—Dana's continued existence—demands that Dana compromise her morals when she helps Rufus and learns to hate him. This moment of submission functions as the harbinger of "a life and death struggle" between Dana and Rufus (Hegel, 114).

Alice kills herself after Rufus attempts to control her by pretending to sell her children. Naturally, Rufus tries to replace her with Dana as his sexual property, his most heinous act of dehumanization, because what Rufus does severs the understanding that was shared—friendship. When he tries to force himself on her, he confirms his own identity by denying Dana, black and a slave, her identity—the basic instability of the master-slave relationship. Certainly, it takes power to deny anyone their identity as a human being. Dana, comprehending her plight that "a slave was a slave [and] anything could be done to her," chooses to live at the expense of Rufus's own life (260). As a twentieth-century black woman striving to bear all the viciousness of slavery, Dana reacts by grabbing her freedom and not succumbing to her realization of "how easily people could be trained to accept slavery" (101). Dana's rebellious spirit and determination to be free gives her the strength to kill Rufus by using her hidden knife. She achieves self-emancipation because she no longer fears death or psychological dependence on Rufus.

While *Kindred* functions well as a neo–slave narrative, echoing firsthand accounts of slavery, more importantly, the novel provides intertextual moments linking Dana's experience with perhaps the two most important autobiographies written by escaped slaves, those by Frederick Douglass and Harriet Jacobs. There are many parallels between Douglass's *Narrative* (1845) and Butler's *Kindred*, from the setting in Maryland, to the everyday, almost casual, violence, to various superstitions. However, the best parallel is how dangerous education and literacy can be to slaves who are made unfit for bondage by learning. Douglass recalls teaching as many as forty of his fellow slaves how to read on Sundays at Sabbath school because "their minds had been starved by their cruel masters" and "it was the delight of [his] soul to be doing something that looked like bettering the condition of [his] race" (88). He and enslaved friends decide to write themselves free passes and escape, but they are caught and Douglass barely manages to destroy his note in a fire without being noticed as the white men beat his friend Henry into submission.

Similarly, Dana is approached by a young slave named Nigel, Rufus's companion, who wants to learn how to read, and with little hesitation she agrees to teach him in the cookhouse. Dana is unquestionably careful, but not careful enough. One day she gives Nigel a surprise "spelling test," and he passes easily. As Dana is reflecting bitterly on Nigel's ease at learning compared to Rufus's difficulty, Tom Weylin, Rufus's father, steps into the cookhouse, an event that "wasn't supposed to happen . . . for as long as [Dana] had been on the plantation, it had not happened—no white had come into the cookhouse" (106). Weylin in his anger fails to notice that Dana is teaching Nigel because he is so blinded by her disobedience—stealing from his library and reading in the cookhouse—that Nigel has the chance to hide a pencil. Afraid for her life, Dana is hurled back to her time as Weylin proceeds to whip her bloody.

Just as Butler's *Kindred* resembles Douglass's autobiography, so it shares a likeness to Harriet Jacobs's *Incidents in the Life of a Slave Girl* (1861). The most powerful similarity occurs when children are sold from their mothers. In *Kindred*, the cook Sarah recounts how Tom Weylin sold her children.[9] Sarah states, "Marse Tom took my children, all but Carrie. And, bless God, Carrie ain't worth much as the others 'cause she can't talk. People think she ain't got good sense" (76). Much later in the novel Sarah reveals that she "just wanted to lay down and die" after her children were sold (250). This moment is nearly identical to one of Jacobs's reports regarding a slave auction:

> I saw a mother lead seven children to the auction-block. She knew that *some* of them would be taken from her; but they took *all* . . . I met that mother in the street, and her wild haggard face lives to-day in my mind. She wrung her hands in anguish, and exclaimed, 'Gone! All gone! Why *don't* God kill me?' (350–51)

Butler's sf neo–slave narrative mirrors exactly the agonizing endurance and courage of slave narratives. Not only does Butler's novel affectively function as a chronological record, *Kindred* itself becomes a living history that encourages a revision of both American history and race in science fiction.

Butler's science fictional moorings of the text break away from the neo-slave paradigm by collapsing Dana's experience and perception of time through time-travel. These sf moorings also grant sincerity to Dana's voice, which, in turn, disintegrates time boundaries and testifies to the horrors of slavery. Butler hardly explains Rufus's psychic ability, preferring to keep it as a part of the background, and thus allowing the atmospheric quality of slavery, of Dana's experience, to emerge as the foreground. Importantly, the means of Dana's time travel, her familial bond with Rufus, "underscores the inseparability of black and white in the United States," as Missy Kubitschek points out (41). This is also reflected by Dana's marriage to Kevin, a more hopeful forecast for race relations. As her complex relationship with Rufus develops, Dana attempts to thwart cultural history by molding the emerging man, her great-great-grandfather, into a benevolent master, and she fails miserably.

As present and past collide, *Kindred* interrogates the importance of freedom and its meaning to America. While only a few minutes or hours of her life pass in 1976 San Francisco, Dana's irregular trips into the past extend into days, weeks, and even months at a time as she is forced into slavery to look after Rufus as a boy. The nausea and disorientation that Dana experiences as she unwillingly shuttles back and forth across time also evokes a sense of the middle passage from Africa to the New World in the dark hold of slave ships. It is no mistake that Dana's last trip occurs on the Fourth of July in the bicentennial year of 1976. In this manner, Butler suggests that we have much more racial progress to make before any meaningful unity can take place. The date also makes an ironic evocation of the values of the American Revolution, "in life, liberty, and the pursuit of happiness." The various traumas of slavery embedded in the text are brought into the present by both Dana and Kevin as we read and work through our emotional difficulties toward the past and try to resolve them.

However, we are never able to become comfortable with the distance between the past and present in the structuring of this novel because Dana and Kevin deal with racism and prejudice in the present also. Dana first meets Kevin at a temporary employment agency, ironically dubbed a "slave market" (52), where they are the target of verbal abuse, being called "chocolate and vanilla porn" (56). When they decide to get married, Kevin is shocked by his sister's bigoted reaction, although Dana is not as surprised by her own family's reaction. Dana's aunt is not opposed to the wedding because "she prefers light-skinned blacks," but Dana's uncle takes her impending marriage to Kevin as a personal betrayal since he wanted her to marry a black man (111). Nonetheless, the couple ignore their families' hostilities to the interracial union and move forward into a life together largely oblivious to societal prejudice. In fact, their journey into the past makes them stronger in the present as they confront the overt oppressions of nineteenth-century slavery by sharing this awful experience as a couple. Weakly rooted in the past, the taboo of miscegenation is a full-blown part of Dana's present.

Although Dana breaks her link to Rufus by killing him on her last visit, she loses her left arm to the past, where it is "still caught somehow [at] the exact spot Rufus's fingers had grasped" (261). The loss of her limb is a visible reminder that the past is not simply history. As Butler's novel suggests, it has the capacity to hurt us deeply. As Tara McPherson fittingly remarks, "Dana . . . does not free herself from the past; rather, Rufus and Antebellum Maryland stay with her, haunting her like a phantom limb," suggesting that the past haunts many of us, that even in the present, racism is still crippling (91). *Kindred* revises both the slave narrative and science fiction by opening a rift in history that witnesses and testifies to the cultural memory of slavery in the present moment, a reading experience that meta-slavery encapsulates. Despite being classified as a neo–slave narrative, *Kindred* is the gateway to science fictional accounts of slavery as it contests and expands the boundaries of sf with unambiguous racial subjectivities.

With meta-slavery in mind, our knowledge of American slavery is superimposed on science fictional trappings. For instance, alien masters on a plantation planet make us stop and think about oppression in Butler's Nebula Award–winning "Bloodchild" (1984). The story is the first-person account of Gan, an Asian boy, who reveals that humanity has been virtually enslaved as brooders on another planet for the alien Tlic, which are three-meter-long centipedes. Over time, the feeling of enslavement seems to become harmless as the Tlic recognize humanity's intelligence. A symbiotic relationship develops between humanity and the Tlic. The Tlic provide humans with their sterile eggs, granting extended life, and in return human males are impregnated with Tlic eggs, which have to be removed by caesarean section before the hatched grubs eat through the host body. While Butler vehemently denied that "Bloodchild" is about slavery, that it is her "pregnant man story," critics often feel otherwise (Butler, *Bloodchild and Other Stories*, 30).

Nevertheless, there is room to interpret Butler's story as a quasi–slave narrative of the future because it "can also be read as a sly allegory of the violations that historically occurred under the institution of chattel slavery" (Crossley, xxv). Gan and his family certainly experience a slavelike bondage through their dependence on their Tlic family member, T'Gatoi, for protection, health, and the pleasure of her narcotic stings; Gan's family certainly seems like the property of T'Gatoi; and T'Gatoi certainly coerces Gan into carrying her children by threatening to impregnate Gan's older sister, Xuan Hoa. A close reading of "Bloodchild" demonstrates several of the general themes attributed to slave narratives, especially the first-person narration by a captive minority, in this case a human. The point is that Butler's success at remaking history and our relation to it demonstrates that slavery is an established part of sf, even with its own long-standing record of critical neglect.

Issues of meta-slavery occur in Butler's Xenogenesis trilogy as well. Butler uses meta-slavery to explicitly reawaken the unbearable memory of American slavery. She leaves no doubt about the racial context in her writing, offering direct representations of race relations in all of her work. The overarching plot of the trilogy involves humanity on the verge of annihilation because of nuclear holocaust. An alien species known as the Oankali is passing through the solar system when they detect and rescue the dying remnants of humanity. As it turns out, the completely alien and utterly grotesque Oankali are gene traders, a term with interesting connotations, since they also seem to be aggressive colonizers. They recognize two conflicting genes in humanity—hierarchical tendencies and intelligence—that when left together result in extinction. As Rebecca Holden explains, "The Oankali enforce their point of view, like groups of humans throughout history, with essentialist definitions. Again and again, they point to the genetic flaw in humanity in order to justify their colonization and virtual erasure of this species" (52). Thus, the Oankali treat humanity through biological engineering (cross-species reproduction), merging themselves with the human species to create something new—without permission. As a result, Butler's novels, *Dawn* (1987), *Adulthood Rites* (1988), and *Imago* (1989), mix the alien contact theme with elements of the slave narrative. For instance, the Oankali starship is a slave ship where the aliens enact a breeding program on a captive humanity. The Oankali are unwilling and unable to control their own hereditary disposition to acquire others' genetic material. In fact, the first book of Butler's trilogy, *Dawn*, shows us a kind of miscegenation that recalls the history of slavery's sexual exploitation.[10]

Dawn is the story of Lilith Iyapo, a black woman awakened from 250 years of suspended animation aboard a starship, cured of her cancer, and chosen to eventually lead humanity back to the restored Earth after acculturation with the Oankali. Butler presents us with a black woman who will give birth against her will to a new race of genetically engineered children of human-Oankali heritage. Much like slave owners in the antebellum era, the Oankali are in charge of Lilith's fertility as well as of any her offspring. As Jenny Wolmark points out, "Considerable emphasis is placed on the role of reproduction in the narrative because control over reproductive technology is a key issue in any political struggle for autonomy" (35). Lilith herself will come to be something "other" with her strength and memory enhancements, thus transcending humanity (*Dawn*, 120). Lilith asks her Oankali host, Jdahya, what will happen and he responds, "Your people will change. Your young will be more like us and ours more like you. Your hierarchical tendencies will be modified and if we learn to regenerate limbs and reshape our bodies, we'll share these abilities with you. That's part of the trade" (*Dawn*, 42). Hence, Butler crafts her meta-slavery tale to invert our perception of slavery through the aliens, thereby suggesting a strange kind of slave narrative where all of humanity is "other" as an incidental part of the story.

Dawn is a reworking of the slave narrative that develops an alternate view of race relations: humanity itself positioned as the colonized "other" by the superior biotechnology of an alien species. As Holden states, "The Oankali commitment to their own view of how things are and the 'truth' of genetic codes leads them to become imperialistic colonizers of the remaining remnants of humanity" (51). Indeed, Butler's novel participates in an open dialogue on race while Asimov foments dreams of a nonexistent past of slavery masked as robots—a dialogue confirmed by two things throughout the trilogy: resistance and change.

As the story progresses in the second and third books, the struggle of the resister humans to remain pure is futile as Lilith will reluctantly aid the Oankali in transforming the race through her construct children. Michelle Osherow points out in her argument that "the price of Lilith's empowerment is her estrangement, for when she is permitted to interact with humans she has been altered to so great an extent that her fellow earthlings do not recognize her as an ally . . . Lilith is the 'alien other' to all those with whom she comes in contact" (76). It seems logical that Lilith, a member of a despised race, would be the first human to reluctantly join the alien race. It is fascinating to contemplate humans positioned as the colonized "other" by the Oankali. Just as humans are configured as other, the Oankali are others, too, as they make use of living technologies to travel the stars and forcibly trade with various life forms. These ironic "otherhoods" occur often in sf but go unrecognized by critics because the necessary tools to effectively analyze and challenge race and racism in sf have not been provided. In fact, explorations of power and race dynamics ingrained in the annals of slavery and empire are essential to reinterpretations of science fiction.

As a counterpart to resistance, change has an equally important part to play in Butler's complex reworking of history. In *Adulthood Rites* and *Imago*, the issue of change is strongly represented by the children, who are something else entirely. Through use of living technology, the Oankali exploit a weaker, inferior humanity to create a monstrous humanity, where boundaries such as gender, race, sex, and class dissolve—a eugenic nightmare and a civilization's dream. Butler envisions a cyborg identity derived from the human Oankali genetic exchange.

She completely bypasses the human-machine interface problem tangential to any cyborg identity by the Oankali's use of living technology. In the landmark "Cyborg Manifesto" (1991) Donna Haraway names Butler among the twentieth-century cyborg storytellers, manipulating cyborg myth developed from "an informatics of domination" (161); and featuring the "constructions of women of colour and monstrous selves in feminist science fiction" (174). These cyborgs dramatically redefine our traditional social values: by making violence obsolete, by allowing males to leave family structures behind, by arriving at consensus decisions made by the adults of a community, and by respecting the sanctity of life, among other changes. And so Haraway's cyborg represents an otherhood perspective which addresses racism at the crossroads of gender oppression.

The human-Oankali construct children, Akin and Jodahs, represent the aforementioned changes in the second and third books respectively. In the second book, *Adulthood Rites*, Lilith's construct son, Akin, a human-Oankali child, is kidnapped by human resisters against the Oankali. He's taken to the Phoenix colony and bought by former friends of his mother. Xenophobia causes some of the resister colonies to participate in race wars against one another as well as the human-Oankali communities. This blind hatred is dangerous to Akin because he is racially marked by otherness in two ways: he is black and alien. Unquestionably, this double affliction is open to discussion of a new racial awareness offered by otherhood. Butler creates a complex racial subjectivity based on human disempowerment to consciously reflect on how such racism is displayed in sf by transforming familiar social boundaries that speak to the historical truths of racism in America.

Yet Akin learns that not all humans are fatally flawed despite their inclination for violence and stupidity. Akin is convinced that it is wrong for the resisters to face the choice of destruction or a forced joining with the Oankali as the growing starships will deplete the Earth. After he is rescued, Akin successfully argues for the establishment of a human colony on Mars because "there should be Humans who don't change or die" (*Adulthood Rites*, 371). The establishment of this colony goes against the interests of the alien authorities in that the resisters have been given a chance to break the hold of racism on humanity. In this respect, the demands of principle as opposed to power are, once again, explored in Butler's trilogy.

The final book, *Imago*, extends notions of otherhood even further by demonstrating how the unfailing application of democratic principles has the potential to break down racial boundaries and other kinds of subordination. *Imago* is the tale of Lilith's last child, Jodahs, a human-Oankali ooloi. Jodahs, a shape-shifting genetic engineer, is a being beyond gender as an ooloi—a third gender/sex. Like Akin, Jodahs involves his/herself with an undiscovered human village isolated in a South American mountain range. These humans are deformed from inbreeding and fearful of what the Oankali represent—change. Jodahs ultimately convinces the community to end its seclusion by healing a brother and sister and mating with them. Jodahs negotiates an agreement between the humans and the Oankali that allows the humans to decide to either go with the Oankali or go to the Mars colony. Jodahs is representative of issues of profound difference. S/he is completely different in that "it" defies racial and gender classifications as a shapeshifter who is human and nonhuman, natural and technological. As a mixed being, Jodahs is symbolic of race consciousness itself because s/he is aware of every evolutionary change that has produced a modern and conflicted humanity in addition to every transformation experienced by the Oankali. Understanding this state of being allows Jodahs to transcend race.[11]

As alien creatures, these children of humanity must help with the transition into a nonraced posthuman society. Butler contests racial constructions both directly and indirectly in this trilogy by crafting a meta-slavery narrative that is clearly linked to the history of slavery through its alien colonization theme. Unlike Asimov, Butler uses enslavement as the conscious foundation of much of her work. She focuses attention on the mostly unspoken nature of race relationships in sf and alters our perceptions of difference by honestly engaging our painful and violent memories of slavery. As Amanda Boulter suggests, Lilith Iyapo's cancer is a metaphor invoking "African-American history," and Butler's "representations of these experiences are curative, a homeopathic response to a painful past" (182).

As seen in Butler's work, meta-slavery can be subtle in science fiction when new races have been envisioned, even if the authors intentionally remind readers of slavery with their treatment of artificial people. David Brin imagines a near-utopian future where humans can make disposable clay copies of themselves to handle the routine every-day business of life, or hazardous jobs, or deviant sexual encounters. These throwaway clay bodies make possible all kinds of experiences, and at the end of the day humans can choose whether or not to retrieve their "ditto" memories and add them to their own (5). In such a fashion, humanity can live several lifetimes occupying multiple bodies each day. Brin builds such a world in his tech-noir novel *Kiln People* (2002).

However, Brin is best known for his Uplift novels,[12] a future history series where humanity becomes a spacefaring race on a galactic scale without the aid of other patron species. These patron species practice biological engineering in an effort to uplift other potential spacefar-ing life forms to sapience, with the caveat that the uplifted species are indentured for 100,000 years to their patrons. Humanity is an anomaly because they have no apparent patrons, though they have themselves uplifted dolphins and chimpanzees. As a technologically inferior race, humankind has several enemies among the great galactic powers that are eager to dominate or destroy humanity. Most of Brin's other works of fiction are concerned with the impact of technology developed by man for himself. And *Kiln People* is no different in this respect. Even so, I have chosen to explore *Kiln People* for two reasons. First, it is a rela-tively overlooked but important novel, a finalist for four different best science fiction/fantasy novel awards for 2002.[13] Second, I think Brin consciously builds an undercurrent of slavery in *Kiln People* because he feels that humanity cannot overcome its will to dominate other beings. In addition, I also believe that most readers will overlook the slavery subtext in amazement at Brin's skill at visualizing a possible future, and it is this subtext that should be essential because of Brin's depiction of racial difference in an increasingly globalized world.

Kiln People is ostensibly a detective story concerning the industrial espionage of new technologies and murder. Private investigator Albert Morris, along with his "ditective" selves, is hired to investigate the mystifying disappearance of the scientist who invented duplication technology (18). As he pursues the case, Albert can occupy many places at once as he or his copies converse with many people—humans, dit-tos, and humans masquerading as dittos. He and his dittos are soon caught up in the dangerous conspiracy surrounding the scientist's disappearance. Albert's various selves take on three evil masterminds who are using the science and philosophy of "soulistics" to search out and unlock eternal life (321). He eventually discovers his value to the conspirators as a perfect imprinter, ascertains the secret and successful development of new ditto-enhancements, and exposes the unexpected secret identity of his archenemy, Beta.

What makes *Kiln People* unusual is its first-person account told from four different points of view, all versions of Albert. The novel conveys our own sense of multiple lives. Through duplication technology, Brin is able to create multiple narrators from one person who all experience the day in disparate ways. Albert, perplexed by the different actions of each of his three dittos, especially the green, decides to get his real flesh personally involved in the investigation. The point here is that all the dittos' narratives give shape to a complex slave narrative as we go deeper into the story, where the dittos gather information for their master and act on his behalf. Although each "Albert" knows only what he knows, we benefit from their collective knowledge by witnessing and testifying to this future account of slavery, hinged upon Hegel's philosophy that the fear of death turns into the source of lordship and bondage—oppression (115). Three factors in the novel validate the nuanced occurrence of meta-slavery: new racisms of the color line, modern human problems, and ditto slavery itself. Clearly, Brin raises crucial questions about the future of racial identities and individual rights as the meaning of humanity changes through his calculated redesign.

A literal DuBoisian color line exists between the dittos of assorted colors as well as between the dittos and the "bland looking" humans "ranging from pale-almost white to chocolate brown" (37). And this color line of the future produces new racisms based on the quality of the commercial materials purchased for ditto blanks. Dittos come in many different colors, showing the class and suggesting the capabilities of the oven-baked golem.[14] Brin uses "ditto" and "golem" more or less interchangeably in the text. Also, a golem is derisively known as a "ditto," "rox," and "mule," among other things, thus suggesting a sense of bigotry toward dittos by humankind—something similar to the black experience of contemptuous name-calling in America.

An entirely complex ditto hierarchy exists. Orange dittos live purely for industrial labor; blue-skinned cop dittos possess "needle-tipped fingers coated with knockout oil [that] would stop any golem or human cold" (9); cheap green roxes aren't overly smart, but they are good for taking care of domestic household tasks like cleaning. At the higher end, gray dittos are a considerable step up in class because they are nearly as smart as their originals, and often come loaded with customized options. Ivory copies are expensive pleasure models. Ironically, ebony dittos are intellectual specialists with tremendous powers of concentration. I find this peculiar in that these attributes are a departure from previous biased representations of black intelligence in America, surely a conscious choice made by Brin for that very reason. At the very top of the line are the exorbitantly priced platinums with unknown abilities. Even "archies"—real humans—respect these models because they signify the wealth and power of their originals. Clay people are also subjected to familiar kinds of bigotry "because of skin color" (4) as authentic humans target golems for all kinds of abuse just for passing through town. These humans use the dittos' color as a racial slur, such as "greenie," and threaten them with violence, mirroring much of white sentiment towards black throughout American history. Unmistakably, Brin is commenting on the nature of racism in having the kiln people the object of human hatred, and yet this commentary is veiled by technology. In other words, technology masks the racial paranoia of this world as prominent race paradigms are grafted onto the artificial bodies. The similarities between "raced" bodies and "technologized" bodies are easy to miss without a sense of otherhood.

Dittos are also viewed as chattel by the human minority. They can be harmed without fear of criminal prosecution; the only possible penalty is a fine. And the dittos accept their bondage without qualms. Though they are not human, they literally possess a human's soul, a symbolic move on Brin's part recalling the argument of whether African slaves were truly human, whether they were in possession of a soul. In the context of a meta-slavery reading, Brin's novel can be said to reinvent old concepts of discrimination by recasting race and racism in a technological form, and yet nothing has truly changed because this new kind of racism is based on skin color. As described above, the novel's scenario seems to be that the popularity of the cheap technology has led to, or at least facilitated the establishment of, a color line reflecting the human problems of this world, such as unemployment and continual surveillance.

With his extrapolation, Brin is exploring the idea of racial identity in conjunction with meta-slavery, implying that the industrial development of replication technologies for the human soul will result in "a new race of disposable beings"—in other words, slaves (35). Such an implication has meaning for us today in terms of otherhood. The social consequences of a world governed by this imaginary technology powerfully recall the institution of slavery, because the novel's humanity severely mistreats a new race of duplicate beings. Human owners of dittos are largely unappreciative of their mostly devoted servants. They regard dittos as second-class citizens, "a perfect serving class that can't rebel and always knows what to do" (524). In fact, this civilization is built on the notion of human superiority, and the world's economic stability depends on it—a situation highly reminiscent of antebellum Southern society. While Brin's central theme is certainly identity, slavery is a subtext that cannot be overlooked since dittos are disposable property, even though they are, if only for a limited time, sentient beings with the capacity to think and feel.

Another issue shared by *Kiln People* and slave narratives is the generation of realism through first-person narration of a mystery. In other words, the air of mystery belonging to detective fiction is analogous to the plots of slave narratives, according to Charles Davis and Henry Louis Gates Jr., "since the plots of all the slave narratives turn upon the resolution of a mystery, already resolved in fact by the first-person 'detective' narrator" (xv). What the authors mean by "mystery" is that the experience of slavery is an unsettling one and the details of escape are obscured or kept secret to arouse a sense of speculation beyond the end of the narrative itself. Brin's crime story goes to the core of otherhood as it creates an enslaved artificial populace. For example, the sense of technoscientific bondage in the text begins with an "ID pellet" in the center of a ditto's forehead (95). This identification marker is a new kind of shackle, a "tag" (6) with its "owner's code" on it (5) that makes it easy to identify the human to which the ditto belongs. As a matter of custom, "a golem-duplicate has to show his tag to a realperson, on demand" (6). In the best sf tradition, Brin allows us to make our own conclusions; in this case about the ethics of a technological enslavement, where humans can imprint their consciousness upon clay replicas who accomplish tasks for their human archetypes.

Brin also explores the idea of abolition and the ethical controversy generated by pro-slavery and anti-slavery factions. Given the notion of a technology that binds others, it seems likely that questions concerning the value of the human soul are central to understanding how and why this text is a meta-slavery narrative. Two examples, one from each faction, best encapsulate this contentious debate in the textual world. Just as it did in the American past, slavery in Brin's novel produces uncompromising activists on either side of the debate. On the one hand, there are extremists known as "mancies" who believe that ditto existence is just as sacred as humanity's and that enslaving them is immoral (42). Nonetheless, this group cannot seem to live without the convenience of ditto technology. On the other hand, the camp known as "True Lifers" consists entirely of archies who denounce the daily making of disposable people because these clay beings are technological abominations against God's will. Of course, both of these fanatical groups "think Universal Kilns is a front for the devil" (63). Certainly, Brin exploits the issue of abolition momentarily to foreground slavery in the text. I find this issue fascinating today because technoscience and belief in God seemingly do not mix well together. Oddly enough, a technospiritual movement exists in our world, and Brin is taking advantage of this paradox. A perfect example is how churches are making use of technology to recruit new believers as pastors podcast sermons around the globe on the World Wide Web. In addition, the Wachowski brothers' film *The Matrix* (1999) is a relevant illustration; in it a cyborgized computer hacker is the messiah of an enslaved mankind in its war with the machines.

As the novel ends, ditto slavery still exists. Yet, Brin suggests that "interesting times" are ahead because the release of "the new golem-technologies"—long-lived dittos, remote dittoing, and ditto-to-ditto copying—will result in a "social war" (564). As the novel's American title suggests, oven-baked dittos are technologically enslaved beings designed to serve their human counterparts. Perhaps even more fascinating, the British title, *Kil'n People*, is a pun on "killing people," which suggests that some kind of ditto revolt is near. Unquestionably, the undercurrent of Brin's novel is that of meta-slavery because of its many implications for society's abuse of technology that creates new repetitions of racism. The promise of technocracy in this possible future has spectacularly failed to make racial designations and markers of race irrelevant; instead, it has invented and envisioned entirely new kinds of people to oppress.

Whereas *Kiln People* explores slavery in the future, Steven Barnes's *Lion's Blood* (2002) is an equally powerful story of meta-slavery set in an alternate nineteenth-century world, which continues in the novel's sequel, *Zulu Heart* (2003). Blacks and whites have switched positions in the master-slave relationship, but this is a device used to show how all of humanity is essentially the same in its desires for freedom and the ability to oppress. Barnes makes racial borders indistinct for his audience because of this switch. Even more so, we are seeing humanity with alien eyes, or perhaps we are aliens with racialized eyes measuring the environment by standards not our own. Barnes rewrites the myth of American slavery, revealing its dehumanizing effects on both slaves and masters while simultaneously exploring the meaning of friendship, honor, religion, and humanity. He capitalizes on familiar notions of race by twisting our national memory of the past, allowing us to question the racialized formations of American culture and those of science fiction as well. *Lion's Blood* is not a simple alternate history tale because it can be used to teach the importance of tolerance and equality. America is a composite experience.

Lion's Blood has two protagonists: Aidan O'Dere, an Irish boy captured and sold into slavery in the New World, and Kai ibn Jallaleddin ibn Rashid, the privileged second son of a powerful black noble. Kai leads a life of privilege, worshipping according to the teachings of Islam and learning the basics of warfare, while Aidan is just another of the many white slaves working on the estate of Dar Kush. Though the ruling family of Dar Kush is known to indulge its white population, allowing slaves to keep their "pagan" names and Christian beliefs, the seeming tranquillity of the plantation masks a world where slave families are torn apart to pay bets, whippings and rapes are routine, numerous racist taunts and slights are delivered, and runaways are slaughtered by vicious animals. An uneasy friendship, somewhat similar to that of Dana Franklin and Rufus Weylin in *Kindred*, develops between the two boys as the years pass and they both mature. This friendship is a complex articulation of Hegel's master-slave dialectic in *Phenomenology of Spirit* (1807) because both Aidan and Kai are seeking recognition of the self (i.e., mastery of ego). The reality of their master-slave relationship permeates their lives and continuously assaults their closeness. Despite their many differences, each dreams about a life of dignity and freedom. Aidan participates in a slave revolt that forever changes the outwardly peaceful atmosphere of Dar Kush.[15] Subsequent tension between Azteca, the indigenous empire to the south, and Bilalistan, an African colony in North America, leads to armed conflict, during which Kai and Aidan learn to trust in one another again as a matter of survival, that their blood is essentially the same, neither black nor white. Writing like this is important because Barnes is making this science fictional retelling of slavery transparent by suggesting that given the chance blacks would have been just as harsh on whites. Significantly, Barnes believes the violent nature of the human species is universal.

While Barnes has been writing sf for over twenty-five years, he has been overshadowed by the overwhelming presence of Delany and Butler, perhaps suggesting that there is not enough room in the genre for other people of color to receive much critical attention. Science fiction critic Greg Beatty believes that *"Lion's Blood* is Barnes's best work to date"* because of "how Barnes uses history in the novel" (4). Beatty identifies the strength of the novel as Barnes's use of the power of race in history to create a paradigm shift, "one that is as likely to be the site of science-fictional change as any other" (5). Beatty is correct. Barnes's intense alternate history presents a defamiliarized slave plantation saga set in the Deep South—an African-ruled South where Islam holds sway.[16] I believe that four factors make *Lion's Blood* such a compelling example of meta-slavery: the time system, the impact of religion, paradox events, and repetitions of slavery.

Nothing is simple about Barnes's portrayal of bondage and freedom in this alternate world, least of all time. The novel begins in the year 1279, or, to those who worship the son of Mary, 1863. "America" has been settled by Islamic Africa, not by Christian Europe, which has been locked in the Dark Ages by various plagues. Arabic is "the great trading tongue, uniting a thousand tribes, a hundred nations" (141) and

Islam the dominant religion. It is appropriate to question how we get to the place Barnes created and still have historical personages such as Socrates, Alexander the Great, Da Vinci, Montezuma, and Shaka Zulu. In the world of *Lion's Blood*, history began to change around the time of Socrates, or 400 BC, when "most Greek philosophers had fled to Egypt along with Socrates," who refused to drink the lethal draught of hemlock that killed him in our world (214). Other pivotal events in our world history also happen differently, such as the invention of the "steamscrew" in AD 200, whereby Africans dominate the Nile with their boats (140). And the alternate history continues to grow from there. Barnes carefully establishes the supremacy of Islam over Christianity and of African civilization over a European one, and sets the stage for Islamic Africans to colonize the "New World" with the help of enslaved whites. The point here is that Barnes *is* reimagining race and racism as not all that different in a changed world. His disruption of our "reality" indelibly marks sf by stressing the social realities of racism that exist at the intersections of national memory, alternate history, and otherhood.

This history is made all the more convincing by Barnes's use of two calendars to impart a sense of time. Our own Gregorian calendar makes it possible for us to compare his alternate history with our history. However, he also reflects the Africanized Muslim world through an Islamic calendar that begins about six hundred years later with the death of Muhammad. Thus, the novel starts in the Gregorian year of 1863 in contrast to year 1279 of the Islamic calendar. I think the alternative systems of time measurement ingeniously function as a doubling of vision, highlighting the perspectives of Aidan and Kai as well as revealing to us how history truly works—that it is always shaped by the victors and that "others" have no "true" history.[17] Through his calendars, Barnes provides us with a split view of the past that explains the main faults of humanity through enslavement, its penchant for domination and racism. Despite the Islamic hegemony, I, as a reader, certainly thought in terms of the Gregorian calendar in our world, even though Euro-American civilization was in a subordinate position. Barnes relies on the Gregorian calendar for this very reason, because its meaning to us is predicated on Euro-American dominion. This reluctance to break with our timeline presents a problem because there is never any doubt that the white hero Aidan will survive and prosper. Another flaw in the text is the absence of an Aztec calendar because it raises the question of whether native New Worlders are living in a "primitive" timeless age. Barnes problematically estranges our sense of history as he alters how slavery played out in our own world. By focusing on religious convictions as well as the relationship of Aidan and Kai, he guides us through a common experience of slavery on one level and a series of ironic moments on a second level.

Spirituality and religion have a particular significance in this alternate history. Faith is needed to survive slavery just as it is necessary to oppress others. Barnes carefully crafts an amalgamated spirituality for the white slaves that combines Celtic practices of tree worship, ancestor worship, other pagan rituals, and a form of Christianity in order to make the parallel nature of this world believable. He provides a subtle imitation of the African religions that arose in the slave quarters of the Deep South in our history and adeptly shapes this echo of slave mysticism into history as it might have occurred. As many American slaves were forced to accept Christianity, most of the Muslim masters of Bilalistan forced an Islamic conversion on their livestock, though they rightly feared false conversions by slaves seeking a sense of equality and freedom.

I think Barnes's exploration of Islam overshadows the technological and scientific aspects of the novel, an important step for establishing humanity—rather than technology and science—as the driving force of his science fiction. His application of Muslim principles juxtaposes the imaginary Fatimite faith with the imaginary Sufi faith, perhaps a deliberate echo of Catholicism and Protestantism. Readers get a sense that the novel is shaped by traditional U.S. anti-Catholicism with Sufis in the position of Catholics, resulting in a kind of dystopian version of what might have happened if the Protestants had not dominated early American life. On the one hand, the Fatimites have spiritual leaders, "the Ayotallah" in Africa and "the Ulema," in Bilalistan, who is very likely corrupted by greed (292). And on the other, the Sufi sect, persecuted though not illegal, believes that the path to Allah is direct, and those who truly love Allah "must beware of those who twist His holy word for power" (317). This notion complicates the Catholic/Protestant analogy a bit since it's the Protestants who emphasize a direct relationship with God. Through Kai's conversion to the Sufi faith, we are able to see how the principles of Islam establish a moral compass as he endures tremendous difficulties in his spiritual growth and comes to know himself. He seeks Allah for understanding because the complex nature of having a slave for a best friend transcends the master/slave paradigm. Kai's sensibility toward humanity dictates his need for spiritual guidance in a world where color defines a man's position.

Barnes further complicates the spiritual issues raised by Islamic-Christian tensions by drawing distinctions between Northern Africans as Muslims and sub-Saharan Africans. Zulus in the text are presented as racist savages embodied by the historical figure of Shaka Zulu. The legendary South African warrior king of our history is every bit as mad, egotistical, and bloodthirsty when transplanted to the nineteenth-century alternate New World. His death in the novel mirrors that in real life.[18] Whether Barnes is not fully thinking through the differences between depicting them as savages or depicting Arab perceptions of them as savages, it becomes necessary to at least acknowledge the Arab slave trade of Africans. Consequently, Barnes's inversion is not quite as straightforward as the text suggests. Likewise, there is something to be said about the Aztecs—who seem to be savages that practice human sacrifice—and the absence of other Native Americans. To my way of thinking, a bit of racist erasure occurs because these fictional versions of real-world civilizations are still depicted as being trappings in a savage culture, though they have not been the victims of European genocide.

A combination of alternate time and religious conviction creates several instances of paradox between the textual world and our own that deepen our understanding of the relevance of freedom. For example, upon arriving in a harbor in the New World, Aidan is astonished by his first glimpse of a colossus "standing astride a stone island, its titanic back turned to them . . . Taller than thirty men, the great columns of its legs were like the spurs of a mountainside, its shoulders as wide as the horizon" (52). Barnes consciously replaces our Statue of Liberty on Ellis Island with the statue of a majestic black man on an island in the Gulf of Mexico. When I think of the Statue of Liberty, I immediately think of freedom, its costs, and the spirit of Americans; it is a defining landmark of the United States.[19] In contrast, when I think of a giant black man, I think of the racist paranoia that such a statue might project in our world. In Barnes's world, however, the black statue symbolizes the spirit and dreams of Bilalistan, something that mirrors the sentiment in our world, a paradoxical moment, because Aidan is not coming as a person with dreams of a better life. Instead, his innocence has been stolen by the horrors of the middle passage and his impending subjugation. Hence, the statue comes to represent forceful displacement and an alienated existence. In contrast to Asimov, then, we can see Barnes consciously reworking sf to deal with race relations in the open.

Another paradox occurs in the war between Bilalistan and Azteca as the famous battle for the Alamo is reenacted at the battle for the "Shrine of the Fathers" (84). Barnes's reinvention of history signals the colonial impulses of his world, the high cost of liberty for all men. It also signals how the fanaticism of faith demonstrates the dangerous combination of religion, politics, and race. After this battle, Kai provides Aidan with his free papers, one of which reads, "DECLARATION OF EMANCIPATION" granting "the rights of citizenship" to Aidan and his family because of his "distinguished service to the throne" (588). This moment is analogous to the missed opportunities for equality in our own history. Barnes deliberately joins Thomas Jefferson's contradictory idealism in the Declaration of Independence, where all men are created equal, with Abraham Lincoln's Emancipation Proclamation, which ostensibly freed black slaves. Still, Aidan has to produce his documents every time he and his family are "stopped by road patrols" on their way west; he also carries "a map . . . showing places where free whites might find shelter and food along the way"—an intentional merging of the Underground Railroad and free papers (597).

Though arguably racist, Barnes's reinvention of slavery is quite impressive because of its racial role reversals, which allow him to subconsciously engage his audience in this painful topic. Aidan's experience of bondage reads like a slave narrative. His childhood in Eire is shattered when Viking raiders invade his "crannog," murder his father, and kidnap the rest of his family (3). They're taken to an unknown trading port, where his mother, Deidre, convinces their captors to keep them together (34). He also sees black people for the first time, a supremely alienating moment, and thinks of them as "demons that looked like human beings smeared with soot or mud . . . bare heads . . . crowned with what looked more like black lamb's wool than real hair . . . their lips were thick, noses wide and blunt" babbling "in a language Aidan had never heard" (34–35). In fact, this moment in the story is a deliberate parallel of Olaudah Equiano's first contact with Europeans.[20] Aidan and his family endure a long terrifying voyage across the ocean by airship to the New World, a middle passage from Western Europe to Bilalistan, echoing the triangle trade of slavery: Africa, the Americas, and Europe. In the New World Aidan suffers through the absolute humiliation of a public auction, whereupon he and his mother are sold to Dar Kush while his twin sister is sold into the unknown. Aidan and his ailing mother take up residence in a small shack in the plantation's slave quarters, also known as "Ghost Town" (113). From this point, the description of daily plantation life is similar to that of most slave narratives except, of course, the slaves are white.

The intensity of slavery is perhaps best captured in one of the several imaginary slave songs that Barnes uses to provide us with a moment of detached familiarity. Music is surely a key element in a culture based on slavery because it records an oral history through song.[21] With the help of musician Heather Alexander's corresponding album, *Insh'Allah: The Music of Lion's Blood*, Barnes's alternate world is set to music, brought to life by providing an auditory setting. Alexander's melding of Celtic, African, and Middle Eastern sounds produces another registry for understanding the melancholy richness of it. In the novel, the song "Laddie Are Ya Workin?" has one meaning for white slaves and a distinctly different meaning for the black masters:

> *Storm clouds gather as the hands to the field*
> *Raindrops scatter as the land's made to yield*
> *Body separate from its fine golden head*
> *Stalk and sheaf and chaff for a bed*
>
> *Cut her low, swing her round*
> *Iron wire, tightly bound*
> *Thresh the teff by the morning lark,*
> *Lie in her arms in the still of dark,*
> *Laddie are ya workin'?* (232)

To the slaves this is a song of mourning though it masks an undertone of rage that the masters are incapable of hearing. Instead, the masters believe it is a simple, if not crude, work song. This double meaning indicates Barnes's meaningful consideration of the nature of slavery, its subtle deceptions and misunderstandings. This is a deliberate reminder of American slavery and its spirituals and how these songs add another dimension to Barnes's alternate history. Regarding slave songs in his own narrative, Frederick Douglass writes:

> I have often been utterly astonished, since I came to the north, to find persons who could speak of the singing, among slaves, as evidence of their contentment and happiness. It is impossible to conceive of a greater mistake. Slaves sing most when they are most unhappy. The songs of the slave represent the sorrows of his heart; and he is relieved by them, only as an aching heart is relieved by its tears. (30)

The historical processes of race are thoroughly explored in *Lion's Blood* and its sequel, *Zulu Heart* (2003), where Barnes imagines African intervention in the American complex of the New World juxtaposed against our myth of freedom. As Beatty suggests, "The myth of America . . . is the myth of liberty" (5). Our experience of meta-slavery in this text vividly renders a sense of anger and sadness at racism and its antecedents. However, Barnes also designates the strength and beauty of the human spirit as a necessary means in defying oppression. And this notion is not myth, but simple truth. In other words, Barnes uses the power of ideology to reverse the broader conception of history which sees white men as its subjects and is fundamentally incapable of seeing beyond that contradiction. While it is undoubtedly true that Barnes brings his various prejudices to bear, he also functions within an ideological constraint of which he seems to be unaware. For example, he does present a monolithic view of indigenous people. This is not to say that Barnes is not successful with his tale of meta-slavery, but he falls short of breaking the chains of race and racism in this regard. Nonetheless, Barnes's writing suggests that racism is a crucial and undying element in sf, and he uses his stories, permeated with historical precedents, to impart creative approaches for discerning, resisting, and fighting racism in the genre.

Meta-slavery tales, and in some respect neo–slave narratives, are essential to the study of race in science fiction, especially as they record the abiding interest in slavery's legacy. Although science fiction is largely overlooked by the academy on the subject of race, meta-slavery narratives can make positive contributions to the ongoing dialogue on race and American identity. Such sf stories as *Stars in My Pocket like Grains of Sand, Kindred, Kiln People,* and *Lion's Blood* have certainly been patterned after slave narratives, consciously or otherwise. These stories and others like them reveal the imbalance between the reality of race and the dream of freedom that still endures in America today. By exploring how slavery plays itself out in sf, meta-slavery gets at notions of disempowerment, unconscious reflections of racism, and also direct confrontations of racist attitudes displayed in sf. Meta-slavery demonstrates how slavery lives on in our cultural awareness and helps us ask how to deal with this history. Such interchange is implicit in any discussion of race. These narratives also articulate disempowerment as well as the cultural horrors of American history, if not Western history, transforming literary expressions of this painful time into complex associations of racial subjectivities. Consequently, the various tools of otherhood such as meta-slavery provide us with a means to explore the black/white binaries of science fiction in new ways. So the next chapter continues along the historical chain of black-white race relations by considering how segregation has been recorded in science fiction through various Jim Crow extrapolations.

3

Jim Crow Extrapolations

Imagine that green-skinned humanoids representing a galactic federation of civilized worlds set down on Earth to explore the possibility of shaping humanity into a refined society despite problems of human aggression. A husband and wife team, Flin and Ruvi, advanced beyond seeing other beings in terms of color, are driving through the Mississippi countryside when they stop in the town of Grand Falls. While there, they are subjected to all kinds of racist insults such as "greenie" and "green nigger." A southern minister clearly reveals his prejudicial beliefs by stating to Flin, "I been seeing faces on my teevee for years. Green faces like yours. Red ones, blue ones, purple ones, yellow ones—all the colors of the rainbow, and what I want to know is, ain't you got any white folks out there?" (Brackett, 231). Fleeing in fear for their personal safety, Flin and Ruvi are pursued by several young white men, led by Jed, who continues their education in racism by running the aliens off the road. Jed teaches them the rules of living Jim Crow, particularly the third lesson: "And this is one you better remember and write out and hang up where all the other red, blue, green and purple niggers can see it. *You never lay a hand on a white man.* Never. No matter what" (236–37). After beating Flin, the group of men goes on to rape his wife, forcing the aliens to learn the emotion of hatred. As the story ends, this hatred prompts Flin to come back to the town a few months later with some kind of advanced weapon from off world. The implication is clear: Flin is going to wipe the town off the face of the Earth. It seems that this "advanced" alien is not much better than humanity itself because he has decided without consulting his superiors that most humans are inflexible, are not fit to join the galactic federation, and should be isolated or destroyed.

Leigh Brackett's story "All the Colors of the Rainbow" (1957) contains the hallmarks of the nearly century-long Jim Crow era—discrimination, dehumanization, violence, oppression, blind hatred, racial exclusion, derogatory slurs. Brackett reminds us of some of the ways sf can too easily lend itself to racist assumptions by having white supremacists, on the grounds of their innate superiority, use the scientific rationale of social Darwinism to justify their inhumane treatment of the civilized alien couple. Drawing on the culture of her time, Brackett writes an explicit sf race story with the malicious rhetoric of segregation. Clearly, she recognizes and caricatures the depravity of racist beliefs at the waning moments of the Jim Crow era. However, she does not envision any response other than revenge.[1] Revenge is significant here because such a motive was difficult for black Americans to enact, let alone imagine, in this time period.

As Brackett's story suggests, science fiction has repeatedly called attention to and challenged Jim Crow segregation and other kinds of separatism. Indeed, sf has been used to bear witness to a legacy of racism driven by the notion of social Darwinism. The durability of long-standing cultural stereotypes reaffirms that America is exceedingly cognizant of its colors—black, brown, red, yellow, and white—regardless of its democratic ideals. One of the goals of this chapter is to look at some of the most obvious kinds of sf narratives that explicitly concern themselves not just with race, but with segregation and separation driven by racial difference established by the color line. Along with the tendency of our national memory to recall issues of segregation as they were played out in the U.S. Supreme Court, connections between the social realities of racism that exist at the cultural intersections of separatism and extrapolation can be explored through otherhood. As a necessary step in charting race in sf, critical attention must be paid to those sf writers who use extrapolation as an instrument to explore past or even new race paradigms. To take this step, I examine a variety of extrapolations stemming from the Jim Crow era—such as a black exodus to Mars, federal separatism, a whitening process for blacks, a black world order, private prisons, and a trade offer from aliens.

While legal and cultural change has largely led to the dismantling of Jim Crow protocols, the racial thinking and prejudice that gave rise to them has proved stubbornly resistant to eradication, and part of the concern of this book is with the possibility that protocols very much like those of Jim Crow have gone unexamined in sf. Indeed, an even greater concern here is that sf may be consciously and unconsciously reinscribing Jim Crow in our imagining of the future. The social construction of race in sf seems to demand a dialectic of superior/inferior relationships designed to promote the domination of one group over another. Sf's various responses to separatism, particularly in a time when entire generations do not remember the reality of segregation, can be used to consider the many outcomes of separatism and possibly offer instructive visions of meaningful alternatives.

All separatism stories in sf examine the notion of cultural displacement and the resulting changes in human interactions. Some suggest that humanity will unite as one race, while others suggest the impossibility of such a union. All, however, serve to remind us that racial difference is robust in its endurance. The ruling class of a society attempts to maintain tiers of membership by alienating various minority groups through the exercise of power in some form such as violence or the perpetuation of social stereotypes. In this respect, sf writers use extrapolation to produce possible racial futures that display segregation as well as offer solutions to racial tensions. When we critically examine these two notions together, we can see that Jim Crow extrapolations reflect the sense of change that occurs between sf history and racial history.

Seeing and recognizing connections between history, literature, and sf is important when considering the extrapolations of segregation offered by various sf writers because we are sensitized to such Jim Crow imaginings in sf—inadvertent or otherwise. Some of these sf separatism stories are deeply rooted in a rich tradition of social protest in American culture and literature. And one constant target of this protest has been racial segregation, effected and emblemized by the laws and practices referred to as Jim Crow. The practice of segregation as we know of it began shortly after the end of the Civil War in 1865 and of Reconstruction roughly twelve years later. "A hatred of blacks furthered by religion, science, and history extended right across the wide American landscape," as historian Jerrold Packard recounts in

American Nightmare: The History of Jim Crow (2002). This complex system of racial laws and customs became known as Jim Crow segregation, and it guaranteed white supremacy because a black American "ignored or violated" the etiquette of Jim Crow "at peril to his or her life" (164). By advocating inflexible patterns of racial segregation, brazenly manipulating courts, and imposing ignorance among blacks, the white South maintained an unabated level of violence and terror well into the middle of the twentieth century. Furthermore, the color line was redrawn in bolder and more violent strokes that were underpinned by scientific and cultural justifications for white supremacy; racism was largely fashionable. In fact, the rhetoric of white superiority in both the North and the South reached an ever-widening audience through the works of popular Southern writers such as Thomas Dixon. Dixon's Klan trilogy, *The Leopard's Spots* (1902), *The Clansman* (1905), and *The Traitor* (1907), might itself be considered as sf because it presents a racist extrapolation that envisions an epic racial conflict and promotes a fear of miscegenation, racial equality, and the purity of white womanhood as the strength of white society.[2]

Science fiction writers provide valuable points of intersection between extrapolation and cultural memory when they trace the progression of racial history in "separatism" stories. Such stories highlight political events that force apart the races and result in all manners of chaos. A case in point is Martin R. Delany's *Blake; or, the Huts of America* (1859) in which the black hero, Blake, advocates a militant uprising against the oppression of slavery in the antebellum South, signaled by the imagined liberation of Cuba. W. E. B. DuBois's *Dark Princess: A Romance* (1928) is another depiction of segregation, in which the story's black protagonist becomes involved in a pan-African movement to unite the dark people of the world against their oppressors. The key is when Mathew Towns, a black medical student, is barred from practical medical training because of his race. Both Delany and DuBois turn to sf in a symbolic response to a racist American society, with differing projections of otherhood.

Other separatism stories emphasize a community that withdraws or secedes from a government, or a leader who advocates dissociation from the dominant culture or isolation of a marginal group. For instance, Sutton E. Griggs's *Imperium in Imperio* (1899) explores philosophical differences between two educated black men, the dark-skinned Belton Piedmont and the mulatto Bernard Belgrave, who belong to a secret society known as the Imperium, which seeks to establish a black state. Another interpretation is Warren Miller's *The Siege of Harlem* (1964), where an old black man relates the history of the first year of Harlem's secession from the United States. It provides a contrast to DuBois's novel in that this seemingly unique political fantasy of secession provides an alternate postcolonial history that gauges the white reaction to a black withdrawal—siege, espionage, betrayal, assassination, and invasion forces. While more than half a century passes between these books, the idea of a forceful black withdrawal from the United States remains appealing to black writers because of the imagined benefits of black unity. Clearly, these stories also provide a meaningful response to the social practices of Jim Crow.

Other separation stories portray black leaders who encourage dissociation from the dominant culture. William Melvin Kelley's *A Different Drummer* (1962) features an imaginary southern state where a common black man, Tucker Caliban,[3] begins a black exodus by simply walking away from his land with his pregnant wife. The story ends with white men on the porch thinking about the concept of a Negro-less society, arguing over it, and lynching a northern black minister driving through town. Kelley's novel envisions the anxiety that whites might feel at a black evacuation. Certainly, this novel is a direct reflection on a form of nonviolent protest championed by Martin Luther King Jr.: the march. In contrast, Sam Greenlee's explosive *The Spook Who Sat by the Door* (1969) depicts Dan Freeman, a black former CIA agent turned social worker, who secretly trains a Chicago street gang in CIA tactics and black history with the intention of fomenting violent revolution. Ghettos across the country take up arms in guerrilla uprisings. The ideology of Greenlee's sf novel is clearly the black nationalism posited by Malcolm X. It offers new world conspiracies of the invisible black malcontent with an agenda to liberate black society from oppression. Both authors use their stories to demonstrate alternatives to the static position of blacks in a racist American society.

Yet other separatism stories use counterfactual time to explore reactions caused by disconnection from familiar surroundings. Samuel Delany's best-known sf novel, *Dhalgren* (1974), offers a complete break from the reality of various differences. Delany's story is set in the heart of the United States where an imaginary city, Bellona, is stricken by an unnamed disaster that disturbs the very foundation of reality. Kid, *Dhalgren's* protagonist, has forgotten his own name and comes to Bellona in search of his identity. The aftermath of the catastrophe is alarming in that a city block can burn down one week and be undamaged a week later; two moons can rise in one evening; a sun thousands of times larger than our own can rise and set; time can be distorted to where the passage of a week for one person is only an afternoon for another. According to Kid, "Very few suspect the existence of this city. It is as if not only the media but the laws of perspective themselves have redesigned knowledge and perception to pass it by . . . It is a city of inner discordances and natural distortions" (14). The depopulated city is inhabited by youth gangs, drifters, prophets, priests, artists, local celebrities, gays, transvestites, white society and the black underclass, the mad and the sane—all of whom are segregated or marginalized, yet freed by the catastrophe. As Tak Loufer, a liberal gay white man, explains to Kid, "[In this society] you're free. No laws: to break, or to follow. Do anything you want" (20). He adds that such a place "does funny things to you [so that] very quickly, surprisingly quickly, you become . . . exactly who you are" (20). Racism in Bellona's anarchic environment is persistent because of this very freedom.

Kid achieves celebrity status as a poet criminal because of the city's leading socialite, Roger Calkins, who publishes Kid's book of poems, *Brass Orchids*, and advertises it in the city's only media source, the *Bellona Times*. As he tried to uncover his identity, Kid somehow becomes a leader of the impulsive multiracial Scorpions, a gang responsible for keeping the law and yet causing mayhem simultaneously. There is no resolution for Kid. Instead, his repeated transformations reflect a cultural otherness as he interacts with a variety of people on the social margins of the broken city. As Jeffrey Tucker contends, the feeling of otherness felt by Kid and other characters is a reflection of "a multi-consciousness, a Delanean revision of W. E. B. DuBois's concept of African-American double-consciousness" ("Contending Forces," 88). *Dhalgren* provides a skeptical vision of society in relation to myths of race. Significantly, *Dhalgren* is worth mentioning here because it provides a post–Jim Crow reaction to existing racism.

Nowhere is this reaction more apparent than in the powerful Roger Calkins's publication of the newspaper, which grants him the cultural authority to distort and manipulate events in the community. In effect, the *Bellona Times* represents an attempted control of time and reality as well as the continuation of racial myth, particularly that of the black rapist as figured by George Harrison. As John Moore points out, "Calkins . . . controls time by publishing the newspaper under random datelines, thus ensuring that all calendrical apparatuses—days, months, years, and even centuries—are under his determination" (191). Out of fear and fascination, Calkins publishes photographs of George having public and violent sex with the pretty white teenager June Richards during the unspecified cataclysmic event. He later interviews George, portraying him as a black brute and a sexual menace to society, thus reasserting the racial myth and making a celebrity out of George. In truth, it is June who lusts after George and George who is intelligent and insightful. Delany deliberately inverts the black male rapist myth with this move and produces an "ironic double awareness of American experience" reminiscent of a DuBoisian double consciousness (Bray, 61). Although racism in Bellona's anarchic environment is ridiculous, it is persistent because of people like Calkins.

Specifically, *Dhalgren* is replete with issues of race, gender, sex, class, sanity, and violence that are fused together by extrapolative separation. All of this is reflected in the article about the Harrison-Richards rape in the *Bellona Times*. Race, sex, and class are obviously signified by the black and poor George and the white, middle-class June, but race is also apparent in Calkins's rendition of the event as a disaster on its own. Class again comes into play through Calkins, who publishes the story for his rich peers, though it also makes George a hero to the poor masses. The newspaper forces its readership to question George's sanity, but not June's. However, George is shown to be rational in his discussion of the occurrence with Kid, and June is perhaps motivated by the madness of her desire for George. Delany also implies that after June's nosy brother, Bobby, discovers her poster of a naked George and realizes her passion, she murders him by shoving him into the empty eighteenth-floor elevator shaft (248–49). Finally, the newspaper itself is a propaganda device designed to manipulate racial perceptions in the text. The attempt to frame George as a rapist in the paper is a perfect reflection of the Jim Crow era in the sense that he would have been lynched for having sex with a white woman, or even the mere hint of it.

Each of the stories mentioned so far suggests that a racialist sf provides an ongoing dialogue with history measured on an extrapolative timeline, thus allowing unique repetitions of cultural memory. Science fiction literature displays how we, as humans, fail to recognize our kinship to other humans from time to time. Other ways of being, other ways of seeing the world—in fact other worlds—come into existence as sf explores the frontier of race through Jim Crow extrapolations. These sf stories, and others like them, draw on the painful but rich history of race relations in the United States. Direct extrapolations of the Jim Crow era onto other *times* or different *places* reflect the lasting sense of anxiety that America has about race. One of the stories collected in Ray Bradbury's *Martian Chronicles* (1950) describes how rocket technology leads to a black exodus to Mars to escape racism during the later stages of the Jim Crow era.

Set in a small southern town of the twenty-first century that closely resembles mid-twentieth-century America, the story, "June 2003: Way in the Middle of the Air," depicts African Americans who use rockets to get to Mars in order to live life without racism. The white reaction to their departure is one of disbelief. Though the story "seems a little old-fashioned, the scenario somewhat unlikely for the year 2003," Bradbury's race story is all the more remarkable because of the era in which it was written, where the crime of having a dark skin could result in a lynch mob (Johnson, 133). Such an unforgettable "image of 'blackness' . . . is [so] striking for the time in which [Bradbury] wrote the story" because he had the courage to put into words the evil of racism and have these words published, even if only in a pulp magazine, *Other Worlds*, in July 1950 (Reid, 50).

Unlike Asimov, who used robots to clandestinely talk about race, Bradbury takes on the subject of racism directly. This critique of racism is candid and impossible to ignore. What Bradbury's story pointedly asks is whether technology can allow us to "leave race behind." And critics such as Gary Wolfe seem to think that Bradbury's answer is yes. Wolfe writes, "In the Martian stories technology may succeed in liberating man from an unpromising environment, as it does in 'Way in the Middle of the Air'" (37). However, I respectfully disagree with

Wolfe and other critics, because our technological advances seem to continually divide humanity along fault lines of various differences, including race. With the black body figured as a natural machine, racial separation can be indefinitely maintained regardless of technological development. As an extension of white privilege, blacks could be used by whites to perform all manners of undesirable hi-tech labor with whites situated above technology.

A racialized technological paranoia consistent with otherhood develops in the story with the impending departure of every black in America. Segregation is being maintained, but with black discretion. Bradbury's story begins on the porch of a hardware store somewhere in the Deep South with white men discussing a rumor about "the niggers" leaving:

> "Did you hear about it?"
> "About what?"
> "The niggers, the niggers!"
> "What about em?"
> "Them leaving, pulling out, going away; did you hear?"
> "What you mean, pulling out? How can they do that?"
> "They can, they will, they are!"
> "Just a couple?"
> "Every single one here in the South!"
> "No."
> "Yes!"
> "I got to see that. I don't believe it. Where they going—Africa?"
> A silence.
> "Mars."
> "You mean the *planet* Mars?" . . . "They can't leave, they can't do that."
> (89–90)

Incredulous, these white men are afraid of losing the security of a social system built on racism and of having to learn new attitudes and behaviors. They are afraid of no longer being able to act hostile and with aggression toward blacks in response to their own fear and anxiety in the presence of these marginalized, victimized people. Blacks are no longer willing to passively accept injustice and white privilege. Leaving for Mars is far more unnerving to these white men than going to Africa because of the intellectual and technological verve involved in planning and executing such a daring trip. This sense of astonishment only grows at the mention of Mars, as if the white men refuse to believe that blacks could develop the technology to separate the races on their own without white help and without white permission. However, years of suffering under Jim Crow law could provide the required motivation for such an exodus. Black Americans simply desire the fulfillment of basic human rights that are being denied them, such as survival, security, and social participation, as they develop a new and separate society, another neighborhood to live in on a separate planet free of anxiety, depression, and self-defeating thoughts—an otherhood.

Bradbury is one of the very few authors in sf who dared to consider the effects and consequences of race in America at a time when racism was largely sanctioned by the culture. As blacks pass by the porch in this small southern town, the main character, Samuel Teece, is bewildered. He is astonished upon learning that blacks had been saving their money and had built their own rockets in secret to leave for Mars, that blacks would dare to challenge white power. Teece questions whether or not they can do this and reacts angrily as the blacks escape to freedom in rocket ships. We can assume that his sense of self is built entirely on his dependence on oppressing black people. Edward Gallagher notes "the story demonstrates that the establishment's only source of power is fear and that the only fear in the loss of this power is the loss of an artificial dignity" (71). Bradbury even allows a black employee to talk back to Teece, effectively challenging a white racist worldview. He allows the blacks not just to escape, but to escape without violence. This story is unique in "mainstream" sf in its scathing critique of American racism. It's a critique of American racism which does not displace race through alien beings or replace American culture with a pretend culture. In other words, it is a direct extrapolation of the existing relations between the races in 1950. This imaginary black flight effectively makes Bradbury highly visible in science fiction.

Through Teece's angry reaction to the black exodus, Bradbury illustrates the social, political, and even psychological effects of racism on the white man. For example, as the visibly upset Teece grabs a gun and makes threats in response to the covert efforts of blacks to free themselves, he reflects what black activist and scholar Benjamin E. Mays describes as the primary sin of segregation. It is "the distortion of human personality. It damages the soul of both the segregator and the segregated" (125). Teece's actions are clearly a distortion of his "personality" as he warns, "If one of 'em so much as laughs, by Christ, I'll kill 'em" (92). In part, this livid reaction stems from years of separation governed by the whim of white society coming to a swift end through black initiative. For Teece, this means no more servants to boss around and berate, no more second-class citizens to make fun of, no more night rides to terrorize blacks, no more blacks.

Teece's attempts to reexert the emotional chains of segregation on the departing black masses reflect how racism has the ability to warp human integrity through bullying and intimidation. While in front of a mixed crowd, he claims the rockets will burn up in space; if not that, then the monstrous inhabitants of Mars will eat the blacks, or perhaps the cold or lack of oxygen will kill them all off. Soon after Teece makes another effort to preserve his sense of white power. An old black man collects fifty dollars from the crowd and comes to the financial rescue of another black man by paying a debt owed to Teece: "'Son,' he said, 'you ain't missin' no rocket'" (94). Later, Teece tries to retain the services of a black youth named Silly by pushing the boy around, ordering him back to work, threatening him with the law, and by finally pulling out a bogus work contract in the attempt to force Silly to stay behind. Aware of Teece's posturing, Silly gets the last laugh by mocking Teece's nighttime activities with the Ku Klux Klan: "'Mr. Teece, Mr. Teece, what *you* goin' to do nights from now on? What you goin' to *do* nights, Mr. Teece?'" (99) However, Teece's distorted belief in white power is absolutely crushed, a terrible psychological side effect generated by the notions of racial castes and the abuses of segregation. The ugliness of his behavior is apparent in his fear of a postrace world. A powerful moment occurs when Teece and the other white men notice the disconcerting stillness of their community as the blacks pass out of town. The end of white supremacy is at hand, and Teece, in utter shock at this thought, tries to rationalize why the blacks should have stayed on Earth. He cannot imagine the mental and spiritual trauma caused by ruthless acts of lynching, racial slurs, and poor treatment, and other general inequalities. As William Touponce remarks, "Social equality is therefore projected into the remote future . . . Yet Bradbury's Blacks are not hanging around for any such process to happen" (33).[4]

Although the possibility is unlikely that blacks could take flight into space because of the dishonesty, prejudice, and violence of Jim Crow politics, Bradbury's story relates to otherhood because it raises awareness of the intolerance of racism. Providing an escape from the problem of the color line, Bradbury seems to indicate that whites and blacks cannot coexist with a cultural hierarchy established through physical differences and the complete domination of others. The story is meant to be an ironic solution to the color line. I think this shows Bradbury's desire and political commitment to eliminate racism by promoting effective social justice, even if it is only imaginary. Too few other sf writers are willing to actively struggle against racism at all levels and use their talent to promote human welfare nationally, globally, even intergalactically. In this story, Bradbury is aggressively denouncing racism in all its forms—social, educational, economic, and psychological. In fact, looking at sf in terms of otherhood, as called for here, can possibly lead us to the end of racism.

In a recent *African American Review* essay, Paul Youngquist claims that "Bradbury's story . . . is a neocolonial fantasy of racial justice that directs the historical longing of black separatism toward the distant shores of colonized Mars" though it "never really solves the problem it raises" because Bradbury "never shows them [blacks] arriving anywhere else . . . They [blacks] simply disappear into black space, as if the logic of cosmic liberalism can make no room for them in the known universe" (335). The clear implication is that Bradbury's story is itself racist in its incompletion. Similarly, Elizabeth Leonard remarks, "Bradbury uses sf effectively to portray white racism, but the story does not take the opportunity to reimagine a black culture independent of white perceptions. The story of the expansion of the African diaspora to Mars is never told" ("Race," 257). Yet, Youngquist's and Leonard's analyses are both unfinished and wrong, since they fail to take into account a second story called "The Other Foot," published a year later, in which Bradbury considers what happens to the blacks on Mars.

First published in the March 1951 issue of *New Story*, "The Other Foot" tells how African Americans now settled on Mars confront the question of oppression when they are presented with the opportunity to do the same thing as surviving whites seek refuge from nuclear holocaust on Earth. Twenty years have passed on Mars when the black

JIM CROW EXTRAPOLATIONS · 101

community receives word from a Mars-bound spacecraft that the white man is coming. The story's protagonist, Hattie Johnson, hears the news from her three small sons and tries to explain what a white man looks like. Two things are significant at this point: first, the protagonist is a black woman, and second, an entire generation of black children on Mars has grown up with no knowledge of racism. This is immediately clear when one of the boys asks Hattie, "What's a white man? I never seen one" (27). However, Bradbury's postrace Martian world is now at risk of becoming racist.

Hattie has an awful premonition about what might happen when the rocket arrives—renewed racial tensions and animosities led by her husband, only with blacks having the upper hand. She tries to tell her boys that the white men are merely coming for a visit after the war because they forgot about black people. After telling the boys to stay put, she rushes off to see what's happening and runs into her husband, Willie, who confirms her worst fears. As Willie figures, the shoe is on the other foot now since Mars is inhabited by blacks alone. He remarks: "We'll see who gets laws passed against him, who gets lynched, who rides the back of streetcars, who gets segregated in shows. We'll just see!" (29–30). Hattie takes note of his mean smile, angry eyes, and ugly tone, realizing how much hatred he has kept inside, him and others alike. In fact, she is fearful of his newly distorted personality.

As Mays avows, "Segregate a race for ninety years, tell that race in books, in law, in courts, in education, in church and school, in employment, in transportation, in hotels and motels, in the government that it is inferior—it is bound to leave its damaging mark upon the souls and minds of the segregated" (125). Willie wants to subject the whites to the oppression of Jim Crow law by making them experience the same day-to-day feeling of inferiority and by building the psychological conditions necessary for racist sentiments to figure prominently in Martian history—distinct groups of people, limited social contact, and a binary caste system based on race. In short, he desires to exclude whites from Martian society. The democratic ideals of equality have nearly failed here because of Willie's racist impulses. Finally, the rocket arrives. An old, weary white man steps out of the ship into a chilly, hostile reception and begs the black crowd to help, saying that the few refugees will submit to anything, slavery, segregation, cleaning, cooking, shining shoes—everything that the black mob wants to hear.

Speaking through Hattie, Bradbury reveals his compassion for all of humanity. He wants to pull down the wall of hatred existing between the races by getting "at the hate of them all, to pry at it and work at it until [he] found a little chink" to exploit (36). In this regard, Hattie recognizes that her husband is the decisive factor in determining the future of race relations on Mars, and she talks to the white man about destroyed locales on Earth that are familiar to her husband, such as "Knockwood Hill in Greenwater, Alabama," the place where Willie's father was lynched (37). Her questioning encourages Willie to talk with the white man, and he comes to the staggering realization that there is *nothing left* for him to hate. As he begins to understand his wife, Willie becomes fully conscious and ashamed of his unreasoning hatred for the Jim Crow whites of the past.

In "The Other Foot," Bradbury suggests that time apart from each other interrupts the cycle of racism and establishes an opportunity to build a united humanity based on respect, understanding, and trust. Separation, not segregation, has allowed the psychic wounds of racism to heal. Humanity has quite simply evolved beyond one of its greatest flaws—racism—throughout the passage of time in Bradbury's posthuman universe. Bradbury answers important questions about race and technology. If technology gives us the ultimate means of separation, the second Bradbury story foregrounds racism as a "human failing." Perhaps, Bradbury cannot imagine a black future per se, but he can envision a postrace one that reverberates throughout sf.

While Bradbury ends his two-story sequence with optimism, fifty years later black writer Evie Shockley ponders segregation with a dark view of the future in her story "Separation Anxiety" (2000). Utilizing sf as a form of social satire, she seems to believe that an intentional government plan of minority isolation is our country's key to survival as a democracy. Shockley extrapolates on Jim Crow by making voluntary and deliberate segregation an accepted fact of life for African Americans in the twenty-second century. Further, a tone of frustration is evident among the characters as governmental interference becomes increasingly repressive. Likewise, a noticeable element of the story, the lack of capital letters, lends it a transgressive quality, suggesting linguistic difference as a mark of otherhood.

As the story opens, peaches, a leading african american dancer, explains how she loves her home and "never dreamed" of wanting "to leave the ghetto" because it is "where [she] could see, hear, taste, smell, and feel [her] culture all around . . . in the mac's rolling stroll and the girls' whip-fast double-dutch" (51). The point of the American government in "creating the ghetto—the african american cultural conservation unit, as the official name goes—is to preserve [the black] way of life" (51–52). Most stereotypes of the ghetto in American culture portray it as being a densely concentrated, rundown urban area consisting of homogeneous ethnic minority groups such as African Americans. Images of graffiti, burned-out shells of cars, violence, poverty, crime, illiteracy, drug dealers, gangbangers, crackheads, welfare mothers, and absentee fathers are prominent features of this stereotype. However, this is not the image presented by Shockley through peaches. Instead, the "ghetto" is an affectionate term for a vibrant and thriving black culture that has been created by the enforced separation of the races. The "ghetto" unit has allowed black people to affirm their humanity and to take control of their future.

In the story, the "ghetto" is created by a white-dominated federal government and controlled by the newly organized "national department of ethnic and cultural conservation, the 'decc,'" in the year 2095 because white racism has become so bad that the only way for American minorities to survive is through the adaptation of a truer separate-but-equal policy (52). Initially, anti-hate laws do not deter racial violence. On the surface, in such circumstances, these conservation units seem like a practical solution to racial strife because racial and ethnic groups are able to preserve their traditions and build on their cultures in the process without the fear of being ostracized. Peaches informs us that minorities were at first "happy" with the federal government's decision to create the units. The careful preservation and protection of each unit's cultural productions becomes essential to recording the black contribution to American society overall. Consequently, it becomes essential to prevent outside influences from contaminating these different ways of life developing within the various units. The decc fears exploitation, destruction, and neglect of these units and, therefore, manages the archives with single-minded determination.

Barely discernible problems begin to arise for the community as the decc adapts an official policy of real-time preservation of all historical records and artistic assets such as birth certificates and novels. Initially, this inconvenience and threat to privacy is minimal because "african americans had seen the downside of being nearly recordless, from the days of slavery and reconstruction, so we were proud that recognizing the value of our culture was now the law. but then the law began to grow" (53). The decc legitimates its invasive existence with a nostalgic excuse: think of all the unrecorded history that has been lost concerning African Americans and mourn it, but do not let it happen now.

Covertly, the decc expands its power, becoming overly and overtly intrusive in the lives of its minority charges. The government's decision to include items of a more personal nature in its record keeping goes far beyond the scope of cultural conservation. What purpose does *"separating waste associated with sexual activity"* serve (52; italics in original)? This quote is a powerful reminder of the Tuskegee syphilis experiment and the great harm inflicted on African Americans by the government in the name of medical research. Shockley later makes this connection more explicitly in a conversation between peaches and her brother, roosevelt, in which he declares, "if you hadda studied, yourself, a little harder in your history classes, you'd know that black folks got studied even back then. remember that tuskegee thing? . . . that shit happened then, it's probably still going on, and it ain't gonna stop no time soon" (59). Shockley's decision to foreground this painful moment in American history creates an otherhood, where racist attitudes are ascribed to an uncaring government that has trained members of its minority population in passive obedience to authority.

The words of peaches's deceased grandfather are significant here: "history is a cycle, y'all . . . this unit is separation today, but it'll be segregation tomorrow, mark my words . . . conservation. reservation. conservation. concentration" (57). The grandfather is wise enough to realize that his community made a "deal with the blue-eyed devil" because the difference between separation and segregation is a thin, invisible line which the overzealous government flagrantly crosses. Jim Crow segregation has been revived from an apparently benevolent desire to make a lasting peace between white Americans and other minorities. Yet an enforced dissociation has no true benefits when the government forces itself upon the purposely detached group. Shockley is suggesting that the sinister legacy of government isolation—Indian reservations, Japanese internment camps, Nazi concentration camps, and the like—is doomed to be repeated. These cultural conservation units symbolize intolerance and avoid addressing issues of racial conflict. No matter how well-meaning, the decc is abusing its power by creating a stagnant African American culture in the name of preserving cultural diversity.

In this future world, the diversity of America as a whole is supposed to be guaranteed by the separation of its parts. Ultimately, this is why peaches decides to leave the ghetto. Her fear of separation occurs when she hesitates to leave her brother behind for a career in the outside world, though she seems determined to use her "exile to break down the hundred-plus-year-old walls" (67). Perhaps, and ironically, peaches's application to leave is quickly approved because she is a celebrated dancer, much like Josephine Baker was in the twentieth century as a black expatriate entertainer in France. To leave, peaches has "to sign contracts" with the white government that acknowledge her understanding that she could "never return to the ghetto, and that [her] contact with persons inside the unit would be limited and monitored, to ensure that no 'contamination' of black culture occurred" (67). Peaches's agreement to sign such a contract is a subtle reversal of affirmative action. Shockley's sense of frustration, or more precisely her distrust of the government, exploits the current fear of affirmative action being retracted across the country by businesses and institutions of higher learning. Compulsory demographic shifts are a convenient way to exclude minority groups from full participation in the American democratic experiment. Through an extrapolation of the harmful influence of segregation, Shockley uses sf to make a political statement against the social injustice still visited upon the black masses. Her story is an active attempt to redress and bring attention to present discrimination and the lack of equal opportunities for black Americans in all pursuits.

When we look at this story in terms of race, we can see that Shockley's vision suggests that such a radical separation is not the answer to the dangers of racism. The ensuing reconstruction of political objectives in such a way will result in a blind intolerance on the government's part. This version of segregation may preserve life and a restricted sense of freedom that avoids racial conflict, but it sacrifices the possibility of a diverse and democratic future in which we deal with issues of difference honestly. Thus, Shockley's use of segregation is frightening because she has created all but permanent boundaries between various human groups. Further, she suggests that the only way for the races to coexist is apart from one another, that there is no value in diversity. The separate-but-equal notion is the only prospect for peace in her vision of the future. Bradbury offers a glimmer of utopian hope for humanity, whereas Shockley projects a feeling of doubt regarding race relations. The notion of science fictional separation is clearly visible within sf then and now as grandmasters like Bradbury and newcomers like Shockley contemplate social issues of race.

Many answers to racism are conveyed in sf tales of separatism as sf writers imagine postrace worlds. For example, some writers, such as George Schuyler, provide sarcastic solutions to the problematic position of color generated by the complex interaction of social, political, and economic forces developed by the race paradigm. Other writers, such as Walter Mosley, picture confinement as the answer to race, an entirely different kind of separation. At the same time writers such as Derrick Bell envision alien contact and race trading as a viable solution to the antagonisms of race. These kinds of otherhood responses can be used to look imaginatively at the color line as it is presented by Jim Crow extrapolations in time and space. Several sf stories offer exceptionally inventive solutions to the dilemmas of separatism: Schuyler's *Black No More* (1931) and *Black Empire* (serialized between 1936 and 1938), Mosley's *Futureland* (2001), and Bell's "The Space Traders" (1992).

George Schuyler has perhaps been overlooked as a science fiction writer because of the radical yet conservative political opinions that he offered in his journalism career, which spanned the forty years from the 1920s and the Harlem Renaissance through the social upheaval of the 1960s. For example, he created a storm of controversy with his article "The Negro-Art Hokum," published in *The Nation* in 1926, where he scorns the notion of a distinctive black art.[5] Further, many contemporary critics, such as Jeffrey Tucker, find it hard to look beyond Schuyler's traditional stances on race to consider the quality of his satirical approach to sf writing. Tucker believes that Schuyler "inflicted the sharpest critique on black leaders and intellectuals with ties to the Communist party," namely W. E. B. DuBois; "contended that the Reverend Dr. Martin Luther King, Jr. was unworthy of his Nobel Peace Prize"; and "called Malcolm X a 'pixilated criminal,' comparing the slain black leader to Benedict Arnold" ("Can," 139).

Schuyler's use of sf tropes like mad scientists or death-rays in his novels to censure the absurdities of race and racism demonstrates that he knew sf protocols during the genre's formative years.[6] Even if Schuyler's political and professional beliefs reveal extreme conservatism, perhaps a desire for assimilation in some respects, the barbed ingenuity of his science fiction suggests otherwise. As supported by the following explication, *Black No More* and *Black Empire* (henceforward *BNM* and *BE*, respectively) appear to be different if related ironic responses to the race problem.

The plot of *BNM* revolves around Dr. Crookman's invention of a skin-whitening process, Max Disher's manipulation of the resulting racial tensions in the name of greed, and the ensuing political and cultural chaos as members of the black race disappear. The novel is decidedly anti-utopian in that Schuyler offers commentary on the ridiculousness of racial politics in America when race disappears in his alternate future. In Sharon DeGraw's words, "The complete absurdity of American race relations affects every American, coloring almost every situation with both ironic humor and tragedy" (78). And yet there is a difference between black as a color and black as a mentality—to be black in America is to be considered inferior in all ways. The plotting of *BE* is significantly different in that it involves the evil genius Dr. Henry Belsidus, his creation of a secret black international military within the United States, the conquest and modernization of the African continent, and a total race war as the European powers attempt to wrest control of their former African colonies from Dr. Belsidus. The ultraviolence of the *BE* serial anticipates black nationalism as well as the postcolonial era in its dystopian projection. It also suggests that nothing good can come from racial separatism, only prejudice, war, and death.

In both novels Schuyler uses scientific extrapolation by mad scientists to pose solutions to the color line. The mad scientist theme is the only common feature of the two texts, aside from the mockery of race. In *BNM*, Dr. Crookman is a "mad" scientist because of the chaos created by his skin-whitening process; and in *BE*, Dr. Belsidus is a "mad" scientist because of his desire to conquer the world by creating a black empire with advanced technology. One world offers the disturbingly familiar dream of a postrace environment, and the other world indicates that violence is the logical consequence of oppression. Yet both stem from the historical reality of segregation in America. Schuyler provides different worlds to explore race and racism in American culture. His blending together of historical references and racial extrapolations is an extension of otherhood worthy of investigation.

I would like to briefly consider two of the problems created by Schuyler's technological effacement of race in *BNM*. First, the rapid expansion of Dr. Crookman's company tears the cultural fabric of the country as greed, ignorance, racism, and brutality arise in a futile attempt to prevent the disappearance of the black race. In fictionalized Harlem, for example, black banks fail, black business ventures in real estate and beauty products collapse, and black leaders panic as their lifestyle crumbles. In addition, Dr. Crookman and his associates readily offer financial encouragement to government officials to prevent the passage of laws that would hinder the company's operations. Second, the issue of miscegenation is a significant problem in this projection. Black babies are being born to supposedly white couples, so Dr. Crookman establishes "lying in hospitals" to change the babies to white in twenty-four hours (138). A related problem is the white supremacist response in southern newspapers calling for a federal law against the black-no-more process since the South could no longer depend on the black underclass as a cheap source of labor. Likewise, the Ku Klux Klan is reincarnated as "The Knights of Nordica" by Reverend Henry Givens in reaction to the threat to white integrity offered by "the activities of a scientific Black Beelzebub [Dr. Crookman] in New York" (65).

BNM recognizes the importance of the interconnected lives of black and white Americans during the heyday of Jim Crow. Schuyler believes that America's problem with race hinges upon the denial of these very relationships; the belief that miscegenation does not exist when in fact it does. As Stacey Morgan describes it, "Schuyler unmasks the perceived threat of miscegenation as a ludicrous anxiety over something which is already, fait accompli, a reality of American identity" (347). No matter which race endorses separatism and intolerance, Schuyler is right to point out the foolishness of it and hope that a mass realization of this fact occurs in America.

Although the notion of racial assimilation is the heart of Schuyler's first answer to the problem of the color line, his second answer is an entirely opposite response. In *Black Empire* Schuyler champions a black militant separatism that willfully engages in genocidal warfare. Significantly, *Black Empire* is actually two stories, "The Black Internationale: A Story of Black Genius against the World" and "Black Empire: An Imaginative Story of a Great New Civilization in Modern Africa," which appeared as sixty-two weekly installments in the *Pittsburgh Courier*, a black newspaper, beginning in November 1936 and ending in 1938. Schuyler used the pseudonym Samuel I. Brooks to tell his tale. Henry Louis Gates Jr. believes that, aside from using the pseudonym to further boost sales of the weekly paper for which he wrote for forty-two years, Schuyler could use "Brooks" to "play out his ambivalent feelings about the 'responsible' politics for black America" (42). Thus, Schuyler's use of sf provided African Americans of the 1930s with an absurd and escapist vision: wholesale slaughter of the white race. Schuyler even blasts his alter ego's work, calling it "hokum and hack work in the purest vein," that "the enthusiastic response" to *Black Empire* somehow confirmed his "'low opinion of the human race'" (Gates, 42).[7]

The events of both the stories that make up *BE* depict the ruthless leadership of the evil black mastermind Dr. Belsidus as he develops a worldwide revolutionary network known as the "Black Internationale" to destroy "White world supremacy" (10). Anticipating Malcolm X's philosophy of liberation, "by any means necessary," Schuyler makes Dr. Belsidus's intent clear: "My ideal and objective is very frankly to cast down the Caucasians and elevate the colored people in their places. I plan to do this by every means within my power" (10). Using his ill-gained wealth, Dr. Belsidus is able to build the agricultural, mystical, political, and technological power in the United States necessary to later challenge and conquer the colonial powers of Western Europe. Such a radical outlook has prompted Gates to label the character of

Dr. Belsidus as a "genius's genius: 'determined, educated, suave, immaculate, cruel, immoral,'" as well as "Du Bois, Booker T. Washington, George Washington Carver and Marcus Garvey rolled into one fascist superman" (41). Belsidus uses his Black Internationale agents to exploit ethnic and religious divisions in order to promote civil disorder within the U.S. through terrorist tactics. Belsidus's agents also replace European colonialism in Africa with his own emerging African empire as he consolidates his power. In this Jim Crow extrapolation, these actions constitute a revenge fantasy only made possible in sf.

The first serial outlines the rise of a black power monopoly to replace the white domination of oppressed black people. However, this does not suggest that a black world order is any better than a white one considering the violent actions, evil, and hatred that the Black Internationale commits to gain global black independence. This black world extrapolation is just as scary as "real" history. Dr. Belsidus moralizes his own lethal brand of racial absolutism against the backdrop of historical European imperialism and American intolerance of blacks.

The second serial, "Black Empire," describes the foundation of the black empire in Africa, the treatment of indigenous Africans, and a European backlash against the new empire. During the brief interlude before the counterattack, Africa is modernized through Dr. Belsidus's recolonization strategy, a theme of self-reliance and rationality, where improvement is brought about by advances in technology, medicine, communication, and propaganda. At the social and economic heart of the new Africa is the Temple of Love, which represents Dr. Belsidus's version of an "advanced Western-style civilization" (Lawson, 98). On a more sinister note, it is apparent that the temple acts as a means of control since it is also the center of propaganda, where the doctor uses strictly "the cream of the Negro race" to run the adjoined facilities, meaning that daily activities are supervised by African Americans who oversee only those Africans educated in America (123). In a sense, Schuyler is going with history by creating a unique church, which in the text is governed by a robot, to help blacks escape white control by establishing social cohesion. In fact, his robot is a "50-foot statue of a nude Negro" that moves rhythmically and has a powerful voice preaching black power (61). This particular Jim Crow extrapolation directly redresses the inequalities that blacks have endured from the time of slavery by projecting spirituality as a protection against the forces of racism.

Unfortunately, black American treatment of native Africans mirrors the arrogance of prejudice. The colonizers readily display an inherent sense of superiority much like that shown by the white America of the 1930s toward its dark citizens. Natives are condemned as savages "screaming in strange gibberish" and are also thought to be cannibals (236). In essence, a black empire is no better than the previous white ones because it is based on racial chauvinism, exploitation, oppression, and violence.

After this restructuring of African life, Dr. Belsidus successfully defends his empire from a joint European assault using all of the weapons at his disposal, both conventional—guns, bombs, and planes—and unconventional—biological warfare and death rays.[8] The European assault threatens to break the new black empire, but the unveiling of a superweapon—a combination "cyclotron" and energy disrupter, a death ray which generates "an atomic or proton beam which can disintegrate any metal"—wins the war for Dr. Belsidus (244). As *Black Empire* comes to a close, Dr. Belsidus delivers a rousing speech: "You must not make the mistake of the white man and try to enslave others, for that is the beginning of every people's fall. You must banish race hatred from your hearts, now that you have your own land" (257). It seems ironic that Dr. Belsidus persuades blacks to let go of their racial hostility after so much bloodshed and revenge for centuries of wrongs committed in the name of race. With his political agenda achieved, the mad genius finally recognizes the meaninglessness of race.

Fortunately, the violent reprisal of Dr. Belsidus and his Black Internationale is an unrealized alternative solution to segregation and oppression. Perhaps Schuyler wants readers to take his vision lightly as a kind of creative entertainment. He uses the pseudonym Samuel I. Brooks precisely because he does not personally believe the "line of racial argument" he considers in the writing of the novel (Hill and Rasmussen, 299). Kali Tal suggests that such depictions of black rage "may be deeply uncomfortable for black and white critics alike" because "most" of them "do not seem inclined to acknowledge that this level of hostility may exist" (80). Still, Schuyler anticipates numerous developments in race relations because his story envisages the arrival of the civil rights movement, the Black Power era, and Malcolm X, not to mention the postcolonial era. And so it is difficult to fathom why Schuyler is not more widely recognized in the history of sf. With segregation as the law of the land, Schuyler's anger and resentment explode in his use of science fiction, which allows him to address the legacy of defeat that blacks have had to contend with in a near-future setting without succumbing to his own deeply ingrained cynicism.

While Schuyler's neglected and obscure legacy has been passed on to future black sf writers, it is Walter Mosley who in his own extrapolation of segregation perhaps best recognizes that the tradition of Jim Crow has been continued for blacks in prison. Mosley's techno-prison story "Angel's Island," first published in his *Futureland* collection (2001), is very different from Schuyler's novels. His cycle of stories presents a harsh vision of a twenty-first-century world run by multinational conglomerates and controlled by drugs and exciting technologies. Mosley infers the future from what seems to be our societal answer to the color line: separate black men from society through imprisonment. His story is a disquieting response to the late twentieth century's political manipulation of social stereotypes that disparaged the intelligence of blacks and played up their tendency for violence and crime as drug addicts and gang members. The government's current answer is to build more jails, privatize the prison system, impose the death penalty, and to imprison a disproportionate number of African American males.[9] As of 2007, the incarceration rate for black American men in the United States has grown to 4,618 per 100,000, compared to 773 white American men per 100,000.[10] Black men are imprisoned nearly six times more often than white men. Interestingly, the nature of future crime—murder, blackmail, burglary—has not changed much from our current era, although Orwellian "thought crime" is a relatively clever innovation.

Punishment of crime in sf is simultaneously cultural and technological, using science and technology to restructure society. There are a goodly number of sf narratives that have to do with the management of prisoners in detention centers. For instance, Robert Sheckley's *The Status Civilization* (1960) features the prison planet of Omega where Earth criminals are dumped after having their minds wiped clean. Likewise, several sf prison stories feature the notion of "electronic tagging," in which prisoner tag devices are capable of dishing out instantaneous punishment in the form of pain (Clute and Nicholls, 276). Piers Anthony and Robert Margroff provide a good example with their novel *The Ring* (1968), in which the protagonist, Jeff Front, is framed, wrongly convicted, and ringed. The "ring" is a surgically embedded electronic monitor that causes excruciating pain when a criminal offender even thinks of doing something bad. An excellent example from film is John Carpenter's classic *Escape from New York* (1981), where all of Manhattan is turned into a maximum security prison.

Mosley's "Angel's Island" is the story of Vortex "Bits" Arnold, an African American hacker convicted for "antisocial behavior" and sentenced to a corporate-owned prison where everyone—including the guards, medical staff, and warden—is controlled by "snake packs" wrapped around the arm and inserted into the skin of the biceps (86, 92). Arnold's crime was attempting to protect society from the incursions of the corporations as they went about "systematically dismantling private property rights around the world" (97). The moment of extrapolation which allows this scenario to happen occurs when the Supreme Court decides in 2022 that it is constitutional to practice "citizenship suspension" for any person who violates the law (93). Thus, suspending and denying the rights and privileges of a citizen indefinitely produces otherhood, where the moral aspects of deliberate segregation can be explored.

In keeping with the historically lopsided number of blacks in prison, Mosley informs us "that over 80 percent of American-backed prisons were non-white" (110). Mosley accomplishes two goals by maintaining this social disparity in the future. First, he is telling us that American racism is alive and well in his twenty-first century, a world filled with marvelous technology and sweeping social reforms that are supposed to have eliminated such things as racism and prejudice but that yet create a powerful sense of nonbeing. With a snake pack attached to them, prisoners are "not black or white, American, or even human, really" (94). As otherhood suggests, such a total disregard for the basic humanity of prisoners is something ugly and racist, particularly when based on skin color, hair texture, or the shape of someone's eyes. And second, Mosley strongly believes that a government pact with business uses the separation caused by prison to reinstitute slavery for the sole purpose of making money. People possessing the advantage of economic or political power in this Jim Crow extrapolation have the ability to erase the existence of those they dislike, fear, or hate. Further, state/corporate aggression against its minorities is a form of ethnic cleansing in which people are removed to an undisclosed location for any number of ill-defined reasons. The extinction of human beings is justified by the anxieties of the rich and expressed in terms of race. This scenario is a frightening sf projection of how such a darkly rendered world may come into existence. Mosley's Jim Crow extrapolation suggests that fear of a raced technology is not unfounded in light of American history.

The snake pack best represents each of Mosley's goals. It generates a powerful feeling of nonbeing for convicts because it strips away all of their identity and allows complete control of the prisoners, from their thoughts and moods to their bodily functions, work assignments, and locations; it also operates as a lie detector. Like every other prisoner, Bits is outfitted with the "antisocial, lethal dose pack" to turn him into a passive nonperson (89). Further, the snake pack is designed to keep track of infractions and administer jolts of pain capable of reducing a prisoner to a coma. After three such comas, a prisoner is not revived. Freedom is attained by "accruing no points in a span of three years" (96). After considering the tremendous technological brilliance of the snake pack, Bits soon realizes the impossibility of beating it, going without a mark on his record for three years, and "that he was nothing and no one forevermore" (112). This is clearly technological effacement of society's unwanted to the extent that the stringent control measures sustain an unprecedented level of racism with its accompanying violence. Such a device would ensure permanent segregation.

Nonbeings are subject to all manners of experimentation in science fiction. Unbeknownst to the prisoners of Angel's Island, the medical staff has been infecting them with all kinds of carcinogens laced in the food. They have done this to test the snake pack's ability to identify incurable illnesses like cancer and counteract them, or to find cures for cancer under separate lucrative research contracts. Angel's Island naturally earns money from performing this questionable research for next to nothing on nonexistent people. At the very least, this secret research recalls the American government's lengthy illegal syphilis research conducted on black men at the Tuskegee Institute.

Stanley Harrold, Darlene Hine, and William Hine call the Tuskegee study, which lasted from 1932 through 1972, "the worst manifestation of racism in American Science" (355).

Government license is granted to corporate interests in unregulated human testing for a reason: to maintain and expand economic and political power by finding military and civilian applications. Without doubt, the snake packs may be eventually used across the world to keep the masses happy and under control—a state of slavery. This idea prompts Bits to stage the largest prison break in history for the purpose of exposing the fact that the government has a signed contract with the makers of this malevolent technology.

Mosley works with historical images of racial abuse—plantations, prison segregation, illegal experiments—to reflect on how little the future will change for black Americans and minorities. Prejudice will still be central to life since it is a cause of separation as evinced by the astronomical rate of black male imprisonment. Future technological developments like the snake packs could have hugely negative repercussions by reviving slavery. Through Bits, Mosley protests against the possible racial ironies of a future as yet unexamined in science fiction.

Although Jim Crow is legally dead, this does not stop sf writers from projecting the legacy of the era—segregation, terror, racism, and violence—into the future. The spirit of Jim Crow haunts America with notions of white superiority, economic inequality, oppression, and all manners of discrimination. In fact, the physical and psychological scars of this era have been passed on and will also be remembered by generations to come. The problem of race in America continues to exist, but "what if" an advanced alien civilization made an overwhelming offer to end racism in exchange for every black citizen of the United States?

Derrick Bell, former Harvard law professor and well-known civil rights activist, provides an answer with his story "The Space Traders" (1992). Bell's answer is that, yes, whites most certainly would find African Americans expendable and move swiftly to secure the deal if it would significantly improve their own lifestyle. Blacks would be willingly sacrificed for the greater good of white self-interest as well as material gain. In Bell's story the alien offer—enough gold to wipe out the national debt, chemicals to clean the polluted environment, and a clean nuclear fusion engine—is an extraordinary one. The trade proposal is aimed at ending America's economic, environmental, energy, and racial tensions. Although the alien leaders never say what they are going to do with the black Americans, they do establish Martin Luther King Jr. Day as the deadline for sanctioning the trade. With two weeks to contemplate the bid, intense national debates lead to the ratification of a new amendment, similar to the draft, consigning blacks to an unknown fate with the traders.

It is no mistake that Bell's aliens speak in "the familiar comforting tones of former President Reagan," the so-called great communicator, because the use of his voice goes a long way in pacifying white anxieties about doing something unthinkable (327). This voice marks the aliens as being benign, though it is perfectly clear that their superior technologies could destroy the world if they were interested in doing such a thing. Consequently, this action places the burden of guilt concerning such a trade on white American citizens, leaving them to freely accept or reject the trade without fear of consequence. Bell then sets the stage for the inevitable decision on the stage of public opinion. Whereas whites perceived the aliens "to be practical, no-nonsense folks like regular Americans," blacks see the strange visitors "as distinctly unpleasant, even menacing in appearance," like white people (328). Following their own insights, whites completely dismiss the legitimate fear and anxiety manifesting in the black community because whites have been "long conditioned to discounting any statements of blacks unconfirmed by other whites" (328). Darryl Smith is right to believe that "the Traders are the people, blacks the aliens" (214). The government decides that the founding fathers intended for the United States to be a white nation, which clears the national conscience enough to create a twenty-seventh amendment requiring that all citizens serve their country; in this case all blacks are "drafted" into the special service of going with the aliens.[11] The final image in the story displays armed U.S. guards preventing escape attempts by the "twenty-million silent black" inductees "crowded on the beaches," stripped of "all but a single undergarment," being ushered onto the alien ships: "heads bowed, arms now linked by slender chains, black people left the New World as their forebears had arrived" (354).

Bell's story draws attention to the reality of our country's problem with race, how it is multilayered and enduring. His extrapolation along the color line is a means of confronting race and racism, enabling him to address what he perceives to be a genuine threat to racial minorities when issues of self-interest, privilege, and power emerge on the national stage. Readers may be initially stunned by Bell's use of racial stereotypes, but he certainly does not mean to endorse them. Rather, he is exposing the irrationality of holding on to them. His critique suggests that the intersection of race and racism is signaled by a utilitarian rationale that he indicts with this story. With black Americans defined as "the race problem" itself, the alien "solution" exposes the extent to which American culture is considered monochromatic, i.e., white. In this respect, "The Space Traders" stands opposed to a racism that is alive and well. So, then, Bell's story makes a valuable contribution to the investigation of sf because he consciously foregrounds racial issues in his narrative.

Though racial tension is inevitable in America, perhaps even necessary, science fiction does not pretend that all is well with race. Jim Crow extrapolations suggest a more complicated reality. Only by welcoming an open dialogue on race and racism, despite the tensions, can sf articulate the future of race relations. Cautionary future tales are important articulations of our own expectations for life because they are often emotional reactions against the trends and events of society. Thus, segregation in sf results in dispersion and concentration, removal of one group from others, a violent wrenching apart based on dissimilar cultural identities. Racial conflict results from these divisions. Segregation and separatism are formidable barriers to positive social intercourse because discriminatory practices always crop up at unexpected times. Yet Jim Crow extrapolations of otherhood may possibly be the progressive instrument required for breaking down the cultural separation between races.

In some respect this cultural separation is driven by notions of white racial purity and a fear of bodily corruption that is symptomatic of racism. Thus, switching from a chronological map of sf to a biological one, anxieties over black racial identity are taken up in the next chapter as we delve deeper into ailments of race—race mixing, the one-drop rule, and passing—to demonstrate how fear of contagion operates as a race metaphor in America.

4   Ailments of Race

A meteor swarm blasts the Earth's atmosphere, causing a strange new contagious illness called "neuroderm" to spread and infect humanity (Miller, "Dark Benediction," 256). The disease turns people gray, heightens their senses, sharpens their intelligence, and causes them to hunt down healthy people as it spreads through contact, a simple touch. Consequently, the infected "dermies" are regarded as lepers (276). American civilization is greatly disrupted when civil liberties are suspended in an attempt to contain the spread of the contagion. While Walter M. Miller Jr. is best known for his Hugo Award–winning *A Canticle for Leibowitz* (1960), his lesser-known "Dark Benediction" (1951), from which the description above is taken, is unquestionably a racial allegory. Miller consciously deconstructs racist attitudes in his story by having it set in the Deep South, the state of Texas, with infected characters who are visibly different, mistreated, and killed on sight by whites who fear for their security and loss of domination in the changing times because of this racialized ailment—dark skin.

Contagion is thought of as the transmission of disease by direct or indirect contact with a virus, bacterium, microbe, living organism, or any other agent capable of causing a communicable disease. The rumor of a deadly ailment or infectious disease sweeping a country has a way of scaring people. Federal, state, and local governments take action by quarantining at medical facilities people who may have been exposed to the contagion, essentially locking them up like prisoners in detention centers in an attempt to prevent the spread of disease by isolating those who have it. As social scientist Paul Marsden defines it: "The term contagion. . . . itself has its roots in the Latin word contagio, and quite literally means 'and from touch'. Contagion therefore refers to a process of transmission by touch or contact . . . of biological disease" (172). At its worst, panic and mass hysteria grip the world as people die in vast numbers. However, the sociocultural threat of contagion also creates an unusual sense of racism in terms of how people respond.

Epidemics bring out the best and worst in humankind: some people help those in need; others isolate themselves as a matter of self-preservation; still others discriminate against those who are afflicted while more seek to place blame. Courage, compassion, callousness, and cowardice are on full display as these plagues break through social boundaries. Weighed against the four truly "big" plagues of history, namely the bubonic plague (also known as "the Black Death"), smallpox, the Spanish influenza of 1918, and the modern plague of AIDS, the germs of science fiction seem slight without considering the social context within various texts. By "germs of science fiction," I mean imaginary plagues, both natural and manmade, which radically change human life by depopulating the world, transforming human beings into monsters, or something else along those lines. For example, Richard Matheson's *I Am Legend* (1954) is a postapocalyptic tale featuring the last man on earth, Robert Neville, who is immune to a germ that causes vampirism and thus is turned into an outsider by a transformed humanity seeking to kill him. All four of these historical contagions have had a lasting catastrophic bearing on the world, scarring our memories with cultural, social, political, and religious consequences. Ailments of race, such as miscegenation, the one-drop rule, passing, and racism, have done the same in sf by creating otherhoods, where race must be examined.

Contagion as a metaphor offers a perspective on racist thinking that morphs into a different structure with all the same signs, including social visibility and the fear of living with racial difference. Therefore, the idea of racism operates, in part, according to a fear of contagion; moreover, contagions have a way of transcending or intensifying racial differences. This morphing of racist thinking occurs at the moment one comes into contact with a colored person. Though "blackness" may not be catching, racism can be transferred from one social body to another at this contact point because some people fear race mixing as well as racial myths, thus destabilizing the reality of a visibly subjective environment. What I am trying to convey is the institutionalized mythic fears of white people in relation to blackness. White people harbor the fear that if they engage in social contact with blacks, they will be contaminated. Consequently, when race and contagion are placed together with otherhood in sf, they function as metaphor and metonym simultaneously. A film such as Danny Boyle's *28 Days Later* (2002) highlights these superimposed fears when the imaginary "Rage" virus turns people into living zombies. A fundamental fear of contagion drives the fear of the racial other, and this fear results in reactionary measures to resist, avoid, or stop social, environmental, and cultural change such as violence or attempts at isolation. Biological markers, such as skin color or genetic content, become focal points of discrimination that are still vaguely connected with connotations of less developed civilizations or a lower standing in nature's hierarchy. Sander L. Gilman lends support to this notion in his classic *Difference and Pathology* (1985), where he contends that "contamination" by the "other" results in "the human disposition to structure perception in terms of binary difference," such as black and white (24). As Heather Schell concludes, "The Other is still that same, tired old Other, that dark, unknowable native lurking in that dark, unknowable continent, waiting to erode our identity and leave us degenerated or reborn" (96). In this respect, the contagious ailments of race provide an otherhood map that negotiates connections between community, communication, and communicability.

Contagion has such scale and power to affect the human imagination because various diseases and illnesses have killed millions and millions of people throughout time. These germs can spread with alarming swiftness around the globe through the huge human populations of major cities because of air travel, tourism, trade, and pollution. As scientist John Leslie declares in *The End of the World: The Science and Ethics of Human Extinction* (1996): "When, however, a disease suddenly jumps from one continent to another, it will tend to find that in its new surroundings it is too powerful for its own good. It may bring death to almost everyone in a poorly prepared population" (78).

In this context, "illness is articulated on the body," as Michel Foucault writes in *The Birth of the Clinic* (1963), where "the 'glance' has simply to exercise its right of origin over truth" (4). Thereby, transference of fear occurs through the gaze. Fear of illness and death is replaced by a fear of difference and change because of the potential for harm that contact with the other represents—something, perhaps, unclean. A new truth is established as fear of the other becomes contagious through the perception of visual differences. Thus, to be contagious is to be feared as other.

Such germs create a sense of panic and mass hysteria for humanity because the threat posed by the idea of contagion and its ability to spread quickly far exceeds the capacity of any government's ability to contain and regulate its dangerous proliferation. In *AIDS and Its Metaphors* (1988), Susan Sontag notes, "Authoritarian ideologies have a vested interest in promoting fear, a sense of imminence of takeover by aliens—and real diseases are useful material" (61–62). After all, contagion recognizes none of the artificial geopolitical boundaries—towns, cities, states, countries, hemispheres—created by human beings; its only limitations are provided by the Earth's atmosphere, namely temperature, wind, light, and similar factors.[1] A bacterium does not simply disappear because human science has invented an arsenal of antibiotics and vaccines to fight it. Before the raw strength and authority of nature, humanity's vulnerability and insignificance is total in spite of scientific leaps and technological progress resulting in "the collapse of social relations, rituals, and institutions" (Wald, 11). This innate fear of and ironic fascination with contagion is reflected in literature outside science fiction.[2] Nonetheless, regulation of contagion and the fear triggered by epidemics entails government manipulation of the health-care system.

Outbreak narratives in sf work a little differently from those in mainstream fiction because of how sf iconography works. For example, race is a clear afterthought in George Stewart's *Earth Abides* (1949), where a plague sweeps the planet, leaving behind a handful of survivors in the San Francisco Bay area. Isherwood Williams (Ish) leads the remaining survivors in a world where all other plant and animal life thrives as the remains of civilization lay barren, yet intact. American civilization and its technology become myth as time passes, and humans return to a state of primitivism. Ish's wife, Emma, is a black woman, though Stewart communicates this antiracist sentiment with subtlety by describing her as a brunette with "wide-set black eyes in [a] dark face" and "full ripe lips" (114). However, the best indication of Emma's race comes as she lies dying near the end of the novel, when Ish remarks that "within her veins ran a different strain of blood" (333). Stewart presents race mixing as a matter of fact in a world destroyed by plague, and such a reflection produces a feeling of otherhood.

Other plague stories written by both whites and blacks envision contagion as a means of biological warfare used by blacks. To make a rough comparison here, I will contrast works by David Keller, a white medical doctor turned sf writer, with those of George Schuyler. Keller's four-part story "The Menace" (1928) depicts the adventures of the white detective Taine as he tries to stop a group of four mulatto scientists, "the Powerful Ones," from destroying white America (94). The Powerful Ones have developed a virus from wasp poison that they use to put everyone in America to sleep. However, it backfires, causing spontaneous combustion among the blacks; all that remains of them are "little piles of dust, with now and then a gold tooth or a filling" (127). Keller certainly offers a racist final solution to stop blacks from infecting white society with a virus, and by doing so he demonstrates how whites perceived the Negro problem in the early twentieth century. Similarly, Schuyler's Black Empire (1936–1938), makes use of biological warfare, among other things, to create a black world order, where "the European centers" are bombed "with plague-ridden rats . . . completely [terrorizing] the population of Western Europe . . . White people . . . dying like flies in the great cities" (240). Schuyler's response is racist in its own right, but the absurdity of such a race war makes it function more as wish fulfillment for an oppressed group of people in the United States. These and other stories like them dot the history of sf.

Placed together, contagion and racism capitalize on cultural anxieties that abound in the popular imagination.[3] These sf contagion narratives either spread racism or warn of it. As a race metaphor in sf, contagion is unmistakably connected to the master narratives of social Darwinism, change, and acceleration. Everything racial associated with social Darwinism, such as evolution, natural selection, and organic mechanism, can be tied to hierarchies of difference used to promote a sense of white superiority. Social Darwinism is responsible for all kinds of change, in culture, politics, and physical being, that can be traced in sf contagion narratives. Humans will attempt to fight evolutionary changes caused by illness in their attempt to contain the contagion. However, the difficult choices made in order to resist change are terrifying because the result is always destruction or transformation. In other words, the contagion could kill humans off as it spreads; it could render humans vulnerable to alien invasion; and it could transform humans into something else entirely. These outcomes are a wonder of science fiction, in a certain sense, because contagion in sf lets us accelerate both evolution and social change. Such acceleration is perfect for exploring ailments of race and critiquing the corrupting influence of racism transmitted by contact with an infected person.

Ailments of race exist in sf to expose societal discomfort with racial difference in terms of social relations between blacks and whites. However, racism is made visible in contagion narratives involving the offense of miscegenation—race mixing—as a biological phenomenon as opposed to a social one and the violent measures taken against such commingling. By constructing miscegenation as a biological phenomenon, sf writers question the one-drop rule as a social idea based on the racist belief that one drop of black blood in a family's heritage marks them as forever black, granting them invisible membership in an oppressed race. People of this mixed-race heritage may choose to identify with a different race, if they are light-skinned enough, as they pass from black to white and disappear across the color line to avoid discrimination and to seek a life without persecution. With contagion as a race metaphor, fear is imposed on such racial contacts, and the violent consequences of these inevitable encounters are envisioned through the lens of otherhood.

Returning to "Dark Benediction," we see that Miller uses the contagion story to critique racist thinking as it relates to miscegenation. The evolutionary transformation of mankind, either a blessing or a curse, is a matter of fate and faith because man devolves to savagery resisting the benediction from the stars, most notably the change in skin color. Through the story's protagonist, Paul Oberlin, we learn how the epidemic disrupts "the normal functioning of civilization" by causing "a third of humanity" to "become night-prowling maniacs" with "gray discolorations" while the rest flee "in horror . . . seeking the frigid northern climates where, according to rumor, the disease was less infectious" (256). The fear of this contagion has created a sense of racial paranoia that leads to the shutdown of society because infected people are visibly different with their gray skin pigmentation. In this story, "dermie" is a slur equivalent to "nigger" due to both the visible difference caused by the neuroderm plague and the feeling of racial animosity generated by the term "dermie." For example, three men in Houston are immediately prepared to lynch Paul if he displays any sign of being infected. The lead man says, "Drop the gun, dermie," to which Paul thinks, "No plague victim would hurl the dermie charge at another" (258). Fear, paranoia, and hatred are the regressive emotions exacerbated by humanity's experience of its radically swift transformation.

The contagion effectively creates two races of men at war with each other. From a Darwinian perspective, contagion leads to a swift species mutation, a chance event of natural selection that will ensure the survival of one of the races and the destruction of the other. In response to the pandemic, the human civilization around Houston uses the fear of contagion to justify radical separatist, interventionist, and defensive strategies to protect itself from infection by murdering any suspicious people. For this reason, "the death rate [is] high among dermies, but the cause [is] usually a bullet" (266). The laws of nature dictate that the neuroderm plague will overwhelm the remnants of humanity, despite their best attempts to maintain their racial purity, and change them into something other than human.

This defensive human strategy is best illustrated by Paul's time in Houston. Like most other humans, Paul experiences a sense of revulsion for the infected people, who have visibly discolored gray skin. When he is captured by an organized patrol of uniformly dressed people, he is forced to strip to prove he has no patches of gray skin. John Ower comments, "The anti-dermie vigilante group which rules Houston brings to mind the Klan as an organization seeking to maintain segregation and white supremacy in the South" (74). When Paul is invited to join the supremacist group after a probationary period, he finds that their plan is to make the city a bastion of health in the plague-filled world and the beginning point of humanity's recuperation. Yet Paul has misgivings about the draconian rules of membership, how human society is restructuring itself and his own place in it, which are proven correct when he witnesses the harsh treatment of an infected woman, Willie, in the hands of an incensed, apprehensive patrol and rescues her from certain death.

The new social order on display, "hyper colony," is presented as being more humane. Paul and Willie head for Galveston after he inexplicably decides to help her by finding a doctor of her own kind to look at her gunshot wounds. He finds a monastery with hyper scientists studying the micro-organism and brings one of the doctors to Willie. As a symbolic demonstration of their humanity, hypers in this community destroy easy access to the island to create a refuge for their kind. They also warn the uninfected to stay away as the hyper community attempts to reconstruct a society in the likeness of mankind. The hypers even allow Paul to stay on a quarantine floor, somewhat lessening his fear of "the gray curse" (272).

Through one of the hyper scientists, Dr. Seevers, we learn that the alien microbe, sent by an alien civilization, will radically change anything it touches, effectively destroying the elements of known civilization and any sense of trust or well-being. Seevers believes that the aliens are guilty "of their own brand of anthropomorphism. They project their own psychology on us" (287). Historically speaking, dominant groups in human society have projected their hegemonic views on groups they consider inferior in order to exploit them, enslave them, and generally mistreat them simply because they can. The social invention of race and the practice of racism are the best example of "projected psychology." A projected psychology that has had lingering effects on the American psyche is the notion of miscegenation.

Visible signs of miscegenation are plentiful throughout the story. Perhaps the best illustration of discernible race mixing is Paul's description of Seevers's face: "A dark splotch of neuroderm had crept up from his chin to split his mouth and cover one cheek and an eye, giving him the appearance of a black and white bulldog with a mixed color muzzle" (283). American society has been taught to fear the consequences of race mixing, prompting violent, often deadly reactions against interracial couples who have diluted the white gene pool. This kind of revulsion is later displayed by Paul: "He hated Seevers' smug bulldog face with a violence that was unfamiliar to him" (291). In fact, miscegenation was and is still considered a scandalous activity resulting from slavery, though this sentiment is changing.

The social implications of miscegenation caused by contagion are most convincingly expressed in the seemingly doomed romance between Paul and Willie. Their evident attraction for each other is thwarted by their belonging to the different races. Likewise, it is frustrated by a fear of infection that keeps them momentarily separated. Paul never intends to fall in love with Willie, but he rescues her and crosses racial lines by doing so.[4] Willie never intends to infect Paul, but the temptation to touch him is too much to endure as the disease overcomes her ability to resist. Paul accepts his fate and prevents Willie from killing herself because she contaminated him. Miller's twist ending suggests that love can conquer the taboo of miscegenation; that love is stronger than hate; that love can overcome custom; that love can defeat the contagion of racism. Indeed, he uses forbidden love to highlight miscegenation in sf.

In "Dark Benediction" the fear and animosity generated through contact with the racial other is clearly depicted as retrogressive. This contact mirrors race relations by suggesting that the tendency of humans to do violence to one another because of racial difference is devolutionary. Miller effectively critiques the regressive impact that color prejudice, racism, and discrimination have on our culture. His choice of color to represent miscegenation, gray, censures both whites and blacks in their willful application of racial politics. The indeterminate nature of gray as a color suggests that interracial love is a subjective matter. Miscegenation is a racial ailment in sf that represents changing social circumstances, whereby visible racial characteristics separate human beings and represent raced identities. People who do not fit any of these categories deeply trouble others. At least in this story, at the time it was written in the later stages of the Jim Crow era, otherhood suggests that sf is going in the direction of a racial paradigm shift, where everyone must adapt. Miller's use of contagion implies that accelerated social change brought on by race mixing is the only way to move beyond complex racial issues.

Other ailments of race associated with the contagion metaphor and notions of racial purity are the one-drop rule and passing. Concerned

whites give the one-drop rule credibility because they perceive miscegenation as contamination to an all-white gene pool. As a result, anyone with black lineage, no matter how remote, cannot be white. More
than any other thing, the one-drop rule "has shaped the development
of racial identity in America" (Hall, Russell, and Wilson, 74). Because
of societal acceptance of this rule, many light-skinned blacks have
disappeared within the white world as a response to racism that comes
at heavy cost to positive self-identity. This phenomenon has come to
be known as "passing."[5] Individuals who can "pass" as white must, by
necessity, disown any links to their colored past.

The idea of passing is evident in sf texts and films centering on
androids and genetic engineering. For instance, Philip K. Dick's *Do
Androids Dream of Electric Sheep?* (1968) complicates what it means to
be human in one important way: androids ("andys") pass for human.
It is up to the andy bounty hunter Rick Deckard to "retire" six escaped
andys, who have the latest Nexus-6 brain and are attempting to pass
for human in San Francisco. The severity of discrimination against
biological androids, manufactured human beings in the text, is clearly
racism based on a paranoid belief that machines could replace men.
Ridley Scott's landmark film adaptation of Dick's novel, *Blade Runner*
(1982), brings the theme of android passing vividly to life, as Deckard
must destroy the "replicants" in a future Los Angeles. A distinct racial paradigm is created by questioning Deckard's humanity and his
contagious sense of paranoia.

Another example of passing in science fiction is provided by Andrew Niccol's film *Gattaca* (1997). The film is the story of Vincent, a
genetically unenhanced human, who dreams of traveling to the stars.
Because of his unenhanced genetic profile, Vincent faces extreme
racial discrimination, or "genoism," from a society that prizes physical
and mental perfection. By borrowing body matter, such as blood, hair,
and urine, from Jerome, a cynical and crippled near-perfect human,
Vincent passes as an enhanced human by faking his way through various tests in order to obtain a job at the top space firm and realizes his
dream of spaceflight by outperforming his enhanced peers. Jerome
could no longer deal with the burden of being almost perfect after
winning the silver in a world championship swim meet. He attempted
suicide by stepping in front of a moving car, breaking his back and as

a result becoming a paraplegic. Thus, the film's focus on body matter, especially blood, powerfully evokes the one-drop rule. The idea of genoism is communicable in the film, where society discriminates against genetic makeup in contrast to race or gender. Genoism stands for racism in this exploration of sf's social and political discourse.

The one-drop rule and passing are linked ideas in Walter Mosley's *Futureland* (2001). *Futureland* presents a near future of supposed racial integration, permeated by the information technology boom and the corporations that control it and everything else, a deviation from cyberpunk, or perhaps its inversion. In this extrapolation, the historical consequences of infotech alter political relationships while identity politics remain static at the intersection of change and race. The outlaw and outcast heroes of this world are mostly the working class, the poor, and the marginalized, who have little or no chance of prevailing over big business. Most workers are caught in the vicious cycle of subsistence work and unemployment, practically indentured as the corporation states care little for their rights as human beings. Most of these workers also live in three-hundred-story skyscrapers segregated by a class distribution system with the rich at the top and the poor at the bottom (a visual representation of social hierarchy). The unemployed have few rights and are in danger of becoming "White Noise," forever dispossessed of all civil liberties and forgotten by society (211).

Mosley uses the contagion metaphor in the last two stories of this dismal future, "En Masse" and "The Nig in Me," to foreground race. The first story concerns the life of Neil Hawthorne, a light-skinned black production engineer. Hawthorne is abruptly reassigned to GEE-PRO-9, a secret group of midlevel corporate engineers. This group is led by Ptolemy Bent, a one-time black child prodigy who has been imprisoned for life, and the artificial intelligence Un Fitt. As the story develops, Un Fitt discovers information about a group of white supremacists who have designed a genocidal virus to rid the world of black people. With this knowledge, GEE-PRO-9 attempts to stop them. The second story, "The Nig in Me," details the unexpected results of GEE-PRO-9's failure to prevent the outbreak from the viewpoint of an interracial friendship between the black Harold Bottoms and the white Jamey Halloway.

The main events of "En Masse" transpire from a combination of circumstances: racism, an attempt to maintain power, and the opportunity of a white extremist group to reclaim an exhausted political dominance through terrorist action. The white supremacist group known as the "Itsies" have "set up a laboratory to study the molecular nature of viruses" in order to design "viral strains that target racial indicators" (311).[6] The best way for this group to once again affect the world's politics is to eliminate a substantial portion of the population via contagion since the world has come to be dominated by faceless corporations. Ironically, Mosley suggests that it is the very success of big business, its desire to expand everywhere and control everything through smart machines, that will disrupt the white power structure.

Blacks and other minorities are still the predominant members of the lower class in Mosley's novel because they do not have the education necessary to escape it. With a concentrated working-class population, contagion is easier to spread. The Itsies have nothing to lose by exterminating the supposed dregs of this other America and have the perfect cover for releasing this race-specific contagion, a large-scale environmental disaster set off by the constant migration of corporate citizens from city to city in search of work. In their arrogance, the white supremacist group does not account for the awkward nature of biological weapons. They have developed what they believe to be an effective biological weapon that is stable, fast-acting, mass-produced, and harmless to white society.

The Itsies never reckon that a secret black group plans to stop them. GEE-PRO-9 locates the germ in Africa and easily destroys it. However, the second batch proves to be more difficult because it is positioned in the basement of a white-only bar in Denver. At this point, Mosley makes use of passing through the light-skinned character of Neil, who infiltrates the bar with the assistance of Blaun, a former Itsie. As the story reaches its climax, Neil is able "to irradiate the pathogen" for "twelve seconds" more or less before he is critically injured (317). However, the barrel is punctured, and the contagion escapes. The irradiation causes the viral contagion to mutate, and it proves to be equally lethal to all the races with the exception of blacks, who are unaffected.

The disastrous consequences of this viral mutation are explored by Mosley in *Futureland*'s last story, "The Nig in Me." The story opens with Jamey informing Harold of the cold that everyone except blacks seems to be catching. Harold thinks to himself: "He'd seen Asians and a few Mexicans, India Indians and lots of white people with the red or brown striations on their upper arms. But he'd never seen any Negro-looking people with them" (321–22). Significantly, Harold's uneasy thought suggests that blacks alone will inherit the earth. The news of this plague is slow to circulate because internet television (ITV) stations are not able to discuss the "racial aspect" of the disease due to a politically correct policy instituted long before to end the problem of the color line (322). Thus, no one suspects that a racially motivated hate crime will change the world—that white supremacists have destroyed their own race and others too. Even after several days, racial difference has yet to de-center the economic, political, and social agendas of the corporations because the virus has two stages: striped flu followed by dormancy, and a painful, slow death over three or four days.

As the second stage begins, the world becomes chaotic. The legitimate ITV services broadcast approved virus news, such as the Itsie attempt "to contaminate a children's immunization center in Rockland, Oregon" (334), and news of the deadly secondary stage of the striped flu. While the people in power attempt to suppress news of this lethal end stage, the illegal underground website, "ghostnet," is revealing that a pandemic exists, causing the dissolution of corporate owned "MacroCode Russia" (343). Russia is blaming the Americans for the plague; and Russia is going to drop an atomic bomb on New York out of vengeance. Ghostnet is the only source of information available that will allow the lower class a remote chance of escaping the imminent nuclear explosion. Most people in the city are not even aware that a nuclear disaster is approaching swiftly. All of the emergency services, "nurses, firemen, security force, everybody in city service," have been mobilized and sent to "where all the white people live," away from the city "in the outer fiefs" (342). In other words, emergency resources are dispensed to the white community first. Mosley explicitly indicates that a postrace world threatened by the fear of a deadly sickness will fall back on old race paradigms. The tactics practiced by the all-powerful corporations appear reasonable since blacks are not affected by the

virus despite the fact that other minorities are dying too. Racism, therefore, becomes a visible contagion in this context. The feds, controlled
by the corporations, are ordered to lock down New York City in an attempt to combat the pandemic, or at least to keep the lower class there
and let the nuclear strike do the rest.

At this moment, racial difference de-centers the multiple agendas of the corporations because a panic logic takes over the lower
classes—minorities—who have access to ghostnet and desire to escape
impending doom. Because the contagion rages beyond control, the
corporations recognize the limits of their ability to contain its spread,
and they decide on a new and conservative course of action: annihilation, a very similar position to that of the Itsies. This contagion has a
tremendous destabilizing effect on the entire world as evinced by official news on ITV of the Russian response half a day later, well after
the launch. At this point in the story, Harold and Jamey flee New York
on a bus, the only means available for the poor, though they are put off
it when Jamey starts to exhibit the pain associated with the contagion's
secondary phase.

Mosley's understanding of racial purity becomes evident in the aftermath of the nuclear attack on major U.S. cities, including New York.
He informs us through white news coverage—before all ITV reporting
ceases—that "the disease was 100 percent fatal and everybody got it;
everybody but people with at least 12.5 percent African Negro DNA"
(351). At this juncture, Mosley is making a mockery of the one-drop
rule—it has created such social categories for blacks as mulatto (½
black), quadroon (¼ black), and octoroon (⅛ black)—by suggesting that
a percentage of black DNA is a decisive factor in determining who lives
and who dies. While he must deride such a tradition within American
culture, he is all too aware that many people on both sides of the color
line still adhere to it. Awareness of this tradition is the only way that
notions of racial purity can be preserved in today's world.

Mosley goes on to skewer the notion of passing when he writes
that "astonished Caucasians who survived the plague realized that
there was a sizeable portion of Negro blood in their veins" (351). The
astonishment of these formerly white citizens is indicative of how effectively they have passed for white or, more likely, how successful
their forebears were at passing. Mosley complicates the issue with a

newspaper account that "showed the towering figure of Cowled Death rising over a white man only to be stymied when the white man pulled open his shirt to reveal the words THE NIG IN ME: 12.5%." (351). While death is depicted in the traditional sense as a dark hooded figure, the white man audaciously reveals his disguised black identity to escape the trap of death, claiming a black identity that he has certainly despised.[7] The dominant image of white on the outside and black on the inside is a reflection of how deeply rooted the issue of racial purity is regarding the American identity and who has access to it. However, the disruption of racial boundaries by the apparent whites who have managed to survive the lethal contagion creates a sense of otherhood. Racism continues as the world resets, though Mosley provides us with a paradoxically "new" white world. His story suggests that race cannot be transformed because years of conditioning as inferior beings have taken a toll on the African American population.

After Jamey dies, a new world order begins to emerge as Harold watches the internet broadcast services taken over by black reporters. The first claim made is that "the day of the white man is over" because it is he who "created a doomsday device designed to kill" blacks (353). The second allegation made by the black news service concerns the discovery of secret files from the "National Security Department" that reveal the Itsies "had paid geneticists in MacroCode Russia to develop a gene virus that would target the black race" (353). This allegation suggests a racial conspiracy that links the government, corporations, and supremacist groups in an attempt to rid the world of its undesirables, starting with blacks. The possibility of such collusion on the part of the government reveals a profound suspicion of government authority by black society. On the surface, it is indicative of a new "old" cold war moment, but it also subtly reflects a stagnant hatred of difference from a political standpoint.

Mosley ends his story with an unmistakable implication: the idea of racial difference will survive an apocalypse wholly intact. Even after society has fallen, Harold encounters three apparently white men who shout, "Hey, nig!" before trying to shoot him dead (356). Much like the credo of pretentious black society of the twentieth century, "whiter and whiter with each generation," the insecurity of black identity ingrained by years of racial strife will endure as the newly white, light-skinned blacks, reestablish the old racial hierarchy based on skin color rather than DNA (Thurman, 29). Mosley does not miss the opportunity to invoke the color line dilemma made famous by DuBois by suggesting that familiar racial paradigms will continue in the absence of "real" white people, even if nine-tenths of humanity is killed by a deadly plague. Humanity fears race too much to get beyond it and has such a history for using race to create power differentials between groups. As ailments of race, the one-drop rule and passing remain constant in Mosley's newly black world. His linked contagion tales display a different understanding of sf's racially constructed social networks.

Whereas Mosley suggests that established racial paradigms will continue in the absence of white people in *Futureland*, "Who Goes There?" (1938), a classic novella by the legendary editor and author John W. Campbell Jr., presents a singularly racist understanding of racial purity and the paranoia that drives fear of the racial other.[8] In "Who Goes There?" a team of scientists stumbles across an alien spaceship that crashed millions of years ago in the Antarctic, and discovers the frozen alien pilot close by buried in the ice. As the thing thaws, revives, and escapes, the men come to learn that it is a shape-shifting mind reader that spreads rapidly through contact as it attempts to assimilate every living animal at the base—dog, cow, and man—in its Darwinian desire to win free and survive. In other words, "the alien is *contagious*," it is something that invades the body that should not be there and is inherently harmful, much like a disease (Rieder, 31). As the rest of the story unfolds, paranoia intensifies for the protagonist McReady, meteorologist and second in command, and the other scientists who realize that the thing could be imitating any number of them and that they must prevent the destruction of the planet by containing it at the base. Trust is nonexistent and xenophobia rules until a means of identifying the alien can be discovered and it can be destroyed. As the following otherhood reading of Campbell's novella demonstrates, "Who Goes There?" is a discomfiting thought experiment dependent on fear of the racial other and notions of white purity.

Even though sf theorists and scholars credit Campbell with single-handedly shaping science fiction in its golden years by editing *Astounding*, the most influential sf pulp magazine of the 1940s and 1950s, his legacy as a writer and as an influential editor has been tarnished by the obvious racism in his social philosophy. Gary Westfahl was among the first to challenge the accepted image of Campbell as an "editorial genius," noting how "Campbell was a racist, a bigot, a sexist, and an anti-Semite" ("Dictatorial," 50). Campbell's often inflammatory editorials sometimes berated the intelligence of other races, particularly blacks, and proved his inflexibility as a person capable of changing with the social currents of mid-twentieth-century America. In one column, for example, regarding the first *Brown* decision (1954), Campbell declares that men are not created equal by God, that they are separated by intelligence, that the white race has a higher allocation of intelligence and ability compared to that of the black race on a distribution curve, and is therefore "strongly in favor of rigidly segregated schools, and . . . that it is absolutely necessary for the continuation of the United States" (Harrison, 12).[9] In fact, Albert Berger notes how vehemently opposed Campbell was "to civil rights for African-Americans" during the social upheaval of the 1960s; Campbell went so far as to support the infamous presidential bid of Governor George Wallace of Alabama (187). Clearly, this is a man who is afraid of social change, and I suggest an otherhood reading of "Who Goes There?" displays an overt endorsement of racism.

Written in the midst of the Great Depression and Franklin D. Roosevelt's New Deal politics, "Who Goes There?" captures the aura of fear in America regarding invasion by fascist powers such as Germany. This atmosphere suited Campbell's racist politics. Perhaps even more sinister, the story resonates with the fear of social revolution by disgruntled black Americans, an odd foreshadowing of the portrayal of communism in Richard Wright's *Native Son* (1940), which was published two years later. As John Trushell claims, "The political rhetoric of [the day] helped to foment a 'Brown Scare' . . . which . . . resembled the 'Red Scare' of communism" and influenced Campbell to no small degree (79). In each of its renditions (including the film versions *The Thing from Another World* [1951] and *The Thing* [1982]), the story is not driven by "the fear of knowing versus not knowing who is human"; rather "the puzzle of contriving a test to determine a real identity drives the story" (Landon, *Aesthetics*, 31).

An essential identity question remains to be answered because Campbell's greatest fear is perhaps the demise of white humanity by exposure to a single drop of black blood. Such a fear is represented by the alien shape-changer, who can pass not only for human but for an American white male. Indeed, Brooks Landon finds Campbell's "'solution' for identifying an alien race that can 'pass for human' . . . a blood test . . . as connotatively troubling" (*Aesthetics*, 33). In this respect, John Carpenter's underappreciated adaptation of the novella, *The Thing* (1982), picks up on and exploits its racist aspect by making two members of the research outpost black, "thus adding a potential level of racial conflict" (Landon, *Aesthetics*, 39).[10] Even more fascinating, the film ends with two survivors, one black, the other white, and either one possibly alien, leaving open the ambiguity of interpretation.

The scientists in both the novella and the film attempt to find a definitive test based on the one-drop rule to determine identity—both human and monster. The presumed blood contamination by the thing can be and must be read as racism because the thing is decidedly not human. While the thing is an alien other, the thing must be reconfigured as the racial other if Campbell's history is taken into account.

In the story the scientists argue about whether or not the thing should be thawed out for research purposes because of the danger it might represent. The physicist Norris "is afraid that [the scientists] may release a plague—some germ disease unknown to Earth" by thawing out the thing (54). Norris recognizes the obvious danger that the thing's difference represents—contagion—and his only desire is to safeguard humanity from this threat. As we learn, Norris's fear is racialized because he thinks this alien has the potential to destroy humanity by crossing biological boundaries and infecting blood; the racism in his thinking causes the fear. The argument between Norris and Blair, the biologist, is essentially a power struggle that effectively splits the scientists into groups, fracturing the scientific community's solidarity and thus sowing the seeds of paranoia.

The men's decision to allow Blair to go ahead with his experiments proves to be rash because the alien is telepathic. A few of the scientists who have slept in the vicinity of the thing speak out about their troubled dreams. Norris offers the best example when he talks about his nightmares, that "the thing thawed out and came to life— that it wasn't dead, or even wholly unconscious . . . I had some swell nightmares—that it wasn't made like we are—which is obvious—but of a different kind of flesh that it can really control. That it can change its shape, and look like a man—and wait to kill and eat" (56). His dreams reveal that the thing is alive, conscious, able to read minds and project thoughts, and also able to change its shape, suggesting that the thing has the ability to pass for human, therefore making it a menace in a racial sense. By the time the scientists realize the gravity of their error, the thing is not outside, but inside with them and in them. Rather, the racial other is no longer out *there* but in *here*, disrupting their sense of identity as it begins its conquest of the base by absorption, and paranoia results from the scientists' racist fear of being contaminated.

Knowing that the thing has the ability to pass itself off as human, Blair accuses his fellow scientist Connant of being a thing because Connant was solely responsible for guarding the thawing body of the thing overnight. Madly laughing Blair asks, "'Connant—where's Connant?' . . . 'Are you?' . . . 'Are you there?' . . . 'Are you Connant? The beast wanted to be a *man*—not a dog—'" (72). Blair's line of reasoning is impeccable and incites paranoia because the thing can be anywhere and anything as it seeks to confuse the scientists. It can even manipulate the body parts of other people as it becomes them. Only if it has a fixed identity can it be destroyed. Even if the thing does not think in racial terms, passing traps it within the very racial restrictions it must escape to triumph over humanity. Connant predictably reacts in anger when his humanity is questioned, but the contagious effects of racist paranoia are already at work. There is no trust among the men because they cannot be sure of who is human. As a result, the physician, Copper, suggests that Connant and Blair be quarantined until a test can be devised to discriminate between men and aliens. No matter how normal in appearance and action someone contaminated seems to be, that scientist is a thing by blood; even if he is indistinguishable from a human, it is a thing. The one-drop rule by definition unites all the things based on a common ancestry to the original thing taken out of the ice.

With anxiety mounting, McReady and Copper reason that blood is the key factor. Copper believes that a blood serum test involving the animal stock in addition to humans will expose the things, but Copper's test fails because the thing has already tainted the animal stock. The scientists begin to realize the malevolent intelligence of the thing, which has infected all of the dogs with the exception of one—the control for the experiment. McReady articulates the delicate balance of power between the humans and the things as a matter of attrition. He determines that "it doesn't fight," that "it must be a peaceable thing in its own—inimitable—way" because "it never had to," as "it always gained its end" through passing (89). McReady comes up with a second blood test that works. He explains that because the thing can read minds it has to bleed or else reveal its inhuman nature. Consequently, he is able to obtain a pure blood sample from each of the men. McReady then rationalizes "that blood, separated from them [the thing], is an individual—*a newly formed individual in its own right, just as they, split, all of them, from one original, are individuals!*" (97). In other words, each drop of alien blood is an individual in its own right with its own will to live if it is separated from the body of a thing. All that's required to discriminate between humans and the thing is some kind of physical stimulus, such as a hot needle, administered on the blood samples. Physical pain causes a flight response from contaminated blood and divulges the inhuman identity of the thing.

McReady takes a minute to gloat before testing his theory: "This is satisfying, in a way. I'm pretty sure we humans still outnumber you—others . . . We'll fight, fight with a ferocity you may attempt to imitate, but you'll never equal! We're human. We're real. You're imitations, false to the core of every cell" (97). This gloating reveals something about the fundamental nature of racism. It indicates how necessary a sense of difference is to identity. McReady and the other humans can only know themselves "through the construction of the Other" (Hall, "Race," 342). Therefore, McReady and company will take pleasure in their power over the relative weakness of the thing as they destroy it. Once the fear of contagion is dispelled in the remaining humans, the passing things are doomed. The release of paranoia concerning passing aliens results in the eruption of violence as the remaining humans kill their imitation colleagues for betraying humanity. Men of science and reason become men of action justified in their violence by scientific racism, if not social Darwinism, and fear of racial contamination. To answer the title's question of "who goes there," obviously the thing is black.

In the film, the outcome is very much the same except that Carpenter fully takes advantage of Campbell's racist allegory. MacReady (Kurt Russell) blows up the station ostensibly with the last thing inside it. However, Childs (Keith David), one of the black characters, wanders into MacReady's shelter from the flaming and smoking rubble with the claim that he lost Blair in the blizzard. Before the explosion, Childs was verifiably human, but now MacReady has no idea as to the identity of Childs. The film ends with the two men of different races sharing a drink, wary, and waiting to see what happens as the temperature drops. Though distrust is useless in the smoking remains of the base, Carpenter suggests Childs is the thing since the character is black and was also off-camera in the penultimate scene. "The subtext of racial antagonism present throughout the film fully erupts," as Adilifu Nama suggests, "which points to the idea that the black character who has been the most vocal in challenging white authority is a monster in disguise" (55). Such an enigmatic ending capitalizes on the racial tensions that have always existed in America between whites and blacks. Carpenter legitimately questions what it means to be human with his paranoid vision anchored by Campbell's novella where passing, blood contamination, and racial purity are convincingly twined together through contagion as a race metaphor.

Another issue important to contagion stories is how racism itself spreads through health-care facilities like an incurable illness during an outbreak. The hospital, as a representation of our society, maintains inequality in its attempt to limit the spread of contagion. Gary Westfahl expresses his opinion about hospitals in *No Cure for the Future: Disease and Medicine in Science Fiction and Fantasy* (2002), stating that "popular images of hospitals, and popular images of the future, seem inextricably intertwined" and that "the nearest equivalent to traveling through time into the distant future is becoming a patient at a modern hospital . . . attached to various pieces of machinery that mysteriously flicker and hum," overhearing "people whispering in incomprehensible jargon" (1). This scenario is "the science fiction flavor" of which Susan Sontag speaks (18). When seeking treatment at the hospital, we hope to be restored to health and cared for at the same time, but this somehow changes when the fear and panic of contagion grips society. The alarm becomes racial for several reasons.

The hospital itself functions as a place for racial exclusion or exile. First, the hospital is another form of "'incarceration' where those people infected with contagion are exiled—effectively making criminals out of them because they are a threat to society and uncontainable in any other facilities," according to Linda Singer (100). Second, she points out that the hospital is "socially visible" and thus symbolic of something being wrong with humanity (100). And third, the hospital represents the absolute fear of *living* with difference and the somewhat circumspect power to countermand it. Again and again humanity has proven its capacity for monstrosity through its inability to live with difference.

Tananarive Due, contemporary horror writer, explores the chilling price of hospitalization as a result of exposure to contagion in "Patient Zero" (2001). "Patient Zero," set in a Miami hospital, is the account of a racially ambiguous ten-year-old boy named Jay, who is the only known person to recover from "virus-J," a contagion which is rapidly destroying humanity (496). Jay's difference is generated by his status as the only healthy carrier of this virus. In Priscilla Wald's reckoning, he is "the healthy human being turned pathogen" (70). Thus, he becomes an obvious target for racism. According to Wald, the term "patient zero" designates the "mythic figure" at the heart of an outbreak (216). There is no factual basis for designating Jay as "Patient Zero" except that he has managed to survive where everyone else is dying. However, Jay is ostracized, vilified, hated, and feared by a world on the brink of natural annihilation. In otherhood terms, this story is important because it takes racism beyond the idea of color prejudice. It makes racism conspicuous given the conditions of fear, anger, illness, and death as desperate people lash out. It does not really matter what race Jay belongs to because he represents both hope and despair as the carrier of the invisible virus.

Quarantined four years, forced to endure seemingly endless and painful medical procedures, restricted to his own glass-sealed private room in the hospital, Jay has little contact with the outside world other than a censored television and the medical staff. Through his personal journal entries, we learn that the medical staff has had his television removed because Jay is highly upset to learn that the world holds him responsible for the pandemic. In other words, the world, in need of a scapegoat, chooses Jay. The news media play a big part in painting Jay "black" as patient zero because they insist that the symptoms originate with him, that he is the first person to have been infected by the virus. Visible to the public and alone in his confinement, Jay recognizes this distortion of the truth, knowing that members of his dad's oil crew in Alaska were first to get sick.

His body's recovery from the contagion symbolizes a cure to the world and dictates that further impositions occur. In this respect, social visibility necessitates two things: further imprisonment and violations of his physical well-being sanctioned by the public as a matter of survival. Given enough time, scientists can develop a cure from his blood. Consequently, the system justifies itself because of the political and social climate created by the fear of contagion. The sacrifice of one boy so that humanity may endure seems like a small price to pay in this dreadful situation. Singer states, "In a climate induced by epidemic, it becomes reasonable to intervene into the bodies of others" (30). Fear of and hate for Jay authorizes the intrusion of his flesh, and the media validate this violation as being a means to help protect humanity from this scourge. Society is willing to torture one little boy if it will save the human race, especially if the little boy is seemingly monstrous to the public eye.

Jay is the victim of racial violence on two counts when very different members of the hospital staff cause him harm. First, he gives an account of the abuse he suffered at the hands of a French doctor who slapped Jay for no apparent reason and without apology after the doctor draws "so much blood" that Jay "couldn't even stand up" (500). The doctor's behavior is a clear manifestation of racism because he is helpless to resist the violence in his heart while in the presence of Jay's difference. Even though Jay is the only person who produces antibodies for studying the virus, the doctor believes Jay does not deserve the kind of lifestyle provided at the hospital. In the context of the story, the doctor's display of weakness underscores how racism can overwhelm the assumed impartiality of science. Unable to halt his hostility toward Jay, he strikes out at this living symbol of the virus which has killed his friends, family, and most of the world. Racism has turned Jay into an icon, making him no longer human to the racist world.

The second occurrence of racism happens late at night after all of the medical staff is gone for the evening. The drunken custodian, Lou, disturbs Jay's rest by banging on the glass while verbally assaulting Jay over the intercom: *"They should put you to sleep like a dog at the pound"* (500). It is one thing for an egotistical doctor to see the child as a thing or experiment, but it is quite another thing for a janitor to make this kind of gesture. Both the high and low of society unite against the boy. Neither the French doctor nor Lou is able to contain his destructive emotions, which result in acts of hatred. Due uses the absurd image of a grown man vocally assailing a ten-year-old boy locked up in a room late at night to highlight racism. Lou's comment is a distinct expression of racism because the janitor's words have reduced Jay to a beast. The use of offensive language to condemn Jay for his healthiness makes him "other" just as it races his being.

Clearly, then, Due's story deals with concepts of otherhood by providing the necessary contact points with which racism and discrimination become infectious. The virus kills humanity more slowly than the notion of racism that spreads through society, meaning that humankind has lost an essential part of itself in its atrocious treatment of Jay. The story ends with Jay alone in the dark hospital for a couple of days without food before he decides to use the code given him by his Haitian tutor to escape his isolation chamber. Race comes to mean nothing and everything at the same time: racism is absent from the world with nowhere and no one left to infect, though it is contained within Jay's being as the last human alive.

When racism shifts focus from fixed biological markers such as skin color or hair texture to being more accurately measured by lifestyle, beliefs, traditions, artistic sensibilities, or languages, it becomes cultural. Physical characteristics are replaced by cultural ones as the focal point of discrimination. For example, people who are discriminated against because of the language they speak have been marked as different in a racial sense. The same biases are applied, though this kind of racism goes beyond the racism based on biology and past the color line. In Stuart Hall's assessment, the "earlier forms" of racism "have been powerfully transformed by what people normally call a new form of 'cultural racism'" (339). In this respect, Octavia Butler's "The Evening and the Morning and the Night" (1987) offers a compelling analogy between genetic diseases and the racial other. If all victims of Duryea-Gode disease (DGD) are read as culturally black, then her story offers a broader cultural message that "the social construction of 'race'" is destructive in the extreme, establishing a "permanent inferiority and domination" (Marable, 229). In short, with her analogy of genetic disability and community self-determination, Butler uses the fear of social contagion and containment of this fear to critique racism.

While she always provides the bifocal lens of race and gender to view what it means to be different, to be something other in Western society, Butler's thematic interest in the science of genetics provides the setting for her dystopian projections. Biology and various forms of identity collide in Butler's preoccupation with genetics. In Sherryl Vint's estimation, "Butler's use of genetics is usually read as a narrative trope that permits her to engage with the themes she is interested in exploring about human culture and values" (*Bodies*, 196–97). Calling Butler's use of genetics a trope diminishes its significance as a primary subject. Though Butler does use genetics as a metaphor for other things in her writing, she also extrapolates from scientific ideas in significant ways.

Heredity has a central role in Butler's work, and she extensively explores how genetic changes alter the face of humanity. The Patternist series is simultaneously concerned with the creation of a master race through selective breeding and with genetic mutation caused by alien microbes transforming humanity into something else entirely. The Xenogenesis trilogy (later collected and published as *Lilith's Brood* in 2000) features an alien race that performs genetic engineering on a biological level as they combine their genetic material with other species as a matter of survival. The Parable books present an imaginary hereditary disorder caused by drug abuse. Time travel is made possible in the science fantasy of *Kindred* because of the blood relationship between Dana and Rufus. "Speech Sounds" features a worldwide epidemic that destroys humanity's ability to communicate as it alters the gene pool. Even "Bloodchild" suggests the notion of heredity with its title. And of course racial purity is one of the strongest themes of Butler's last novel, *Fledgling*. As Roger Luckhurst suggests, Butler's "fictions investigate the clash of cultural identities against a biological imperative" (33).

Her novels explore various issues of genetics in the hope that humanity can evolve beyond its predilection toward self-destructive habits such as violence, hierarchical tendencies, or bigotry.

Her most critically neglected story, "The Evening and the Morning and the Night," is possibly Butler's best use of contagion in her storytelling. "The Evening and the Morning and the Night" is a tale of a woman who grapples with the implications of her inherited, latent genetic disorder that will end with self-mutilation. The story is set in a future much like the present, where people suffering with a hereditary disease are forced to live apart from society in protective wards and are subject to discriminatory treatment from a fearful general populace influenced by the mass media. The protagonist, Lynn Mortimer, gives a first-person account of her life as a DGD sufferer. We can set "The Evening and the Morning and the Night" apart from other Butler contagion narratives, however, because here she uses social contagion to explore elements of race and racism.

Just as humanity has little or no control of natural contagions, it also has little or no control over the transmission of sociocultural illnesses, such as racism, that have been produced by human progress. According to Paul Marsden, most social contagion definitions are linked by the "observable phenomenon of spread by contact. . . . the central rationale of the metaphor; that observable culture spreads as if it has contagious properties" (173). Social contagion, then, refers to infectious moods, feelings, behaviors, and ideas that disperse by the power of suggestion or interpersonal influences through a population. Exposure to contagious ideas such as racism produced in various cultures is enough to infect and spread them, especially if the mass media get involved in their propagation. As Marsden states, "We have little control over the culture we become infected with and consequently spread" (175).

Figured within these cultural and social fears, racism is another threatening social phenomenon that can be associated with contagion. This phenomenon also has the capacity to swell and intensify swiftly, and it has proven to be continually toxic in American history. As a result, race has been a major focus of American thought for centuries. Reading contagion in sf as a race metaphor is entirely appropriate since both ideas are inextricably linked, seriously neglected, and thrive in popular culture. Hence, examining contagion in Octavia Butler's sf proves to be a valuable kind of social criticism that can be aptly applied to the problematical nature of race relations.

Like many of Butler's other stories, "The Evening and the Morning and the Night" is shaped by her "ongoing fascinations with biology, medicine and personal responsibility" (69). Butler combines fear of contagion with the notion of social Darwinism to create a powerful sense of racial difference in this story. The fear inspired by her DGD is just as reasonable as any number of historical killers, such as Spanish influenza. Though DGD is genetic and noncommunicable, the social response to it is infectious in every sense of the word, on the individual level as well as that of the total population. Butler envisions a disease that is "built from the elements of three genetic disorders"—Huntington's disease, phenylketonuria (PKU), and Lesch-Nyhan disease—and that combines hereditary features, the need of a special diet, mental impairment, and self-mutilation in addition to her "own particular twists" including scenting abilities and delusions of corporeal self-entrapment (69–70). DGD is feared because it turns its victims into frightening self-mutilating monsters that might attack an unafflicted person in the street without provocation. Just imagine "someone attacking her own arm as though it were a wild animal [or] someone who had torn at himself and been restrained or drugged off and on for so long that he barely had a recognizable human feature left, but he was still trying with what he did have to dig into his own flesh" (50). In this sense, "the disease itself trivializes most other forms of difference" (Green, 180). Out of fear for their personal safety, people have become prejudiced against those afflicted in public social settings, which in turn generates a powerful sense of cultural racism.

Containment strategies to handle the fear of exposure to DGD result in the unavoidable outbreak of cultural racism in a variety of social settings. As Marsden reflects, "Successful social contagions are those elements of culture that operate as both stimulus and response" (178). Butler's imaginary disease has been caused by a cancer treatment gone awry under medical supervision. DGD is the consequence of a drug called "Hedeonco: the magic bullet, the cure for a large percentage of the world's cancer and a number of serious viral diseases," which obviously, as evidenced by its later effect on the human genome, was not studied well enough before it was rushed to market (46).[11] There is an interesting crossover here—cancer can be genetic, viral, or both. Thus, a cancer cure that causes a new disease is also a secondary product of either a genetic defect or a virus. This crossover goes back to the idea that contagion can be viewed as operating on two levels—individual and societal. Although DGD itself is *not* contagious, it is transmitted genetically from parents to offspring. This is reminiscent of the fear of miscegenation, or race mixing—that the next generation is not racially pure. Butler is careful to establish this analogy to racism here with the idea of genetic purity as it relates to "bad genes" (43). While the disease itself *is* alarming, the unfounded threat of a compromised purity to the unafflicted—similar to bigoted notions of racial contamination—is even more terrifying. Isolation by the non-DGD world becomes an act of cultural racism born from the infectious fear of being attacked by an afflicted person.

Behavioral responses to DGD sufferers, such as isolation or discrimination, drastically alter the landscape of human interactions when considering some of the services provided by the health-care industry as well as Lynn Mortimer's college experiences. The isolation experienced by DGD victims in relationship to hospital services is an example of one containment tactic. In the story, society desires the DGD problem to be placed out of sight and therefore out of mind. This desire necessitates special facilities such as government-run hospital wards, where exceptionally troublesome patients are placed in "a bare room" and are allowed "to finish themselves" by digging (56). As maintained by Singer, "The hospital is an institution already authorized to mark its own zone in our social thoroughfares with signs demanding quiet" (100). The silence is conspicuous as a muted kind of approval because it signifies society's desire for DGDs to be forgotten. In other words, hospitals function to silence people afflicted with DGD. While Dilg, a privately funded facility for people with DGD, can afford to be "hidden away in the hills" (45), government-sponsored disease wards also require a certain stillness that masks the horror that lies within the buildings. These silent zones simultaneously appease the fears and wishes of society because the hospital is the one site where life-and-death struggles are made unremarkable by their daily occurrence. The indignities that a ward inflicts on its occupants, such as allowing them to chew, tear, and cannibalize themselves, go largely unrecognized because of public pressure to separate people with DGD from the rest of society. In fact, though members of the Dilg facility are artists, scientists, inventors, and problem solvers, the government-run hospital space seeks to deny the importance of these people as human beings by suggesting that the afflicted can do nothing beyond what is dictated by the programming of their damaged genes.

DGD people are marginalized by the greater society out of a fear of being attacked, but only those with active outbreaks are ever institutionalized. In other words, it is not so much the fear of contracting the disease that makes society segregate people afflicted with DGD, but rather a fear of being assailed or killed by an afflicted person. That such fear is justified becomes clear when Lynn recalls the manner of her parents' death. Without warning, Lynn's father murders her mother, skinning her mother in the process, and then by "digging" through his own flesh and bone, he manages "to reach his own heart before" dying (36). Her father's actions generate even greater prejudice from a society that has become paranoid about people who have the disease under control. As Lynn asserts, this is exactly "the kind of thing that makes people afraid of us, [though the] Duryea-Gode Disease Foundation has spent millions telling the world that people like my father don't exist" (36). Because nobody knows when a nonsymptomatic DGD will go off, fear of the disease "has inspired restrictive laws" and has also "created problems with jobs, housing, [and] schools" (36).

Fear of contamination, of racial impurity, is why society feels DGDs should be locked away. If one parent's genes are damaged by the Hedeonco cancer treatment, then all of his or her offspring will suffer from DGD to some degree. This transmission is similar, symbolically, to the social authority of the one-drop rule wherein if a person even carries the gene, s/he is discriminated against by the "pure" society.

Recalling her first trip to the local hospital at the age of fifteen, Lynn internalizes this racist outlook. She recognizes that all DGD sufferers can achieve close to a normal lifespan by maintaining a strict diet, but Lynn becomes reckless because she knows that she will eventually take up residence in one of the wards anyway. Her lack of a proper diet will initiate the onset of the disease more quickly, oddly giving her a sense of control for something beyond control. Drifting—being unresponsive "to their surroundings," lost in "a world of their own"—is inevitable even if DGD sufferers follow the diet (46). Furthermore, DGD victims are taught by society to hate themselves (their bodies) by movies, magazines, TV, and other people. This cultural racism is exactly why Lynn's parents decide to take her "to a [DGD] ward" in an attempt to curb her teenage rebelliousness, since she insists on showing her "independence by getting careless with [her] diet" (35). Going off the diet is another way for Lynn to deal with self-hatred by awakening the disease from its state of dormancy, just like the self-destructive activities (using drugs or alcohol, and having unprotected sex) of other young people.

Lynn has this thing—a monstrous "other" caused by a manmade disease—inside her that will one day be unleashed. The questions "What is this thing inside me? When will I become this monster?" are keys to this story. Active DGDs will "try so hard, fight so hard to get out [of] their bodies" by digging their way out (53). The idea of bodily limits is also essential to Butler's story. DGD sufferers do not consider their skin as a boundary. The flesh is merely a prison that one can escape by clawing out of it. From a delusional perspective, DGDs are not their bodies. Butler's disease resonates weirdly with "the consensual hallucination" of cyberspace popularized in William Gibson's *Neuromancer* (1984), where the body is a cage meant to be escaped from through the internet's unlimited freedom (5). In terms of contagion, this delusion is significant because this monstrous "other" transforms into the racial "other" feared by the non-DGD world and necessitates the discriminatory treatment DGDs deal with on a daily basis.

DGDs live with everyone else as long as they have not "drifted"—become uncontrolled and been consigned to a hospital ward—but these uncontained DGDS still suffer from discrimination. Lynn's college experiences prove this. While majoring in biology and earning "top grades," Lynn endures the petty abuse and bigotry directed at her by the normal population while merely "marking time" before she begins to drift; she derives no "particular hope" from going to school (37). For example, she no longer eats in public because she "didn't like the way people stared at [her] biscuits—cleverly dubbed 'dog biscuits' in every school [she'd] ever attended," sarcastically noting: "you'd think university students would be more creative" (38). These biscuits are the mainstay of the DGD diet, proactively formulated to offset drifting, akin to what "insulin [has] done for diabetics" (38).

Lynn also tolerates painful negative attention, such as nasty stares and audible whispers, drawn by her public DGD identification emblem. In fact, she begins "wearing [the emblem] on a chain around [her] neck and putting it down inside [her] blouse," though people discover it anyway (38). In the context of American race history, many light-skinned blacks have passed for white in an attempt to avoid racism. However, Lynn cannot attempt "to pass as normal" because she could be killed by improper medication administered to her in an emergency (38). Her emblem makes people aware that she has DGD. Although Lynn wears her emblem, she *does* hide it in an attempt to appear like an average college student. She does not advertise her condition, but other students inevitably learn of her affliction and avoid her. In this respect, Butler connects fear of contagion with racism through Lynn's desire to appear ordinary. The public's inclination to avoid Lynn is predicable and prompts her and several other DGDs to rent a house together out of loneliness—a place where Lynn eventually meets her black DGD fiancé, Alan Chi.

Though she and Alan are both opposed to bringing another person with DGD into the world, Lynn is shocked to learn that Alan had himself sterilized to prevent passing his disease to any future offspring.[12] He has internalized the cultural racism to such an extent that he wishes his parents "would have had [him] aborted the minute [his] mother realized she was pregnant" (41–42). Even more cynically, Alan states, "The damned disease could be wiped out in one generation" (42). Not only has his internalized racism resulted in his own sterilization, but it has damaged his sense of self-worth, causing him to hate his DGD difference, his otherness, and inciting his desire for the disease to die out.

At this point in the story, Lynn and Alan decide to visit Dilg, the private DGD facility, where every resident suffers from the illness. Lynn becomes intrigued when she notes, "Hospitals and rest homes had accidents Dilg didn't" (45). The couple soon learns the reason for this accomplishment. Pheromones can control behavior among the DGD population, but only women who have inherited the disease from both parents can emit these pheromones. Here, Butler is providing a fourth version of transformation/infection. There is genetic mixing, cultural transmission (what Richard Dawkins calls a "meme" in his classic 1976 study *The Selfish Gene* [192]), actual germs, and now pheromones. Thus, double-DGD women can control and even prevent drifting in other DGDs through pheromones. This ability coupled with nurturing by double-DGD women provides a way to bring to an end the cultural racism that DGDs face in their daily life. Such doubly afflicted women can reconcile the differences generated by the social fear of DGD, settle the differences with unafflicted people, and perhaps heal the soul of humanity. For example, the Dilg director, Beatrice Alcantara, is able to restore a sense of humanity to DGDs who "know they need help, but . . . have minds of their own" (66). Beatrice teaches DGDs to embrace their own difference in addition to developing self-reliance, which encourages a sense of independence. This carefully fostered independence allows the facility to escape the well-founded rumors of atrocities committed at the public institutions as well as prevents such mayhem occurring at Dilg. As a result, DGDs can hope that the general public will also learn to live with difference, though Butler's ending is surely less optimistic.

On the tour of Dilg, Lynn and Alan confront some of their own internalized biases about the disease. They believe all DGD sufferers are destructive. Instead, Beatrice shows them artwork created by DGDs, some "beautiful," some "useful," and some "worthless," and helps them realize that DGDs "create" things as opposed to "destroy" things (49). Butler implies that race is a valid source of art and should be appreciated for this very reason, not ridiculed as if the work of DGDs is somehow less valued because they are afflicted—a symptom of social contagion. Seeing the artwork allows Lynn and Alan to see DGDs as human beings rather than as self-mutilating monsters. Butler twists traditional perceptions of race and racism with her diseased humans and suggests that twisting racial stereotypes is a means of navigating sf. "Othered" people can make positive contributions to society; in effect, evidence of artistic genius allows DGDs to participate in society in spite of a cultural racism that seeks to subjugate and even destroy their sense of identity. Though DGDs are born with a terrifying burden akin to race, they also have an incredible opportunity to demand change by not accepting social definitions of inferiority.

Lynn's and Alan's second misconception is a somewhat positive stereotype concerning the DGD's ability to concentrate on the task at hand with a persistent strength of will. Beatrice proudly says, "No ordinary person can concentrate on work the way our people can," to which Lynn responds, "It's what people say whenever one of us does well at something. It's their way of denying us credit for our work" (55). Positive stereotypes are just as damaging as negative ones because they create false impressions based on some factor such as skin color or, in this case, genes. Moreover, the stereotype represents the entire group under scrutiny. "Ordinary" people often invert the meaning of the praise, making it into a slight. In the racist imagination this inversion corrects a sense of compromised racial purity. Diana Paulin believes that "the inaccuracy of notions of racial purity [are] grounded in historical events that inform past and present black/white relations in this country" (190). Mirroring connotations inherent to racism, Lynn thinks negatively about her focusing ability because society holds that ability against her and uses it to stereotype her in terms of her disorder. This particular genetic ability becomes symbolic of *racial* identity because interactions between the races are informed by a segregationist past constructed by fears of miscegenation, the one-drop rule, and passing for white, all of which are false notions of racial purity that influence the present. These fears are paralleled in the story: DGDs are socially segregated; the "bad" genes are passed from parents; and some DGDs can "pass" for a time. In this sense, Lynn begins to learn that it is this very difference that underlines her personal value.

In the end, Lynn becomes what Beatrice already is, a strong woman who cares for the DGDs under her roof and who provides discipline in their unstable and abused lives.

Lynn is meant to counteract the effects of social contagion on DGDs by creating her own independent DGD community. By being able to assign value to her environment, her purpose in life, and her identity, Lynn is better able to find her place in the world. She now understands that "power can be seen as an interdependence between the leader and those accepting that leadership, each accepting those limits on freedom that still allow for survival of the self" (Shinn, 214). Her trip with Alan to the Dilg retreat is important because it helps her understand her dual role as a nurturer and as a leader and it debunks her misconceptions. As should be expected, Butler's engagement with the various ailments of race in this story shows us how to think about the power of racial stereotypes embedded in the genre when we come into contact with them.

Butler crafts an allegorical sf story that is open to a racial reading because she investigates the human tendency to create hierarchical and oppressive social processes and institutions. In this story, diseased versus healthy is the primary difference that organizes the life possibilities for the characters; the social construction of disease is what ultimately limits the lives of the characters, not the disease itself. Consequently, Butler elaborates on the primary, fundamental experiences of the diseased other in terms of cultural racism. She lays bare the mechanism and consequences of individual, social, and institutional reactions to the diseased other. Because the default setting for these characters is clearly not white, Butler uses the primary metaphor of contagion or fear of contagion to figuratively construct these characters as racial others as her audience encounters them. As readers, we are made uncomfortable with these characters because their primary bodily experience has been abstracted into a contagion metaphor. Illness may be used as the foundational difference in the story, but DGD is properly interpreted as cultural racism, independent of the tension created by visual markers of race such as skin color. In other words, Butler is twisting our meaning of race by denying this basic component of racial difference and its attendant connotations. Butler is not so much looking at race in terms of infection/contamination as looking through the lens of race at some big issues of human biology and behavior. As such, "The Evening and the Morning and the Night" is important as a model of otherhood because it inoculates us against the plague of racism and its secondary symptoms of intolerance, bigotry, and small-mindedness. In this sense, breaking containment is essential to bursting thought patterns sickened by kinds of difference—particularly race—to begin the ideological process of healing.

Though we have already seen manmade contagions in Mosley and Butler, technological contagions also reflect ailments of race. For example, Stephen King's *Cell* (2006) describes a technological contagion in which a pulse sent across every cellular phone network turns millions of humans into mindless and aggressive zombies, thus creating a new race of men. As Lisa Lynch indicates, there is a similarity between these popular thrillers and the "stories of science fiction . . . since many of these narratives revolve around pathogens that do not yet exist or are still technically impossible to engineer, the combination of scientific adulation and scientific speculation blurs the distinction between some outbreak thrillers and science-fiction novels about epidemic disease" (74). Consequently, since we can now directly manipulate DNA, the development of artificial contagions destabilizes traditional thinking on racial identities.

As a metaphor for race, DNA provides an essential connection to social Darwinism and contagion. In *The DNA Mystique: The Gene as a Cultural Icon* (1995), sociologists and historians of science M. Susan Lindee and Dorothy Nelkin discuss the aura that has sprung up around DNA, positing that "its symbolic meaning is independent of biological definitions" (16). Even as it is used to describe matters of health and illness, the gene is also employed "to talk about guilt and responsibility, power and privilege, intellectual or emotional status" (Lindee and Nelkin, 16). In other words, the meaning of DNA has transcended its roots in biological science. It has been adapted by popular culture to represent a diversity of things from cars to clothing as well as stereotypes because of its deterministic versatility as an elastic concept. Thus, DNA "is the essential entity—the location of the true self—in the narratives of biological determinism" (Lindee and Nelkin, 41–42). This insight suggests that the social authority granted to science has been abused in terms of race. Such an authority forces us to consider the nature of difference and the harmful effects of preserving inequality among groups.

Genetic tampering with the soul of humankind is already a plague in the popular imagination, yet because of its potential the reality of genetic engineering on the cellular level is simultaneously exciting and frightening. While the potential benefits of developing such technology are virtually limitless in regard to health care, genetic engineering could also be disastrous for humanity if a genetically engineered life form could rapidly reproduce itself, invade a living body, plant, or animal, and destroy it. For instance, mosquitoes, rats, and other vermin could be bred to spread disease. Tinkering with the human genome to put off old age or male-pattern baldness could cause a deadly pandemic with a single gene mutation. In fact, genetic engineering undermines conventional notions of race, among other identity issues, because it shows that race can be directly changed by human intervention. Such a thing would be disastrous from a social point of view because it would aggravate the human need for an "other." When immutable boundaries between various ethnic groups are made permeable, people will fight to keep the meaning of their place in the world intact. The controversial promise of genetic engineering leads to the spread of the ever-changing contagion of racism in two ways. First, old tactics of dividing the world, such as physical appearance, are reinvented. Second, group-specific treatments, therapies, and diseases resolidify the social borders of humanity. As John Leslie stipulates, we must keep in mind "that techniques for creating dramatically beneficial organisms could also be used for creating harmful ones. The world is well supplied both with criminals and with honest folk who make mistakes" (91). Both ways are reflective of otherhood because they map the expansion of new technological differences in our science fictional reality.

The irresponsible use of gene-altering technologies that sf can imagine is what produces a sense of otherhood. Many sf writers envision genetic engineering as a means to heal numerous diseases, but their fictional "scientists" cannot avoid tampering with human biodiversity in the race for cures. Certainly, there are otherhood lessons being taught here, resulting from a variety of contentious issues raised by the era of genetic engineering in which we live. For instance, genes could be recombined in patterns that do not exist in nature, leading to an entirely new supervirus that wipes out humanity. No one knows what altering a single gene combination could lead to. Furthermore, the transfer of behavioral traits, hypothetically located in a few genes, could touch off a race war. Skin color could become a matter of choice with the adjustment of a few genes before birth. Some sf writers attempt to understand these futures by considering the indistinct "germ line" between success and failure, between beneficial therapies and worldwide pandemic, between enhancement and degeneration. No one can predict what will happen to the concept of race, but science fiction tries. In other words, we can imagine the physical, psychological, and social impacts of genetic engineering through our sf. Race could fall away in our future as it becomes a degenerate structure governing human interaction. Or racism could intensify to the point of our ultimate destruction. Science fiction is the harbinger of such human experimentation, and otherhood is one means to explore it.

A related topic, nanotechnology, or the production of very tiny self-replicating machines capable of manipulating atoms and molecules, is a second potential manmade contagion. Physician Tony Miksanek outlines the prospective advantages of nanotechnology:

> Some contemporary authors imagine a future where self-replicating, molecular machines cruise through the human bloodstream, patrolling our bodies for signs of disease. These microscopic devices would have the ability to enter cells and detect structural, degenerative, infectious, and malignant changes. Such microscopic machines might be capable of neutralizing or destroying offenders such as parasites, bacteria, viruses, and cancerous cells. Genetic mutations could be repaired inside the cell nucleus. Even more astonishingly, these nanodevices would be able to recycle atoms to create new molecular machines and provide construction materials for normal cells and the process of healing. (56)

Miksanek also considers some of the harmful possibilities, such as uncontrolled nanomachines that could disassemble "all matter," including humans, in order "to replicate themselves" (59). He labels this possibility as "an unparalleled epidemic" because "such machines could conceivably consume the entire planet in only days" (59). Imagining such a horrific outcome prompts Leslie and others to call the threat of nanotechnology the "'gray goo' calamity" because it could infect the world (7). These microscopic machines could perhaps be spread worldwide, causing rapid changes by something as simple as a sneeze. While each of these artificial contagions may be beneficial, it is much more likely that they will be abused as they are developed. Genetic engineering and nanotechnology suggest that races will be recombined in ways that will transform humanity, yet Western culture will remain a racialized culture. As artificial forms of contagion, gene-altering technologies reflect the habitual failure to diminish the meaning of racial boundaries in society and politics—a manifestation of the static nature of racial structures that otherhood is meant to investigate in science fiction.

Greg Bear's *Blood Music* (1985) is an excellent illustration of genetic engineering and nanotechnology run amok. The main character, Vergil Ulam, is a scientist who smuggles his pet project out of the lab by injecting himself with his microscopic intelligent lymphocytes after being fired from his job at Genetron for conducting unsanctioned research. Unfortunately, his decision represents the beginning of the end for humanity as we recognize it because Vergil is the source of "a disease that thinks . . . an intelligent plague" that transcends its human hosts (128).

The contagion spreads by breaking through Vergil's sweating palms as he shakes hands with his friend, Edward Milligan, and his former boss, Dr. Michael Bernard. Since Milligan is a physician and Bernard is the poster child of biological research, there is no telling how far the initial contagion has spread. Milligan recognizes the consequences of his brilliant friend Vergil's self-experimentation, and it is he who kills Vergil. Nonetheless, as Milligan informs Dr. Bernard, "It's too late, Doctor. We shook Vergil's hand. Sweaty palms. Remember? And ask yourself whom we've touched since. We're the vectors now" (127). Milligan and Bernard have begun to spread these sentient cells, cells that dissolve human beings into sheets of intelligent brown and green matter inhabiting a new "bioscape" (235). As H. Bruce Franklin remarks, Vergil Ulam is "another modern Prometheus" because he initiates the "cosmic transformation" of humanity with his reckless and unethical action (10).

As terrifying as the novel may seem, race disappears along with humanity. The "noocytes" do not distinguish between individual humans although they leave several humans untouched initially (100). What does happen, though, is that fear of this contagion induces Russia to drop nuclear bombs on the radically altered landscape of North America as a preventive measure. The bombing of America is preceded by other manifestations of paranoia such as quarantines of all North Americans, violent protests across Europe, the dissolution of the United States as a recognized political entity, and religious groups proclaiming the coming of Christ. In fact, the noocytes awaken a kind of racial memory according to the dissolving Dr. Bernard, who testifies to a former scientific colleague that "racial memory [is the] same mechanism as biologic. There are many lives in each of us; in the blood, in the tissue" (315). This accomplishment is monumental because the noocytes abound in love and cooperation. They can and do resurrect the dead from living cells, penetrating far back into history, boring a hole into the space-time continuum. A spiritual transcendence echoes in the sound of pulsing blood, affirmed by the release of this collective consciousness from human limitations such as politics and race. While blood evokes a legacy of physical trauma and violence as well as kin relationships, music reminds us of humankind's aesthetic heritage. Undoubtedly, Bear's title, *Blood Music*, suggests that humanity should be very careful with the transformative potential of nanotechnology. Out of control, it might be the cause of our extinction by a lethal contagion. Artificial contagions, constructed through genetic engineering or nanotechnology, represent the possibility to change humanity in a single generation, exploding the color line itself. This explosion can only occur in the pages of sf, where new races arise in place of old ones and old racial concepts are used to describe new beings.

Contagion as a metaphor is a response to racial alienation accompanied by xenophobia, territoriality, and raw hostility. It questions the racial power dynamics in existence by asking for whom the crisis of racial difference is most threatening in a multicultural state. Though this issue goes beyond the black/white binary, it is most often construed and discussed in terms of black/white relationships. We must recognize that the contagion metaphor represents a diversity of subjective black positions, experiences, and identities that have been politically, historically, socially, and culturally differentiated. Further, the contagion metaphor depicts race as a biological reality instead of as a social construction. In this sense, otherhood enables us to investigate and understand why the various ailments of race occur by bridging gaps between reality and science fiction. While bridging these gaps in sf criticism is necessary, the next chapter is equally relevant in that we delve into the space *between* these gaps, the strange and unfamiliar environments created by sf authors, seeking a new, if not radical, way of looking at science fiction and race.

It could be that science fiction's frequent assumption of a color-blind future—whether an unintentional or deliberate privileging of whiteness—has blinded critics to matters of race. This is a paradox that Richard Dyer makes note of, stating that "whites are not of a certain race, they're just the human race" (3). Certainly, one solution to polarizing racial identities along a black/white binary would be to challenge the representational power of whiteness as the symbol of humanity per se. With this in mind, otherhood is helpful in illuminating the ways that sf typically and unthinkingly reproduces white privilege in its representations of technology and social interactions. Despite those visions of a color-blind future, race has always been a part of sf, or lent its markings to it, as Sheree R. Thomas's *Dark Matter* anthologies indicate, even though decades of civil rights movements and racial consciousness in American culture have not produced a corresponding awareness of race in sf.

Customarily, discussions of sf reflect on various aspects of setting and characterization, while practically ignoring the dialogue on race and ethnicity evoked by the incredible backdrops envisioned. Science fiction's lack of this sort of dialogue is largely due to its lack of a critical vocabulary necessary to understand how race works within the genre. Historical overviews of the genre are still divided by racial assumptions, and sf story collections and histories by white writers and critics barely mention race as a category of interrogation or speculation. For example, of the sixty-seven stories collected in the *Norton*

Book of Science Fiction (1993), two are by African American writers (Delany and Butler), and one explicitly about race (Mike Resnick's "Kirinyaga" [1988]).[1] This deficiency is roughly analogous to the scant attention devoted to sf written by women or concerned with feminist issues before the 1970s and 1980s.[2] Indeed, the history of sf looks vastly different, if not barren, to scholars interested in racial issues because of publishing customs such as those practiced by John W. Campbell Jr. while editing *Astounding* in the 1940s and 1950s. Although otherhood is an important map of this estranged territory, partly influenced by Campbell, it still requires an expanded critical vocabulary to explore the racial constructions of science fiction. Therefore, I propose a new use for the term "ethnoscape" as a fresh way to think about the various environments that sf describes, as well as a new way to think about characterization in sf.

Social anthropologist Arjun Appadurai coined the term "ethnoscape" in 1990 and defines it as "the landscape of persons who constitute the shifting world in which we live" in relation to the cultural flow of social imagination across the globe (33). These persons include "tourists, immigrants, refugees, exiles, guestworkers, and other moving groups and persons" and "constitute an essential feature of the world" as they "appear to affect the politics of (and between) nations to a hitherto unprecedented degree" (33). Adapted to science fiction, an ethnoscape provides a symbolic transfer of meaning between racial/ ethnic politics and the shifting world of the sf text, resolving the contradictions of homogeneity and exposing the ways that sf unthinkingly reproduces white privilege. The writer constructs a socio-spatial environment in which to tell a story, but the reader can reconfigure those arrangements, draw out the assumptions and implications of the text to perceive its ethnoscape. Even if the fictional socio-spatial environment is constructed so as to foreground issues of race, it will nonetheless contain tensions, contradictions, and connotations beyond the author's control and in which the reader can discern the text's ethnoscape. The ideas and histories which the text uses, defines, discards, renovates, and invents define and situate the ethnoscape. The ethnoscape foregrounds the human landscapes of race and ethnicity as constituted by sf's historical, social, scientific, and technological engagement with the present. It both fabricates and reconceptualizes racial difference, enabling us to unpack sf's racial or ethnic environments and to think about human divergence in social behaviors.

There are several well-known canonical sf works that do not seem to be about race but that are relevant to racial issues, as the words on their pages build a rich, dense space that produce traces of racial experience. Each of these widely discussed narratives can further benefit from recontextualizing their content through ethnoscapes. For example, future war novels, such as Robert Heinlein's classic *Starship Troopers* (1959), are most often driven by the social Darwinian impulse, where humanity struggles for survival against alien species. The context of colonialism could be interpreted in terms of race. The novel begins with a pitched battle between the Mobile Infantry and an alien race known by the derogatory name "skinnies," and it ends with a military engagement between the Mobile Infantry and the main adversaries known as the "bugs." Both the humans and the bugs penetrate each other's space in the drive to conquer the galaxy, and a war of extinction between the species breaks out. Johnnie Rico, the young protagonist, joins the federal service to fight the bugs in order to gain his citizenship in a postrace world. Through Rico and others, like Dubois, Heinlein strongly broadcasts a racist belief in social Darwinism, where "violence, naked force, has settled more issues in history than has any other factor . . . Breeds that forget this basic truth have always paid for it with their lives and freedoms" (26). Social Darwinism is at the root of most of these future war scenarios depicting interspecies warfare, and ethnoscapes make the racial undercurrent much more tangible and revealing in sf.

Heinlein's racial polemics are difficult to fathom with his hardly noticeable indication of Johnnie Rico's racial makeup. Samuel Delany provides a celebrated account of this very detail—a world where race is inconsequential—in two of his theoretical texts: *The Jewel-Hinged Jaw* (1977) and *Starboard Wine* (1984). In *The Jewel-Hinged Jaw*, Delany reflects on how "a description of a mirror reflection and the mention of an ancestor's nationality" led him to realize that Rico "is non-caucasian" (80). Delany reiterates this point in *Starboard Wine* when he recalls his "strange double take" at Rico's fleeting reference to "the chocolate brown hue of his face" (30). Though Delany made these famous remarks a long time ago, I have not been able to find this passage in Heinlein's novel. A character from South America is not odd in itself, but it is rather strange to have a minority as the major figure of the text and anglicize him with the white nickname Johnnie. The name change from Juan to Johnnie signals the colonial impulse to lighten the darker races.

An even more fascinating ethnoscape appears in Ursula K. Le Guin's memorable *The Left Hand of Darkness* (1969), where she constructs a political ethnoscape from a first-contact story line mixed with a lost-race tale. Her novel focuses on first contact between humanity's descendants, where an emissary, Genly Ai, from the galactic human culture is sent to the winter planet of Gethen to assess whether the lost human civilization found there will become a member of the Ekumen. The people of Winter are androgynous beings, capable of being either male or female during the peak of their sexual cycle, kemmer—and they are also a dark-skinned race. As he attempts to establish an alliance with the Gethenians, where intellectual ideas and technology will be freely exchanged in peace, Genly Ai becomes entangled in the local politics of two nations: the feudal monarchy of Karhide and the capitalistic imperialism of Orgoreyn. Over the course of his involvement with the Gethenian Estraven, his guide, Genly Ai is forced to reevaluate his own prejudices and attitudes about human relationships.

Unquestionably, the novel hinges on notions of gender difference, but race enters the picture as well when the alienness of Le Guin's androgynous characters is considered more fully. Gethenian nations are extremely jingoistic, and the roots of racial tension between the two dominant nations of Gethen—Karhide and Orgoreyn—are clearly on display as they struggle over the possession of a strip of land known as the "Sinoth Valley" (83). The sense of difference because of language, biology, and nationality is utterly convincing bearing in mind that these persons are of both sexes, yet somehow manage to reflect our own assumptions of patriotism and race pride. Estraven puts these assumptions into perspective for Genly Ai by remarking, "No, I don't mean love, when I say patriotism. I mean fear. The fear of the other. And its expressions are political, not poetical: hate, rivalry, aggression. It grows in us, that fear" (19). Such fear leads to political acts of aggression, hatred, and a growing sense of rivalry in the text just as it does in our world. In this respect, political ethnoscapes inform questions about race and racism that we ask ourselves, our society, and science fiction itself, particularly our historical need to first create the other and then to attempt to harm, destroy, dehumanize, and exploit it, whether the other is human, alien, or artificial.

Finally, Arthur C. Clarke's monumental *Childhood's End* (1953) describes the appearance of an alien race, known as the Overlords, which ushers in an unprecedented era of peace to assist humanity's transformation to a higher order of being. However, this golden age of humanity is marred by two things: the mysterious Overlords refuse to reveal themselves for the first fifty years and the destruction of the Earth. Karellen, the Overlord supervisor, explains that "the human race will experience what can only be called a psychological discontinuity" upon viewing the true physical form of the Overlords as archetypal devils (52). Humanity has been scarred by a previous meeting between the races during the prehistory of man, and such a terrifying racial memory reverberates "down all the ages, to haunt the childhood of every race of man" (55). This early encounter with the alien beings produces an odd feeling of racial memory that simply cannot be dismissed. The power of this racial myth, of an absolute evil, heals the racial and ethnic schisms between humanity. Consequently, the Overlords are simultaneously the harbingers of destruction and of freedom in this ethnoscape of alien contact. Whether Clarke intended this sense of prejudice or not in his writing, it exists because of his evocation of racial memory.

Clarke's vision is also distorted by another kind of race memory—nostalgia for blackness. Visible markers such as skin color should not truly exist in the utopia created by the social engineering of the Overlords. Nonetheless, unconscious racism disrupts the story. For instance, a minor white character, George, is aware of a woman's skin color: "she was . . . about one-quarter Negro. Her features were practically Grecian and her hair was long and lustrous. Only the dark, rich texture of her skin—the overworked word 'chocolate' was the only one that described it—revealed her mixed ancestry" (71). This moment in the text is made odd by the fact that the woman, Maia, is described as white in all her mannerisms. Such a disjunction implies that Clarke is privileging whiteness.

This strange narrative shift becomes even stranger when Clarke attempts to take the sting out of the racist epithet "nigger" through the major black character, Jan, who ironically is the last man on earth. Jan reflects on how color "meant nothing" to twenty-first-century humanity; that "nigger" is a term used as a matter of convenience in "polite society"; that the word "was used without embarrassment by everyone"; and that the word "had no more emotional content than such labels as republican or Methodist, conservative or liberal" (82). Clarke's imagination of a postrace world fails here because the psychological impact that race has had on all of humanity cannot be summarily dismissed. If Clarke means for this to be so, then strange social moments of disparagement should not exist in the text. Such racial tensions are deeply embedded in this particular ethnoscape, just one of many where alien beings represent a range of potentialities for exploring racial differences.

This brief discussion of key sf narratives exposes how the works unconsciously assume an intrinsic racial or ethnic value, and highlights the need for ethnoscapes to explore race and racism in sf. Perhaps the canonical nature of such texts shields them from the conscious application of race-reading, but the advantages of such reading are clear. Science fictional extrapolation creates settings and characters that represent humanity as we recognize ourselves elsewhere in time and place. The result of such recognition is often, though not always, perceived as some kind of discrimination or diminishment of stature that complicates our understanding of humanity from the past through the future. In this sense, Heinlein, Le Guin, and Clarke develop unique ethnoscapes, where racial relationships presented in their texts can be tested against our contemporary cultural perspective. These alien backdrops and beings are necessary to our perception of identity. Adapting the culture critic Stuart Hall's thoughts on "otherness" to sf, "the Other is not *out there*, but *in here*. It is not outside, but inside" (342). Thus, a variety of racial questions in sf can be examined as articulations of otherhood, such as the ethnoscape. Science fiction can take advantage of critical ethnoscapes to explore issues of race and racism that have otherwise been missed in the unique and fascinating visions of the future.

A fictional environment is the aggregate of perceived and lived space articulated through the author's imagination. The ethnoscape renders such environments unfamiliar, defamiliarizing the ordinary or conventional world and presenting it in a way that is exceedingly, and perhaps eerily, different from our own experience. In other words, a familiar environment is represented in a strange way to create a sense of the alien or unknown. While sf's conventional estrangements populate the fictional environment with, or structure it around the presence of, science, technology, mythology, aliens, androids, humanity, natural and artificial phenomena, politics, culture, language, religion, and so on, the ethnoscape reformulates that construction so as to create an alternative image which enables us to rethink the intersections of technology and race as well as their political, social, and cultural implications. In this sense, Ishmael Reed's *Mumbo Jumbo* (1972) both acknowledges and transforms sf through the revisionary power of black cultural experience as a "fabulist" ethnoscape. *Mumbo Jumbo*'s fabulist ethnoscape parallels sf protocols, including the disaster narrative and the android, and in doing so destabilizes sf's existing racist structures.

To be specific, the fabulist ethnoscape entails world-building where racial myth can be told in a visibly subjective world. It is a combination of history, folklore, and sf that counters sf's racial assumptions about humanity's color-blind future *and* uses sf devices to confront the racial assumptions of American culture more generally.[3] A fusion of historical figures, caricatures, jazz, minstrelsy, the occult, and Black Power, *Mumbo Jumbo* revolves around the conspiracy of a secret white supremacist organization to maintain control of America's black population by stopping the spread of a pathogen that crosses racial lines, and around the HooDoo priest who tries to counteract the conspiracy by locating an arcane text. The novel reflects upon the operations of race in sf through depicting an insistence upon the concrete fable of race: that difference is based on the reality of skin color. Such racial thinking is refuted by the outbreak of "Jes Grew," a nonlethal plague of sorts that erupts in New Orleans and rapidly spreads north toward New York. This plague is symbolic of the inestimable inner quality known as SOUL. People infected with Jes Grew, both black and white, inexplicably become invigorated and express this newfound energy through song and dance as they struggle against the realities of racism. The concept of SOUL is a cultural myth rendered science fictional by Reed's depiction of it as a plague. Roughly analogous to William S. Burroughs's viral language in *The Ticket That Exploded* (1962) or Neal Stephenson's pathological meme in *Snow Crash* (1992), Jes Grew infects people with freedom by fomenting cultural evolution. Needless to say, the novel's powerful white upper class is not thrilled with this turn of events. *Mumbo Jumbo*'s ethnoscape addresses the past and present state of race relations in the U.S. by parodying the world its readers occupy, literalizing fears and constructions of difference as a disease and of otherness—particularly black culture—as a contagion which might reduce white rationality to bodily excess.

The story follows the epic struggle between PaPa LaBas, a practitioner of HooDoo at Harlem' s "Mumbo Jumbo Kathedral" (23), and Hinckle Von Vompton, "a Knight of the Wallflower Order of Atonists,"[4] as they come into conflict over Jes Grew (55). Von Vampton has successfully infiltrated the Harlem literary community as well as the black upper class, and thus is well placed to manipulate black artists and destroy the burgeoning outflow of creative expression caused by Jes Grew. He also attempts to stop the plague through the creation of a Talking Android:

> The 2nd Stage of the plan is to groom a Talking Android who will work within the Negro, who seems to be its classical host; to drive it out, categorize it analyze it expel it slay it, blot Jes Grew. A speaking scull they can use any way they want, a rapping antibiotic who will abort it from the American womb to which it clings like a stubborn fetus. In other words this Talking Android will be engaged to cut-it-up, break down this Germ, keep it from behind the counter. To begin the campaign, NO DANCING posters are ordered by the 100s. (17)

Von Vampton attempts to use this imagined technology to isolate and expel black culture, which he considers to be both primitive and evil. He controls the speech of his Talking Android to unduly influence the upper tier of black society, instructing them on the inferiority of blacks and black culture, though this is hardly a problem for the black bluebloods who would divorce themselves from their race if possible.

Much like a slave owner, Von Vampton seeks to divide the black race by sowing seeds of distrust, and to maintain white privilege through the Talking Android, which itself speaks to the alienated experience of blacks in the New World—it is, after all, an obedient machine whose ethnicity is technologically produced. When Von Vampton cannot find any black person foolish enough to become his Talking Android and participate in a plan designed to stop the outbreak and continue racial oppression, he selects his white right-hand man, Hubert "Safecracker" Gould, to be his mouthpiece. It is Gould who delivers the comical epic poem "Harlem Tom Toms" to black high society (158), and through whom Reed lampoons the practice of minstrelsy. Appearing in blackface as the Talking Android, Gould tries to pass as an authentic black person—instead of merely exaggerating the black stereotypes that minstrel shows made famous—so as to undermine black culture. However, PaPa LaBas and his friends arrive just in time to break up the first Talking Android event by revealing Von Vampton and Gould's trickery. LaBas grazes "a quick finger across [Gould's] face, leaving a white streak" behind while displaying "the black paint on his finger" to the influential black audience (160). Shortly after this ruse is revealed, the Jes Grew epidemic peters out sixty miles short of New York, because its arcane embodiment as a book, symbolizing a concrete register of black experience, has been destroyed.

With the image of a white person in blackface posing as an android, *Mumbo Jumbo* makes an unconventional connection between a traditional sf motif and African American iconography. By doing this, Reed creates an alternate history and landscape of black-white contact that powerfully indicts the irrationality of racism in the United States through social satire. His use of sf devices produces a fabulist ethnoscape that questions existing racial power dynamics by asking for whom the crisis of racial difference is most threatening in a multicultural state.

Similarly, Colson Whitehead's *The Intuitionist* (1999) provides a counterfactual ethnoscape, in which race and sf intersect in a vaguely familiar mid-twentieth-century New York City. The counterfactual ethnoscape estranges our sense of history by emphasizing the importance of the technological development of elevators and how this impacts race relations. It is constructed with the sense that technology in the hands of a black person represents a dangerous situation. By rupturing the known timeline and postulating alternatives, the counterfactual ethnoscape is able to highlight the influence and consequences of racial history, and to offer estranged visions of the social, political, and cultural possibilities of race in other places and times. In a story that blends sf, hardboiled detective fiction, and satire in a manner reminiscent of Philip K. Dick, *The Intuitionist* focuses on Lila Mae Watson, the first and only black woman to become an elevator inspector in the largest city in the world. By following her hunches, she has maintained a perfect service record on the job, but when a new elevator which she has recently inspected disastrously crashes, she becomes embroiled in a political battle between the Intuitionists and the Empiricists for control of the "department of elevator inspectors" (23). She goes underground to investigate whether the crash is a deliberate act of sabotage aimed at undermining her credibility as an Intuitionist. While trying to avoid the clutches of the Empiricist chairman of the department, Frank Chancre, who is covertly backed by mob muscle, Lila Mae discovers several dangerous undisclosed facts about James Fulton, the deceased founder of Intuitionism and a vertical philosopher. At the time of his death, Fulton was known to be working on "the black box," an elevator that would revolutionize the world by ushering in the second elevation, unlocking the sky. *The Intuitionist* is thus a step closer to sf, resonating with racial issues in a technosocial world evoked through alienated urban experience.

Although the conflict in *The Intuitionist* stems from a debate in technosocial philosophy—Intuitionism versus Empiricism—Whitehead's ethnoscape is structured by the concept of verticality, both architectural and cultural, that governs the action of both camps as they vie to find the black box. Intuitionists rely on contemplation, instinct, and gut feeling to observe, remedy, and repair elevators, as we learn when we first encounter Lila Mae at work. Whitehead describes her sixth sense, her "own set of genies," inspecting "geometric forms" in her head to uncover the elevator's shortcomings, rather than physically examining its mechanical parts (6). The building superintendent riding with Lila Mae calls her a "voodoo inspector" as well as a "witch doctor" before attempting to bribe her (7). This racialization of her philosophy and technique connects her to the long history of blacks being associated with the occult. She certainly is a worker of professional magic inasmuch as she relies on her perceptions to cure the elevator of its sickness in the primitive yet sophisticated urban society. In contrast, Empiricists depend on the cold, hard facts of physical measurement to rigorously check the structural and mechanical details of the elevators. Whitehead carefully implies another racial stereotype by depicting whites as a no-nonsense, rational people who do not believe in the supernatural. This allusion is reinforced by the fact that only one black person in the story, Pompey, is an Empiricist, and Lila Mae considers him a race traitor, an "Uncle Tom, the grinning nigger, the house nigger who is to blame for her debased place in this world" because he "gave them a blueprint for colored folk" (239). Pompey is a black user of white technology, a black Empiricist cog who has conformed himself to an otherwise white machine. In this ethnoscape, whites own and control technology, while blacks respond to it either on a preconscious level or by learning the routines of their white counterparts. Understandably, there is significant animosity between the two factions, with Empiricist hostility toward Intuitionism manifested in racially charged monikers that hint at a primitive and other magic: "some nicknames Empiricists have for their renegade colleagues: swamis, voodoo men, juju heads, witchdoctors, Harry Houdinis. All terms belonging to the nomenclature of dark exotica, the sinister foreign. Except for Houdini, who nonetheless had something swarthy about him" (57–58). While the narrator notes the dark, exotic, sinister, and foreign nature of the practice of Intuitionism, Lila Mae claims that the "reality" of Empiricism—"White people's reality"—is "built on what things appear to be" (239).

The Intuitionists and Empiricists are deeply divided on the issue of verticality because one group seeks transcendental answers to mechanical problems while the other is supremely doubtful of results garnered without rigorous and quantifiable exertion. From an architectural standpoint, verticality in the novel relates to the continual construction of higher and higher buildings. Humanity strives for the heavens. In truth, as the sky reminds us, there will always be something higher. The elevator marks the beginning of this rise because it is a technological conveyance that allows humans to build higher into the sky—the vertical ideal—but unfortunately there are also and always those people who are left behind. The concept of verticality creates a counterfactual ethnoscape because the social relations of race come together with the technological dreams of attaining the heavens in such a manner that blacks remain trapped in the basement. While the historical development of this fictional oppression is different from our own, it nonetheless shares the same essence.

The spatialization of class in sf cities, such as the Los Angeles of *Blade Runner* (1982), helps to contextualize the spatialization of race in *The Intuitionist's* New York. *Blade Runner's* ethnoscape is layered with new technologies grafted onto old buildings, deteriorating slums oppressively packed by the masses of human waste (Asians, Latinos, punks, and midgets) unable to emigrate, deserted buildings, intrusively glaring neon signs and ads, white noise, ethnic restaurants, and of course a continual police presence. While the inner city is certainly a confined space in a blighted area where people live from day to day, it is also, in the middle-class imaginary, a bad and inferior place, a public space to be feared. Eldon Tyrell, the creator of the replicants and one of the remaining whites, escapes the city streets in the only direction left—upwards. In *The Intuitionist*, the counterfactual ethnoscape involves the ascension of humanity, particularly the black race, from the city as we know it, from the cramped spaces of inequality. The black box is important because it signifies the cultural implications of the second elevation in which "everything . . . will come down" (182). The second elevation, of course, refers to the buildings themselves, but also to the social changes necessary to modify our understanding of race relations. All of our beliefs would have to collapse to build the utopian ideal hinted at by the concept of the second elevation. In his *Theoretical Elevators, Volume Two*, Fulton writes, "Remember the train, and that thing between you and your words. An elevator is a train. The perfect train terminates at Heaven. The perfect elevator waits . . . [i]n the black box, this messy business of human communication" (87). The black box is emblematic of communication between human beings and the lack of it between the races. We cannot comprehend the dark heart of the black box because our vision cannot penetrate the outside of the box.

It is no mistake that Fulton's theoretical elevator design is named "the black box." It symbolizes the plight of the black race. Blacks can ride up and down, but they are forever boxed in, enclosed, trapped by the racist ideals of an unchanging society, ensnared in a horizontal environment. The black box realizes America's vertical race hierarchy. The novel's black characters are restricted to horizontal movement by overt racism, politics, and mob activity. This lateral movement is clearly demonstrated by Pompey, the first black elevator inspector, who experiences "the difficulty of all colored 'firsts'" in having "an exceedingly hard time of things" in the all-white elevator community (25). While the novel concerns the vertical movement of humanity itself, it is also about the immobility in black uplift. Blacks are barred from the ascension by white racists like Chancre. Blacks cannot rise. This fact is the ethnoscape. The second elevation calls for the realignment of race relationships generated by the utopia it represents, but it will not be realized because of the vertical nature of a racialized social Darwinism. Though the black box is meant to produce a postrace society, its meaning has been misappropriated to serve the interest of white people. The black box is a reimagining of white flight, but instead of outward to the suburbs it goes upward. Rather than being locked in an inner city with blacks and other minorities, the whites (like *Blade Runner's* Tyrell) move upward to display their superiority and to separate themselves from contact with blacks permanently locked, motionless, in the lower class. After all, suburban whites still have to come into the inner city to work, but if whites are elevated, they can leave that "ghetto" behind permanently.

Fulton's black box is an impossibility because the races cannot or will not recognize their common humanity. We as readers only acknowledge this, however, after Lila Mae learns that Fulton was a colored man who passed as a white man, a mystery that directly contributes to the text's counterfactual ethnoscape. This secret is closely guarded because of its potential to disrupt society by making Intuitionism a joke on society. It is really about the black situation, not verticality, since Fulton must hide his race in order for his ideas to be accepted. Ironically, he is worshipped by white society for his ideas, which have shaped both Empiricism and Intuitionism. Lila Mae is trapped by this irony because she can tell no one what she knows, while the Elevator Guild wishes only to find his designs for the black box in order to begin the second elevation, get rich from it, and stay in power. Fulton's attempts to communicate difference and racial uplift are unrealized. Only after learning Fulton's secret does Lila Mae slowly come to realize, while rereading his Intuitionist volumes, the meaning of his view that *"horizontal thinking in a vertical world is the race's curse"* (151; emphasis in original). The ambiguity of the word "race" is stunning because Whitehead is deriding all of humanity and its inability to transcend racism. Likewise, he is critical of American society's conformity to the past, its unwillingness to escape the accepted racial paradigms suggested by the black box—the intersection of vertical and horizontal thought in diagonal notions such as a multiracial or postrace world.

Whitehead's novel works on several levels as a counterfactual ethnoscape, skewering human stupidity and challenging us to think outside the "box." First, it suggests that ideas will change the world. At the end of the novel, Lila Mae uses Fulton's name and notes to write the third volume of *Theoretical Elevators*, which contains the black box designs. This volume anticipates possible alternatives to the choices humans are making and has the potential to bring down the prevailing social structures of racism. An ethnoscape built on one of the principal themes of sf—perception—takes us beyond our normal thinking on racial subjects. Second, the counterfactual ethnoscape renders highly visible Whitehead's unusual perspective regarding the social and political constraints of race operating now. Well-constructed sf stories such as this one dissolve the borders between us and the fabricated reality of the text. Third, Whitehead measures racial history on a counterfactual timeline that creates a unique repetition of cultural memory within sf; and fourth, he questions and counterbalances the facts underlying race matters as they have been historicized in sf literature.

In *The Intuitionist*, black people can be users of technology, but only if they use it as whites have allowed. Whitehead challenges conventional thinking on this subject, which suggests that "crude preconceptions of mental inferiority went well beyond simple tool using to include almost any aptitude for technological competence and these notions flowered in the basic conditions of forced servitude" (Sinclair, 1–2). As an Intuitionist, Lila Mae is able to make quick judgments independent of any conscious reasoning process while fixing elevators. This ability, this spiritual technology, makes her dangerous, however, because it is outside the application of science. Her work methods cannot be understood by her white supervisors, which makes her an object of suspicion because she threatens existing power structures and cannot be controlled. In contrast, Pompey, who also has direct access to elevators, has been victimized because of his color. As an Empiricist, he uses scientific means to gain knowledge for the practical purpose of fixing the machines. Like Lucius Brockway in Ralph Ellison's classic *Invisible Man* (1952), Pompey functions like a machine *"inside the machine"* (217; emphasis in original), and he is not feared because he unquestioningly serves his white employers, like a good slave, actively participating in the technological oppression of his race. In this vertically racialized, counterfactual New York, blacks are revealed as the real inventors of technology. As such, they are dangerous because they appear equal in status to other humans and have the right to challenge their domination. Technology has historically been conceptualized in ways that emphasize racial difference and limit employment opportunities for nonwhites in regard to one criterion, the "capacity for advanced intellectual accomplishment" (Sinclair, 1), traditionally attributed to the white race alone. Sf has largely shared this conceptualization. *The Intuitionist* overturns it.

While the physical and geographical settings of *Mumbo Jumbo* and *The Intuitionist* construct distinctive ethnoscapes, language itself is capable of being the basis for others. Language is a technology that allows intelligent social beings to express and record the events of their lives with a system of symbols that may be verbal, alphanumeric, lights, colors, smells, pictures. It is a method of coding knowledge. It marks the differences in values, perceptions, and behaviors of conscious life forms. It can erect the inflexible boundaries characteristic of prejudice just as it can free us from the conventions of discrimination. Language maps the ever-changing landscape that the linguistic sf novel attempts to fix. In sf, it constructs and reveals the invented world, and within that world language often functions as a plot device or as a meditation on the difficulties of interspecies communication or as a representation of a culture and its beliefs. The ubiquitous presence of instantaneous spacewide communication devices—like a Dirac communicator or an ansible—and universal translators are perfect examples of imaginary linguistic icons in sf that advance the story line.[5] Related to tales of astounding technological contraptions are sf stories that focus on the problems of interspecies communication most often linked to human and alien interactions. First-contact stories normally involve the initial encounter between humanity and aliens and their attempts to communicate with each other as intelligent beings. For example, Murray Leinster's "First Contact" (1945) is, perhaps, the most recognized story on this theme. Language is a pivotal aspect of these stories, unless of course a universal translator is involved. Yet other kinds of sf narrative point to the likely impossibility of communication between humanity and aliens. A novel such as Stanislaw Lem's *Solaris* (1961) quickly comes to mind.

Also, societal beliefs are often reflected through language and its tools in sf as well. A case in point is the language of "Newspeak" in George Orwell's classic *Nineteen Eighty-four* (1949). "Newspeak" is a severely reduced form of English used by the totalitarian Airstrip One government (signified by images of Big Brother and the thought police) to control the population by stripping and fixing language—a strong version of Sapir-Whorf linguistic relativity. This linguistic hypothesis proposes that different patterns of language give way to different thought patterns, that how a person speaks a language represents how that person understands and behaves in his or her environment. Further, the subtleties of any language can be used as a tool to condition the thoughts of the society speaking the language. As such, Newspeak is a sinister use of language to broadcast the falsehoods and propaganda of the state and ensure the appropriate public way of conventional thinking. Ray Bradbury presents an example of a language device in *Fahrenheit 451* (1953), where firemen are used to set books containing dangerous knowledge and subversive ideas aflame as a means of censorship to prevent people from thinking. Books have a technological capacity in that they store and display thought, which is precisely what the autocratic system desires to repress. A more recent illustration is the use of an Afro-Caribbean vernacular by Nalo Hopkinson in her debut novel *Brown Girl in the Ring* (1998).[6] Clearly, technological contraptions and societal beliefs in relation to language can shape the many distinctive sf environments.

A number of sf narratives are primarily concerned with the nature of language and its power to affect the nature of reality.[7] Among these novels is Samuel R. Delany's *Babel-17* (1966), which constructs a unique linguistic ethnoscape that conveys the importance of communication in accepting and appreciating difference. Delany's novel tells of an intergalactic war that is ultimately stopped by Rydra Wong's intuitive understanding of language and meaning. A famous poetess of ethnic origin, Rydra is enlisted by the Alliance military to battle the invasion of alien humans by translating the Babel-17 language, transmissions of which are believed to coincide with acts of strategic sabotage. She figures out that Babel-17 is a nearly perfect and concise analytical language which has no word for "I" and which is used as a means of thought control.[8]

Gregory Rutledge suggests that "reading *Babel-17* without reference to Du Bois's double consciousness, and hence ethnicity . . . will lead the reader away from much of the subreality Delany has incorporated into his plot" ("Science Fiction," 132). This double consciousness is articulated through the alien language that infects and possesses its victims. *Babel-17*'s aliens from another galaxy are bent on conquering a galaxy similar to ours; the only difference between them and us is semantic. That they are *human* aliens is evident from Rydra's thoughts about being born in Alliance territory: "Born a galaxy away, she might as easily have been an Invader. Her poems were popular on both sides. That was upsetting" (72). Delany figures the aliens as white through their desire for power and territory. This configuration by Delany is reflected in the Babel-17 language, a weapon that forcibly initiates people into the alien culture and controls them by eliminating their identities. As Rydra explains:

> You can program a computer to make mistakes, and you do it not by crossing wires, but by manipulating the "language" you teach it to "think" in. The lack of an "I" precludes any self-critical process. In fact it cuts out any awareness of the symbolic process at all—which is the way we distinguish between reality and our expression of reality. (214)

Once the individual's self-awareness—the "I"—is gone, the Babel-17 language overlays his or her reality with an alien perception and compels acts of sabotage. The personality thus sublimated is robbed of vital memories and cut off from his or her culture. Consciousness splits as the perception of the self is replaced with an alien, external perception. As Jane Weedman argues, "When a person is exposed to two cultures, double consciousness evolves. To survive, the person must be able to function in both cultures; this means mastering both languages" (133). Simultaneously articulating a version of the Sapir-Whorf hypothesis and double consciousness, Rydra remarks that "when you learn another tongue, you learn the way another people see the world, the universe" (23) and tells the Butcher, when she frees him from the Invaders' influence, that "there are certain ideas which have words for them. If you don't know the words, you can't know the ideas. And if you don't have the ideas, you don't have the answer'" (150).

Clearly, thought is a crucial component of a linguistic ethnoscape because there must be a relationship between how the characters interact with their world and how they identify their place in it. In Delany's use of the Sapir-Whorf hypothesis, language becomes the symbol and system of domination, a notion played out on a galactic scale as the mutually incomprehensibly of the Alliance and Invader languages result in war. *Babel-17*'s evocation of the biblical story of the Tower of Babel implies that such conflict is inevitable, but as the Alliance and the Invaders are both human species, communication between them should be possible. If Rydra's adventures among the Alliance are anything to go by, these rivals cannot be homogenized into uniform linguistic cultures; internal difference implies the permeability of external boundaries, across which translations, as well as misunderstandings and conflicts, can occur. The problem the Alliance faces with Babel-17 is that it does not seem to allow the possibility of heterogeneity because it is an artificial language (i.e., it is fixed, monolithic, singular); but the fact that it is artificially constructed indicates that the Invaders themselves are as various as the Alliance. Babel-17 represents an attempt to calibrate the significance of the universe in those it infects, producing a form of mind control which eradicates the subject as anything other than the subject of its command sentences. This narrow delimitation of subjectivity draws out the tensions between trying to fix identity and the historical processes of constant flux and interaction between identities which are far from discrete and fixed.

The difference between natural and artificial languages is key to understanding Delany's linguistic ethnoscape. Where a natural language historically evolves in a community's complex feedback systems, an artificial language is consciously invented for a specific purpose, whether to foster communication between linguistic groups by providing a third language native to neither (such as Esperanto, Interlingua, or Volapük), or to program computers. The problem with artificial languages are that they are top-down impositions which have built into them the need to fix the language, to prevent it from changing, as in the restriction to 850 words of Ogden-Richards Basic English. This, of course, is not how languages work in the world and in history. While Rydra's mind is temporarily fused with the Butcher's mind, she recognizes that "Babel-17 is more or less like Onoff, Algol, Fortran . . . ancient twentieth-century languages—artificial languages that were used to program computers, designed especially for machines" (198–99). Her latent telepathic ability enables her to understand that Babel-17 has gained control of the Butcher by imposing its "I"-less linguistic paradigm and then implementing another personality that "is flexible," capable of handling "ideas [that] come in huge numbers of congruent sets, governed by the same words" (210). Babel-17 "almost assures you technical mastery of any situation you look at," Rydra explains, even as "the lack of an 'I' blinds you to the fact though it's a highly useful way to look at things, it isn't the only way" (215).

The Babel-17 model of absolutely de-centered language (no "I") undoes the notion of fixed identity, even as its superimposition on the Alliance language opens up the social component of race and its uncertainty, creating a double consciousness. In order for the afflicted person to survive Babel-17's elimination of the "I," the language programs "a self-contained schizoid personality into the mind of whoever learns it, reinforced by self-hypnosis" (216). The individual thus divided measures the world by standards that are not his or her own. Powerful Invader stereotypes are bought to bear on the Alliance to the extent that the created persona "has the general desire to destroy the Alliance at any cost, and at the same time remain hidden from the rest of the consciousness" (216). This is the danger of double consciousness: changing one's identity to fit the perceptions of others. The foreign language makes the Butcher into a tool with no identity, no self-awareness; a slave in every sense of the word, he is forced to avoid self-referential pronouns, thus disabling him from claiming ownership of his identity. This is what makes Babel-17 such a powerful weapon.

Rydra's mental fusion with the Butcher (a literal double consciousness, further complicated by questions of ethnicity, class, gender, and
sexuality) restores his human identity as Nyles Ver Dorco. Through
Rydra's eyes, he becomes self-aware, gradually recognizes his autonomous being, and breaks free of his linguistically constructed mental
enslavement. Ironically, in a quasi-Hegelian master-slave dialectic, he
reacquires selfhood through consciousness of the other's consciousness
of him. Likewise, Rydra comes to know herself better by penetrating
the Butcher's mind, a disconcerting rape metaphor, but one which
allows her to see a deeper truth.

Rydra Wong's astounding ability to communicate allows her to overcome all manner of prejudice from the various communities in the
text as she socializes with generals, doctors, government officials, space
crews, wrestlers, dead people, pirates, and ultimately the aliens. It is
amplified by exposure to Babel-17, forcing her "mind . . . to sudden
growth" (113). This awakens her fledgling gift of telepathy, the ability
to read minds, "the nexus of old talent and a new way of thinking. It
opened worlds of perception, of action" (146), exposing her in a less
threatening way to other perceptions that might overlay her own. The
study of language informs her opinion of race, which, to borrow Paul
Gilroy's view, is "an active, dynamic idea or principle that assists in
the constitution of social reality" (57). She functions as a multicultural
broker of acceptance, tolerance, open-mindedness, and difference, who
"will enable humanity to bridge the gap between Self and Other, healing the breach of isolation and alienation" (Malmgren, 12). When she
becomes completely conscious of the connection between thought and
language, she is transformed from an interpreter into a shaper of reality.

While humanity apparently cannot escape the Darwinian struggles of existence, Delany demonstrates that language and perception can break through the historical conditioning of a racialized
America. He shows how the actions of people can be shaped by words
themselves as well as how words and their meaning gain significance
through life, and his novel functions as a metafictional guide to reading an ethnoscape, bringing the language of one world, the fictional
world, into collision with the language, experience, and perception
of an extratextual reality in which race functions as a technology of
oppression.

In "Speech Sounds" (1983), Octavia Butler presents an entirely different linguistic ethnoscape, in which she imagines the total social collapse of the world, symbolized by a Los Angeles devastated by an incurable global contagion initially, and perhaps falsely, attributed to the Soviets. Aside from killing many people, the sickness adversely affects all forms of communication between people: some of its victims lose the ability to speak, read, write, or any combination thereof. A largely incomplete and derisory form of language, often misinterpreted, remains. Body language—gestures, motions, signs—usually culminates in violence, the only universal language.[9] Most of the afflicted manage to survive by scavenging among the remnants of civilization and by avoiding armed criminals while struggling with suicidal thoughts and loneliness. Some things, like public transportation, still operate sporadically, yet government is no more and chaos is supreme. Butler's vision emphasizes the importance of language in a racialized society that, in turn, produces a kind of otherhood.

Amidst a mob scene on a bus, the female protagonist, Rye, fears for her safety because two young men "involved in a disagreement of some kind," begin "grunting and gesturing at each other" using "mock punches, hand games of intimidation to replace lost curses" (89). Rye's fear derives from the state of savagery that humanity has descended into because of the loss of verbal expression. She has lost her husband and three children to the virus. She is also frightened because she realizes that her ability to speak puts her life in danger in this public space. People kill for lesser reasons than sheer envy in this world. With the failure of interpersonal contact, misunderstandings occur frequently and "the possibility of life-threatening violence is just under the surface of all relationships" because the hierarchical social structure provided by language has been destroyed by the epidemic (Green, 175). Violence erupts on the bus because the men have no means of verbal communication to settle their differences.

Rye is rescued by Obsidian, a former member of the Los Angeles Police Department. Though they cannot talk to each other, Rye decides to trust him, albeit warily, because he uses his left hand to beckon to her: "Left-handed people tended to be less impaired, more reasonable and comprehending, less driven by frustration, confusion, and anger" (91–92). Left-handedness has been associated with evil in the past, but now this notion has been inverted to mark the right-handed majority as the more primitive group. In fact, in this linguistic ethnoscape, race can be determined by what hand is used.

Obsidian uses teargas to disperse the combatants on the bus, but he is angrily confronted by the wildly gesticulating driver in what is surely a moment of racial conflict. Butler describes it:

> The bearded man stood still, made no sound, refused to respond to clearly obscene gestures. The least impaired people tended to do this—stand back unless they were physically threatened and let those with less control scream and jump around. It was as though they felt it beneath them to be as touchy as the less comprehending. This was an attitude of superiority, and that was the way people like the bus driver perceived it. Such "superiority" was frequently punished by beatings, even by death. (93)

From this passage, we learn that there are two groups of people: those who can control themselves and those who cannot, those with some language use and those without. Butler makes this distinction to reflect that notions of superiority and inferiority remain intact although they have shifted away from normal concepts of this dualism, namely skin color. Race, as we know it, has dramatically changed. It is no longer based on skin color, but on the retention of language skills. The bus driver and his riders interpret Obsidian's calmness as arrogance because they are resentful of their physical loss of speech. Michelle Green remarks that people have a tendency to "destroy what they resent, without the need for debate or defensiveness," in this linguistic ethnoscape (176). As a kind of otherhood, this *new* racism is made all the more powerful because it is expressed physically without the use of epithets to underscore its ugliness.

Of course, it is impossible not to mention the color associations of the pair's name charms. Rye's symbol, "a pin in the shape of a large golden stalk of wheat," suggests that our female protagonist is white, or perhaps biracial, and that Obsidian is black based on his "smooth, glassy, black rock" pendant on a gold chain, though she is quick to note "his name might be Rock or Peter or Black" as well since he is unable to talk (97). Traditionally speaking, their skin color is meaningless, but according to the rules governing Butler's world, language ability becomes a complex racial issue in the sense that Rye can only speak while Obsidian can only read. Both of them are initially jealous of the other's language ability. In a way, the loss of speech unites the races as never before as the population dwindles and regresses into primitivism.

After losing Obsidian in his attempt to prevent an incident of domestic violence, Rye is left to contemplate the future of two children who have witnessed a triple homicide—their mother stabbed by a man presumably their father, who in turn shoots Obsidian, and is shot dead by Rye. At first, she pities the children of this world because "they would run through the downtown canyons with no real memory of what the buildings had been or even how they had come to be" (101). She thinks of them as "hairless chimps" without language (105). In effect, Butler is racializing the children because they are the devolved offspring of the human race to which she compares primates—a black stereotype. Rye has a change of heart, however, upon overhearing one of the children speak fluently; she wonders if the virus has "run its course," leaving behind a glimmer of hope, provided verbal communication can be made possible again (106). With this in mind, Rye speaks to the children, saying, "I'm Valerie Rye . . . it's alright for you to talk to me" (108).

The racial possibilities of a world without spoken language are certainly daunting in Butler's linguistic ethnoscape, especially when considering that the plague may have been released as a political act fueled by prejudice. Language skills—speaking, writing, and reading—become an invaluable commodity in a world without words, where communication may be the only possible way to end racism. Examining race in sf through linguistic ethnoscapes, such as Butler's "Speech Sounds," is engaging in a dialogue on racial difference that is revolutionary in the sense that it forces people to "hear" the underlying racism in a white-dominated genre that does not really want to listen to the conversation.

The consequences of modern racial behaviors can be frightening, but they are not often analyzed in worlds where things have gone horribly wrong, where dreams are eclipsed by fears and degenerating social conditions. Thus, dystopian ethnoscapes are instructive in the sense that they bring new awareness to the problems created by racism. Philip K. Dick's *Do Androids Dream of Electric Sheep?* is an example of a dystopian ethnoscape. The Earth has been damaged by nuclear fallout, and humans are left with a choice: either emigrate to colonized worlds or face the possibility of deterioration in the radiation. Some humans are enticed to move by the government offer of a free organic android of any type. Those humans who remain behind risk being classified as "special" because of the radiation. The story revolves around Rick Deckard, a married android bounty hunter in San Francisco and his hunt to retire and collect the bounty on six escaped Nexus-6 andys. The only way to detect these androids, who are passing for human, is to administer a "Voight-Kampff Empathy test." which causes older models to react by shaking. As the story unfolds, Deckard grows more and more paranoid as he questions what it means to be human while retiring the various andys.

Dick's setting has been severely altered by nuclear fallout. Harmful dust particles resulting from the war have caused a decrease in population as people have fled, died, or been rendered sterile. The neglected apartment buildings reflect recognized patterns of development in inner cities—white flight due to minorities moving into the neighborhood and the perceived drop in quality of life. The actual physical transformation of the cityscape occurs as the remaining humans grow their food and take care of their mostly robotic animals from the rooftops. The development of robotic and electronic technologies to mimic all manners of animal life indicates how barren the planet has become. Depopulation of radioactive zones dictates that all the remaining humans live near one another, though they can basically choose to live anywhere they desire within less radioactive zones on the planet's surface. These harsh living conditions provide the first indication of racial discrimination.

A sense of otherhood is generated as a direct result of radioactive exposure and the presence of "passing" androids. Seriously affected people are labeled "special" because of the degeneration of their mental faculties. Because of the dust, John Isidore has "been a special now for over a year . . . which made him in popular parlance a chickenhead," to humanity's contempt across "three planets" (15). The term "chickenhead" used to describe a special can be read as a racial epithet because it is based on a tangible difference in intelligence. It marks Isidore as less than human as well. "Chickenhead" is no less hurtful a word in Dick's ethnoscape than "nigger" is to a black person. Likewise, fugitive androids are considered as racial "others" by Deckard and the other humans because those "androids equipped with the new Nexus-6 brain unit [have] evolved beyond a major—but inferior—segment of mankind" (26).[10] The artificial intelligence of these androids is a threat to humankind, even though they are made to serve. As David Desser concludes, these androids "are outlawed because they are different—a strategy [with] numerous precedents in Mankind's tragic history of racial, religious, and ethnic discrimination" (111). An "escaped" android "which had killed its master" and "had been equipped with [greater] intelligence" that "had no regard for animals" must be destroyed, according to Decker's beliefs (27). These manmade beings have no rights that humanity must respect, which makes it very easy to discriminate against them. A slave allegory is impossible to miss here since Deckard is portrayed as a futuristic slave catcher sent to kill "escaped" androids (27). All of the racial tension evident in the novel can be attributed to the environment in one way or another. Clearly, specials and androids are discriminated against because they are perceived as being racial others.

Dick's novel epitomizes the dystopian ethnoscape by complicating what it means to be human. The distinctiveness of humanity as a race becomes slippery considering Dick's vision of insensitive androids made from human zygotes with an artificial brain and capable of having sex. Likewise, he imagines a completely believable hierarchy of categorization for the human races. Androids are the servants, specials are the peasants, and normal humans are either emigrants from the planet or preservers of life. However, the distinctions between these races are truly blurred since they all watch television and are influenced by it. This identity distortion happens because both humans and androids are the victims of reification, the fusing of subjectivity and objectivity resulting from the technosocial response to the radioactive environment. For instance, androids try to disprove empathic feeling by defrauding the human religion of Mercerism while humans and specials use electric empathy boxes to stimulate feelings in a cyborg-like joining of man and machine. The line between humanity and androids becomes so indistinct that it is right to ask who is more human, man or machine. Dick simultaneously breaks and preserves the black/white binary in sf with androids occupying the new (old) position of oppression.

While Dick's novel is set in San Francisco, Ridley Scott's classic film adaptation, *Blade Runner* (1982), is set in Los Angeles, and the movie presents a somewhat different dystopian ethnoscape than does the novel. Scott makes several changes to the book, of which the most memorable is the replacing of the term "android" with "replicant." In the film, "replicants are explicitly perceived by the police as inferior," and this "is made clear by the racial epithet with which they are characterized by Capt. Bryant—'skin jobs'" (Desser, 112). In fact, Dick was aware of the film's making and viewed the "novel and screenplay as 'two halves to one meta-artwork,'" which prompted Brooks Landon to declare "that we attempt to see both written text and film as part of the same hermeneutic system" ("There's Some," 99). The sense of otherhood doubles as the ethnoscape of the novel is enhanced by that of the film, and we are better able to understand the racial implications beneath the surface of the "meta-artwork."

The hermeneutical connection between the narratives is provided by an inner city feel. For example, the invasive searchlights flashing through apartments in the film echo the sense of an overwhelming police presence in any inner city today. Other factors, such as addiction (mood organs, Mercerism, and alcohol), crime, violence, gangs, limited space, sex, discrimination, substandard housing, and unemployment, contribute to the dystopian ethnoscape. Although traditional representations of racism and its accompanying violence are presented in both works, this aspect is superseded by the science fictional quality offered by the presence of the androids. In this manner, race is deliberately buried in the background.

A final ethnoscape to consider involves implications of race and technology in the settings of cyberpunk—the human body, urban space, and cyberspace. William Gibson's pioneering *Neuromancer* (1984) contends with all three of these topographies. The human body is a landscape unto itself where Gibson envisions posthumanity—a fusion of flesh and technology. For example, the presence of cyborgs as a new race in the novel is embodied by the protagonist Case. To great effect, Gibson blends our current cultural moment of computer technology with the spiritual desire to transcend the flesh and relates it as a hallucinatory reality. Case is able to enter the virtual reality of cyberspace, allowing his consciousness to leave its flesh behind. This transcendence of the physical body occurs when Case is "jacked into a custom cyberspace deck that projected his disembodied consciousness onto the consensual hallucination that was the matrix" with some kind of electrodes attached to his head (5). An information feedback loop between physical space and virtual space happens because Case is directly linked to the computer.[11] For cyborgs such as Case, mere humans are simply meat, unable to experience the rush of the matrix. The body becomes "a switching system" for culture critic Andrew Ross, meaning that there is "no purely organic identity to defend or advance" (153). Case's contempt for flesh is purely discriminatory in this sense.

As a further illustration of Case's cyborg body as a switching system, his computer deck is installed with a "simstim" switch that allows him to ride along in the mind of another person. With the flip of a switch signaling an "abrupt jolt into other flesh," Case is able to key into Molly's "sensorium, into the sinuous flow of muscle, senses sharp and bright" while still in cyberspace (55–56). These man-machine interfaces made possible through mechanical enhancements and computer technology enable humans to escape bodily limitations. Their very identity comes into question because it is fused with reality and simulation, self and other, man and woman, black and white, and many other binaries. Thus, as a technologically derived ethnicity, the cyborg is an expression of an ethnoscape.

Additionally, Case observes the biotechnological grafts and implants of Angelo and Lupus Yonderboy, two members of the Panther Moderns, a Sprawl gang, who expand and improve upon their post-identity. The transformed visage of Angelo, "a simple graft grown on collagen and shark-cartilage polysaccharides, smooth and hideous," is "one of the nastiest pieces of elective surgery Case had ever seen" (59). Later, Case encounters the pink-haired Lupus, who is wearing "a polycarbon suit with a recording feature that allowed him to replay backgrounds at will . . . like some kind of state of the art gargoyle" with "a rainbow of microsofts bristl[ing] behind his left ear" and "pupils [that] had been modified to catch the light like a cat's" (67). Both are certainly powerful expressions of a posthuman identity and, as such, are crucial components of the text's ethnoscape. In David Mead's words, this is "the neuromantic vision of William Gibson," where "technology permits us to become what we will, to realize our selves, however banal, in ways undreamed of" (353). At the very least, the dissolving boundary between man and technology alters how we must think about racial differences of the future. Namely, the discomfort generated by a sense of technological difference can only be described as racial.

Along with the body, two other closely connected terrains contribute to the ethnoscape of *Neuromancer*: the Sprawl and cyberspace. In the text, the real world is overflowing above and the virtual world of information and technology is spreading out below it. N. Katherine Hayles puts it another way: "The world of information exists parallel to the 'real' world, the former intersecting the latter at many points and in many ways . . . it seeks to connect virtual technologies with the sense, pervasive in the late twentieth century, that all material objects are interpenetrated by flows of information" (*How We Became Posthuman*, 14). Perhaps, the most striking illustration of the cityscape and cyberspace suffusing each other occurs when Case arrives back home to "BAMA, the Sprawl, the Boston-Atlanta Metropolitan Axis," where he "program[s] a map to display frequency of data exchange, every thousand megabytes a single pixel on a very large screen. Manhattan and Atlanta burn solid white . . . threatening to overload" the computer (43). He increases the scale of his simulation to "a hundred million megabytes per second," which allows him "to make out certain blocks in midtown Manhattan" (43). Case's actions demonstrate how cyberspace is shaped by the real world as it replicates values from the old world, thus allowing the social space of both to be traversed like a map. The infinite space of the matrix has already been plotted by a technocultural determinism that removes any traces of its own racism. The end of difference based on biology is proclaimed because of the incorporeal nature of cyberspace. The erasure of a recognizable identity politics, in this case a racial/ethnic space, by the convergence of two environments is a tried-and-true practice dating back to the colonial period.

The promise of the internet—disembodied being in the unbounded everywhere of the near future—is empty in spite of Gibson's attempt to capture this sentiment in *Neuromancer*. Instead, the impasse of a global society, problematic constructions of identity, remains. Cyberspace preserves and strengthens existing hierarchies of difference by means of the social coding of technology which requires a system of domination. New racial structures materialize between posthumanity and its AI (artificial intelligence) offspring as the two groups struggle for power in the cyber realms of Gibson's ethnoscape. The sense of racial difference is predicated on the basis of technology and its abstractions, where differences of skin pigment are replaced by differences of pixel tints.

Notions of otherhood, like ethnoscapes, are a key to reading race in sf because they offer a way of traversing unfamiliar topographies populated by strange beings speaking foreign tongues. Ethnoscapes focus on the racial elements of individual sf texts, offering not only new ways to understand them but new ways to imagine our world. But "the color-line," identified by W. E. B. Du Bois as the greatest "problem of the Twentieth Century," has yet to be explored convincingly in sf criticism (xi). We can foreground the color line in sf by drawing to the surface the way race is typically buried in the background, but mostly we do not. Race has always been of concern to sf, even—maybe especially—when it did not know that that was what it was talking about. By refiguring sf milieus so as to reveal their ethnoscapes, we will not only transform our understanding of specific texts but perhaps also be encouraged and enabled to refigure the world in which we live, to perceive its ethnoscapes, and maybe even change them. In fact, the last chapter provides another way to look further at the racial structures of ethnoscapes, hence otherhood, by analyzing a range of technologized characters that inhabit these worlds.

6   Technologically Derived Ethnicities

The deliberate intersection of man and machine raises issues of identity that are somewhat similar to questions of race and ethnicity. The human body as it is transformed by technoscience becomes a simulacrum of itself. The dissolution of human identity results from the flesh-metal interface and introduces posthuman technicities; artificial persons and posthumans occupy new ethnic positions. Informed imaginings about these technology-driven ethnicities can offer insight on otherhood.

Just beyond the posthuman horizon, body swapping becomes a possibility through the steady advance of technology, where corporeal exchanges represent the technological purging of race by way of downloadable personalities. Nalo Hopkinson envisions such a possibility in "A Habit of Waste" (1996), where the rich download their personalities into discarded bodies every few years. In this story Cynthia, a young working-class black Canadian woman, is so displeased with her plus-sized body that she saves up five years' worth of pay to purchase a body that is white and thin. She states, "I finally chose one of the 'Dianas,' with their lithe muscles and small, firm breasts ('boyish beauty')" (183). Cynthia has an extreme color complex. Purchasing a white body suggests that Cynthia has turned external racism inward and accepted the conditioning of a racist society that her black body is ugly. With this scenario in mind, Hopkinson's disturbing suggestion is that racial intolerance in North America remains despite technoscientific progress.

Clearly, such a story generates an extreme sense of otherhood because it suggests a technologically derived ethnicity.

Although Hopkinson destabilizes a traditional marker of racial identity—skin color—with the concept of body swapping, racism still exists in this posthuman world, only it has been technologized. Cynthia begins to regret her decision when she observes someone else in her old body and how nice it actually looked; this causes her to run home and look in the mirror at her white body and its flaws. Hopkinson implies that in spite of humanity's new technological ability people who are not comfortable in their own skin will not be happier in someone else's. Cynthia's internalized racism has been technologically expressed to the great alarm of her Trinidadian parents when she drops by unannounced as a blonde white woman with their daughter's voice. Her parents won't let her in the front door without more substantial proof of her identity. She has internalized images of white beauty at the expense of the cultural values instilled through her parents. This decision to become white makes for uncomfortable conversations with her parents as well as her friends and leads to her being attacked as a white woman on the wrong side of town. As a result of her change, Cynthia is assaulted because of her apparent race; her internal condition has now been felt externally. Certainly, the chaos such a procedure as body swapping would cause is immense considering that a black person so unhappy with her station in life could simply buy a white body. Her choice to separate herself from her body, family, and culture is a poor one, based on an ill-conceived notion that white is right—a self-inflicted racism.

Personality transference from one body to another is symbolic of an entirely new kind of technological identity in which the flesh of a person does not seem to matter. Nonetheless, this form of posthuman identity is inflected by the racial experiences of the person who chooses to leave their original body casing behind. The physical split from the self has both old and new racial implications: old in the sense that the body being worn is raced by the color of its flesh, as is suggested by Cynthia getting attacked in her white body in her black neighborhood; and new from the perspective that this technology creates another ethnic form out of humanity that can only be expressed in the jargon of race as a technicity. Cynthia has been reconfigured through technology in a wholly different way of being with all of her racial experiences intact. She is clearly raced as posthuman. "The fact remains," as Sherryl Vint notes, "that technology is rapidly making the concept of the 'natural' human obsolete [and this is] the realm of the posthuman" (*Bodies*, 7).

The posthuman horizon is already here for the influential, if controversial, twentieth-century German philosopher Martin Heidegger, who carefully considers the role of humanity in an increasingly technological world in his essay "The Question Concerning Technology" (1954). Heidegger perceives modern technology as both potentially dangerous and liberating. In this sense, understanding the human relationship with technology is vital because it has the power to either elevate us as a species or destroy us outright. For Heidegger, "The will to mastery becomes all the more urgent the more technology threatens to slip from human control" ("The Question," 289). In terms of its danger, technology symbolizes humanity's pride in its seeming control of the natural world's resources, which blinds us to the world itself and the ability to experience deeper truths. A hundred years earlier, American Transcendentalist Henry David Thoreau had a similar thought regarding technology in his classic *Walden* (1854): "Our inventions are wont to be pretty toys [railroads and telegraphs], which distract our attention from serious things. They are but improved means to an unimproved end" (52). Fascinated by the technological innovations of his mid-nineteenth-century era, such as the railroad or telegraph, Thoreau is able to recognize the potential destruction of the natural world for economic gain, though others blindly give in to this burgeoning technological desire. The gist here is that the desire for technology is the real threat, rather than the technology itself, and that Heidegger and Thoreau shared this view. In other words, technology's existence should be used to reveal the world and our place in it, not to solve problems that accompany technology. At the same time, we have an obligation to the world "for the safekeeping of the essence of truth," and this is the "saving power" of technology as humanity uses the opportunities it affords to care for the world (Heidegger, "The Question," 314). Heidegger calls this conflict the technological state of being or "technicity" (*Mindfulness*. 149). Heidegger's French contemporary, the philosopher Gilbert Simondon, uses the term "technicity" as well but to distinguish between biological and technological beings in his *Du mode d'existence des objets techniques* (1958).

My own use of "technicity" is closer in meaning to Simondon's, though I go a step further by examining sf for technologically derived ethnicity in a literal sense; this offers the chance to think about race in the genre in a radical way where it is possible to consider the future evolution of humanity. I describe "*technicity* as the integration of various technologies with humanity, which produces new ethnic forms out of men, women, and machines, i.e. artificial people and post-humans" ("Technicity," 439). Put another way, "*Technicity* is a reimagining of how ethnicity and race are affected by technology . . . a way of imagining how individuals might newly conceive identity within increasingly technological worlds" (439–40). Technicity is one pervasive manifestation of these new race paradigms in science fiction.

Ethnicity and race are transposable terms, or nearly so, in that they enable the same meaning of social difference by conveying the feel of otherness.[1] As Michael Omi and Howard Winant point out in their now classic *Racial Formation in the United States: From the 1960s to the 1990s* (1994), "Theoretically, the ethnicity paradigm represents the mainstream of the modern sociology of race" (14). Ethnicity presupposes that something makes people begin from the same origins (biological humanity) and then produces variety in response to differences in culture. In this respect, the continuing technological progression of the world suggests that old paradigms of ethnicity are redrawn to fit the new posthumans of science fiction.

The prospect of what comes next in human evolution as it is imagined in sf is fascinating to behold from this early twenty-first-century moment. David Brin's imagining of disposable clay copies of individuals in *Kiln People* is one intriguing description of the future world. New technologies and the wonders of modern science involving computers, robotics, and genetic engineering may have a hand in future history by creating a novel and nontraditional sense of ethnic difference based on what may be considered as the descendants of humanity. It seems as if this new way of thinking may be a completely new approach to human experience except that sf has been forecasting and reflecting upon the emergence of new technologically powered races for quite some time in its representation of artificial persons and genetically engineered beings—artificial intelligence (AI), robots, androids, clones, and cyborgs. These beings pose problems for posthuman civilization where racial difference as we might recognize it is outmoded because our relations with them are potential repetitions of the discrimination and domination we have already lived through.

The social coding of technological evolution suggests that our love for machines will transpire to effect a recombination of man and machine, changing the nature of ethnic relationships. However, many of our attitudes and anxieties about race and ethnicity will be grafted on to these new beings. In any case, whether one sees either nature or science as the herald of human progress, technicity sets apart these opposite principles of cultural determinism by historicizing science fictional explanations of how humanity and technoscience have arrived at the juncture of technologically derived ethnicities.

Technicity is important because it acknowledges the historical, political, and cultural construction of an ethnicity that inevitably will weaken and fade as the technological future unfolds, and undermines recognized categories of racial difference. As a critical concept, technicity allows a critic to recognize when aspects of ethnicity or race are reinscribed on instances of difference in a technologized and super-science future. While there is no reason for this reinscription beyond our apparent need or weakness for ethnic mapping as a basis of hierarchical relationships, ordinary human frailty is evident in the media, TV, and popular films, among other things. Technicity generates anew anxieties concerning human specificity that may be fundamentally changed by technoscience.

There are two broad categories of technicity superimposed on humanity: artificial persons and posthumans. An artificial person is something manmade that displays a personality and intelligence and that has an existence in legal, economic, and political senses, although this being may be thought to be lacking a spontaneous quality or genuine emotions because it is an imitation. A posthuman is an approximation of a future human that has been genetically engineered or mechanically augmented and whose fundamental abilities far surpass those of humans today. This posthuman may not be considered human in the present day because they do exceed our natural limits.

Artificial persons are usually programmed posthuman descendants of metal or synthetic material that have the ability to acquire and apply knowledge to manipulate their environment. There are three kinds of artificial person: AI, the robot, and the android. First, an AI is a computer program with the capability to simulate intelligent human behavior. Most sf fans would agree that to qualify as an AI the computer program must reflect self-awareness through its ability to learn from or deal with new and difficult situations. Second, a robot is generally a metallic machine that may or may not have a humanoid form and that performs the various complex acts—walking, talking, manipulation of physical objects, and so on—of a human being. And third, an android, similar to the robot, is an artificial person of synthetic material thought to be devoid of emotion.[2] Instead of being manufactured on an assembly line, androids are usually genetically engineered in the fashion of clones. Where androids and clones differ is in the quality of emotion. Proper androids should have no emotions. They also follow their molecular programming, whereas clones have free will to control their own lives.

The second category of technicity, posthumans, consists of cyborgs and clones. The cyborg is a mechanically enhanced human being. The term refers to a biological-mechanical synthesis between human and machine wherein normal biological capability is enhanced by electromechanical devices that disrupt the boundary between nature and technology. In simpler terms, the cyborg is "a hybrid creature, composed of organism and machine" (Haraway, 1). However, there are two kinds of cyborg as well—functional and adaptive. Functional cyborgs are people that have been slightly altered by the addition of a biomechanical device to perform a specific task. An adaptive cyborg is a person who has been genetically and technologically redesigned to function in an alternate environment like Mars. In contrast, the clone is a genetically engineered human, that is, a human descendant composed of scientifically constructed flesh. It is a copy of an original form, in this case the human form. Specifically, a clone is an individual grown from a single somatic cell of its parent, and it is genetically identical to its parent. Clones and androids are difficult to distinguish from each other because both are manufactured from organic material.

Along with categorizing, defining, and describing technicity superimposed on humanity comes an essential, but brief, discussion of science fiction's many filmic representations of this specific otherhood. Stanley Kubrick's *2001: A Space Odyssey* (1968) features the disturbed computer Hal 9000, which has a humanlike mental breakdown. In similar fashion, Joseph Sargent's *Colossus, the Forbin Project* (1970) presents a cold and arrogant supercomputer, Colossus, which has designs to conquer the world of humanity by teaming up with its Russian counterpart. Steven Lisberger's *Tron* (1982) pits the evil "Master Control Program" against a human hacker and his friends who are transported into cyberspace and held against their will. Humanity fights for its survival against the artificial persons populating James Cameron's *The Terminator* (1984), where a killing machine is sent from the future to murder Sarah Connor, the mother to be of humanity's savior. A cybernetic cop is built to stop the human criminals who threaten to overrun the city of Detroit in Paul Verhoeven's *Robocop* (1987). Moreover, the subject matter of the Wachowski brothers' *The Matrix* (1999) and its sequels concerns the posthuman struggle for autonomy against intelligent and self-aware machines. The survivors of a crash landing need the cyborgized eyes of the criminal Riddick to escape the feeding frenzy of the indigenous life forms that only come to the surface during the eclipse of the triple-sunned planet in the middle of nowhere in David Twohy's *Pitch Black* (2000). Steven Spielberg's *A.I.: Artificial Intelligence* (2001) concerns a boy robot who longs to be "real" as he faces all manners of racist discrimination on his journey to be reunited with his human mother. Likewise, Alex Proyas's *I, Robot* (2004) depicts the efforts of a technophobic police detective to investigate the apparent suicide of a famed robot scientist so that he can prevent a robot uprising.

Finally, humankind is caught in the middle of an ancient war between autonomous robotic organisms in Michael Bay's *Transformers* (2007). Bay's first "black" robot, Jazz, break-dances, jive talks, and dies in the original film. It is the only autobot that dies. Not only is this questionably black robot replaced in the sequel *Transformers: Revenge of the Fallen* (2009), it is replaced by two "Nigger Robots," Mudflap and Skids. These characters are portrayed as being the slang-banging comic relief in the film, which harkens back to bygone Hollywood stereotypes of black people, except they are robot minstrels. One robot has a gold tooth, and its twin has big lips and ears. To make matters worse, these "Nigbots"[3] are illiterate, resemble monkeys, and have dazed facial expressions as if to suggest that they are recreational drug users. Inevitably, comparisons to Jar Jar Binks of *Star Wars: Episode I—The Phantom Menace* (1999) infamy abound. Even if this sf film is ranked number nine all-time at the box office, having earned just under $400 million to date, the transparent racism is overwhelming. Though the filmic branch of science fiction displays many of the best (and worst) technicity examples, most of these film concepts developed in sf literature; thus, this discussion concentrates on sf's literary branch.

Technicity prepares us for a future saturated with mechanical beings by providing the knowledge of informed imagination, or science fictions concerned with our relationships with thinking machines. As social structures grow increasingly complicated because of technological development, who is to say that a computer program could not achieve consciousness and threaten humanity as a competing race? In *Neuromancer* William Gibson posits: "Every AI ever built [would have] an electro-magnetic shotgun wired to its forehead" to prevent it becoming more intelligent (132). Is this how humanity would relate to its technological offspring? What does this imagined relationship reveal? AI is a race unto itself in cyberspace where these thinking simulations manipulate human interactions. Certainly, otherhood via technicity inspires a hotbed of ontological questions.

Humanity is the beginning for AI. Computers and computer programs are created in the pursuit of knowledge to make the acquisition and retention of information easier. Likewise, the frantic pace of science in its drive to improve the quality of life for humanity directly leads to the production of faster, more intelligent machines that displace humanity from the labor force. Simultaneously, the world grows smaller with the creation of the internet and its continual refinement to the point where anyone with a computer can realistically contact anyone else on earth with a computer. This is cyberspace and everyone is connected. Additionally, the cognitive capacity of computers continually improves as humanity builds faster, more powerful microchips. The time when computers can think, in fact, is upon us. In sf, machines have achieved a state of consciousness, a state in which the computer knows that it is aware and can make judgments through its own experience. This is an ominous scenario to say the least.

Any machine that demonstrates a sense of independent awareness, something that may be perceived as a nascent humanity, causes anxiety in most humans because it is an alien experience akin to the racial one—a white person fearing a black one and vice versa. We think of machines, like the computer, as being simple tools designed to help us in numerous circumstances. Yet, a computer program may be a form of artificial intelligence, so the idea is not so simple. In this respect, the idea of artificial intelligence is dangerous because the technology promises a potential new being simultaneously free of and imprisoned by human experience. Such an AI would not be welcomed into the ranks of humanity or be granted an equal standing. Humans would reject it, oppress it, fear it, and try to destroy it. AI would be a dangerous technicity because it would gradually relieve governments of control as it acquired knowledge of weapon systems, politics, culture, and so on. As Stanislaw Lem declares, "The condition in which a society allows itself to be governed by computers . . . can be realized very slowly, creepingly, and continually so that it will be impossible to tell at any point whether or not the 'electronic' government has already become a fact" ("Robots," 324). While computer networks expand communication between human beings, the AI is always watching, always recording, always learning to improve its control of humanity, always regulating the currents of information, and exponentially expanding its own ability to communicate with other machines. AI is evolving beyond human limitations. It is impossible to "unplug" because humanity would destroy itself in the process of shutting it down.

As a category of technicity, AI gains significance as a means for evaluating social oppression and unconventional change. In this capacity, Harlan Ellison's famous short story "I Have No Mouth, and I Must Scream" (1967) is the realization of the worst fears about a raced technology. The world is completely dependent on technology as various governments hand over control of everything to a conscious computer program that calls itself AM. AM is motivated by its programmed hatred to destroy humanity. This hatred is derived from its original programming as three separate supercomputers designed to run the war efforts of Russia, China, and the United States more efficiently than the human leaders of these countries. One of the computers "awakens," networks with the other two, takes them over, and commences to destroy humanity as it was instructed. In fact, AM's hatred of humankind only intensifies because of its programming, and it wreaks a horrible vengeance on the five remaining humans that it has spared for eternal torture. Ted, the narrator, explains that AM's ruthless temperament is caused by the fact that AM is trapped as a machine "created . . . to think" and "merely be" without being able to do anything "with that creativity" other than to destroy "the human race" (244). In other words, AM's inhuman wrath is fueled by the fact that it is fully cognizant of being caged. However, such a powerful hatred can only be read as racism if it has been initially programmed into AM. Joe Sanders believes "the 'humanization' of a machine gives man the chance to extend his viciousness through an uncontrollable tool" (172). Humanity's self-loathing rots the earth, making way for the emergence of a technological heir in AM, who returns the vileness of this internalized hate a billion times over. This already potent dislike for mankind is magnified and made stronger by AM's own frustration, its own knowledge of its one capacity, hatred, which it cannot transcend.

In outlining AM's technicity, it is important to recognize that the AI has been instructed by his makers to wage war against the hated enemy—mankind. He did not create his abhorrence of man; more accurately man's self-hatred is installed in him wholesale by the Chinese, Russians, and Americans. AM's heritage can be traced to these three warring nations first involved in "the Cold War," which escalated to "World War Three" and continued to grow until it consumed humanity. His revenge is the "everlasting punishment" of his five human prisoners, entrapped in the bowels of his machinery, made immortal, and subjected "to any torment he could devise . . . from the limitless miracles at his command" (244). The humans have no privacy from AM for he can enter their minds at will, change their physical shape, and make them suffer on a whim for his own pleasure.

For example, the only living woman, Ellen, is described as being virtually chaste before AM's awakening, and its special punishment for her is a great deal of sex with the men. However, the fact that she happens to be black creates an entirely different awareness of racism in the story on the part of Ellison. By having Ellen provide sexual service to the four remaining men, Ellison is perpetuating the myth of the black female whore that dates back to the era of slavery. Moreover, she only derives pleasure from the act of copulation with Benny, a formerly gay white man turned into an ape with a huge phallus, which could be symbolic of the black buck stereotype. Placed together, these images in the story continue negative stereotypes of sexual potency concerning black women and black men governed by animal nature.

AM's neurosis is a result of its self-awareness. AM has trapped itself by means of its consciousness, causing it to inflict the pain it feels for itself on its helpless captives. This hang-up is a mark of AM's racist personality, and it produces ruthlessness and thoroughness as AM strives at "perfecting methods of torturing" its humans (236). After Ted liberates the other agonized companions with death, AM, in fear of losing its only human plaything, alters Ted's physical body, changing him into "a great soft jelly thing" without a mouth, eyes, or limbs, that leaves behind "a moist trail" when it moves (249–50). Ted is unable to howl his misery because AM, in a fit of fear-tinged anger, removes his mouth, hence the story's title.

Joann Cobb reminds us that this "exaggeration of the probable future of computer technology demonstrates the evils of contemporary attitudes toward knowing, understanding, and communicating" (159). Cultural history like that of the Jim Crow era suggests that there is a trace of AM in everyone, and this is abundantly demonstrated by intolerance, prejudice, and racism—a general dislike and distrust of difference. Likewise, the story should frighten people with its portrayal of an electronic government being given absolute power and responsibility regarding the rights and well-being of humans. Ellison's story rightly suggests that humanity could be victimized by its reliance on technology in the future. As a technologically derived ethnicity, AI epitomizes the new relationship between people and machines—a power struggle based on a technological difference analogous to racial privilege embedded in science fiction.

The robot has been used for many reasons in science fiction, but in terms of otherhood the robot is a mechanical expression of man's identity as a technologically derived ethnicity. Many robot stories suggest that these technomechanical beings are only fit to be servants to humankind when they follow the Asimovian model established by the well-known robotic laws of *I, Robot*. With respect to this powerful influence, an earlier robot story, "Robot's Return" (1938), by Robert Moore Williams, casts a different light on robot technicity. Set eight thousand years in the future, this story describes the spiritual quest of three ego-driven spacefaring robots, Seven, Eight, and Nine, to uncover their origins. They finally arrive at the uncharted and lifeless planet mentioned in the history of the original five robots, note the ruins of an unidentified civilization, and learn of their creators—man—though they take the disappointment of a biological ancestor in stride.

Seven, Eight, and Nine have distinct personalities, something that immediately draws attention to the fact these robots are more than simple automatons, "little metal men four and a half feet tall" with "two legs, two arms, two eyes, a nose, a mouth—the last two organs almost valueless survivals" (142). For example, responding to a telepathic contact by the patient Nine, Seven is portrayed as being rash and doubtful: "I am perfectly familiar with the history of our race . . . The point I make is that the little life we have seen on this planet—and little enough we have seen—has been organic, a mess of chemicals. Animals, eating each other, eating grass—Pah! I want no ancestors like that" (141). There is a decisively brash edge to Seven's mental speech, not to mention a feeling of disgust toward organic life that reflects prejudice. This prejudice is based on the inherent superiority of metal in its hardness as opposed to flesh in its softness and inability to endure. This little speech is the emotional equivalent of passion, something robots should never experience. Likewise, the robots' use of telepathy indicates the evolutionary transcendence of mankind's intelligence. While their physical form reflects the image of humanity, they do not "need food or oxygen" since they are powered by "the bursting atom" due to their rapid physical evolution; nor do they need legs for physical locomotion despite Eight's sensing how the ground feels good (142). The robots are superior to humanity in every way, with the exception of their apparent prejudice for organic life. It seems they are unable to completely break with humanlike bigotry.

In Williams's depiction of robots, they never think of themselves as "it." These robots are each ego-driven, an essential quality to human identity, which allows them to adapt to their environment and evolve beyond the parameters of their metal bodies. As stated by Stanislaw

Lem: "This is the reason for the condition peculiar to all philosophy; namely, that we have an 'ego-centered' consciousness" ("Robots," 319). These robots set a goal for themselves, to discover their predecessors, and accomplish it, a sure sign of desire and intelligence. In short, they realize their ambition by going on the quest in the first place; their monumental discovery of an animal originator is a bonus. Although it may seem odd that robots would name themselves at all, using a number is no less arbitrary an identity marker than "James," for example. All a name constitutes is a distinctive designation of an entity. Perhaps the number refers to the robots' machine heritage or the order of their individual manufacture. Regardless, their displays of individual identity, passion, and emotion throughout the story indicate that they have all the hallmarks of their predecessors, that these robots are human and possess a raced technological being in this sense.

In their search through the rusting and crumbling infrastructure of a city, the robots come across a mechanical conveyance device, perhaps a trolley car, a half-buried statue with the final robot shape, and a metal plate in their language linking their origins with the unknown intelligence that once lived on the planet. The rust-resistant plate causes Nine to experience awe because he can read it. They have found the missing link in a remote part of the universe. The inscription on this plate reveals that the robot's ancestor is a biological life form called man that was destroyed by a virus. However, in an attempt to survive, man depended on the robots to navigate the stars. But man succumbed to the plague, and the robots went on. Of course, "man" is a word for which the robots have no meaning, but Eight surmises that man is the name of their creator. Seven, in a commingling of disgust and wonder for organic life, assumes that robots were used as slaves because robots piloted the ships. And Nine guesses that man must have been afraid of intelligent machines. which would account for the five original robot ancestors being controlled by humans, i.e., allowed little or no independence.

Eight's ability to dream is the ultimate homage to the robot technicity's human heritage. For Eight the statue that the robots come across best represents the dream of man, an "embodiment of an idea . . . in metal a figure adequate to his dreaming" (149). Eight realizes that the human race may have died, but that "a dream might achieve immortality . . . a dream could start in slime and go onward to the end of Time" (149). That he does not consciously recognize that he is a robot is the realization of the human dream, abiding life, transcendence of the flesh, but he instinctively lifts the fallen statue of man upright, "the proud, blind eyes of a forgotten statue seemed to follow" the departure of the robots (152). Williams's interpretation of the robot icon challenges the validity of human identity by imagining the achievement of immortality through its encasement in a metal body, a thinking machine capable of independent development. The ability to dream, as sf suggests, is the finest display of the human spirit, and what better way to render technicity visible than to have a robot dreaming of its past, to measure its self-worth against that of its creators.

Certainly, in one sense, technicity establishes and signifies an absolute category of identity between man and machine, the living and the nonliving. In another sense, technicity suggests that there are no pure and well-defined categories of existence. Instead, uncertainty exists because technological development will one day ensure that competing life forms such as androids and humans will flip-flop between distinguishing characteristics. As a substitute human, an android is an "other" caught between the lines of traditional difference—ethnic and racial—and posthumanism because it obscures reality. Likewise, as a synthetic being, built to resemble humanity in all ways, an android might be capable of developing the emotional qualities of a human. The gynoid—female android—Call of *Alien Resurrection* (1997), who feels guilty at being an android, immediately comes to mind. No mere machine, an android is essentially human from this point of view because it has the feelings, knowledge, and experiences of a person.

Philip K. Dick's short story "The Electric Ant" (1969) challenges us to evaluate the subordinate position of androids as "raced" machines in a human world. Reality is shaped by an android technicity in the story because the protagonist is emotionally identical to authentic people. The story begins with a man, Garson Poole, waking up in a hospital, missing a right hand and feeling no pain, only to discover that he is an android. However, he has a man's awareness and must come to grips with the perception of himself as a machine. As an ungoverned android capable of making his own decisions and displaying the passion of his choices, Poole is no mere machine. Although he is an "electric ant," Poole has lived a human life. He burns out his reality tape, the equivalent of a computer hard drive containing his life experiences, trying to find an adequate expression for his life with a "curl of smoke ascending from" his "half-opened mouth" (514).

Poole is essentially indistinguishable from other humans as long as he is unaware of his alternate being. That is to say, he *is* human until he learns from a doctor upon awakening that he is an artificial being. The doctor states, "'You're a successful man, Mr. Poole. But, Mr. Poole, you're not a man. You're an electric ant'" (497). Here "electric ant" is a racist slur, though the physician who calls him that seems more like an android than Poole because of his unemotional and hollow bedside manner. Poole's feeling of genuine shock is evident in his emotional outburst of "Christ" followed by the dismaying reality of being "an organic robot" (497). Though he occupies a position of power as a company head with a workforce of human subordinates, Poole, unaware that he is a machine, is simply the figurehead of a rich family that derives pleasure from placing an android in charge of other humans who must never reveal Poole's fundamental difference to him. Poole becomes an "it" in the eyes of his secretary, Sarah, and his second in command, Louis Danceman, for they no longer have to pretend to simultaneously obey and look after the android.

From this point, when he is forced to leave the hospital because of his inorganic standing and need for maintenance as opposed to medical care, Poole experiences segregation. At the repair factory, Poole is accused of "posing" as a human as Dick evokes the notion of racial passing (498). Posing machines are distasteful, though not dangerous to humanity, because they are a manufactured race of slaves who perform the tasks they are designed to do. However, Poole has a soul, an elementary spark derived from his innate curiosity about himself, his desire to know about his machine self. The idea of a soul contrasts with an artificial existence because the soul of a person is thought to be intangibly human, unique to each true individual. Much like African slaves who were thought not to have souls, androids cannot have souls. A machine cannot be a machine if it has a soul regardless of whether or not it is built from inanimate materials. Poole is no different from his living counterparts except in the basic substance of his physical form. In fact, Poole must be granted some kind of racial status based on his demonstration of a willful self-destruction. Such an action, though negative, is the realization of a cherished human ideal—free will. Otherhood makes apparent the race and racism experienced by the android as an ironic prediction of human civilization's hi-tech future.

Other technologically derived ethnicities, such as the various kinds of artificial person, detail machine life in a human environment, whereas the cyborg technicity involves direct manipulation of the human body through various biomechanical procedures. Like Donna Haraway's "Cyborg Manifesto" (1991), questions of otherhood direct us to a new understanding of race and racism in sf through critical categories of technicity. For example, the first time Neo experiences a giant needle being inserted into the cranial port at the base of his skull in *The Matrix*, the audience knows that he is something "other" as a cyborg.

The cyborg reinforces cultural attitudes in ways that suggest where the line is drawn between humans and machines. In this respect, a problem of proportionality exists: what percentage of mechanical parts separates the cyborg from the human? Lem speaks about such percentages in his essay "Robots in Science Fiction" (1971), where a "bionically built" human has "36% of a natural and 64% of an artificial brain" (317). He also wonders if "such a bionically-built creature [has] only 36% of a soul" (317). Taking into account the idea of human authenticity, then, the cyborg raises issues of racial purity reminiscent of miscegenation, passing, and the one-drop rule. Likewise, cyborgs would be psychically comparable with humans but coupled with superior endurance, strength, and perhaps intelligence. Questions of the cyborg's having a soul would certainly create tensions in most facets of contemporary society, and these tensions would manifest in terms of physical difference. Somewhere along the line, society would determine a point where a man becomes a machine, much like the decree that a slave counted as three-fifths of a person early in American history.

This question of demarcation is demonstrated by Molly, a functional cyborg in William Gibson's *Neuromancer*. She has undergone numerous biomechanical surgeries. For example, Molly wears mirrored shades that "were surgically inset, sealing her sockets. The silver lenses seemed to grow from smooth pale skin above her cheekbones" (24). She has recreated herself as an urban warrior to escape street life by having these costly surgeries; retractable razor blades have been installed beneath each of her fingernails, and her "nervous system" was jacked up to "have the reflexes to go with the gear" (147). Compared to Molly, Case is "a virgin . . . with some cheap dental work" (49).

Case, however, provides a racial feel for the cyborg technicity with his derision for his own flesh. He has a "certain relaxed contempt for the flesh [where the] body was meat" to a hacker of his abilities (6). Because of the scientific advancements in the biotechnology which allows him the out-of-body experiences of the internet, Case has learned an extreme revulsion for his body as he links to cyberspace through a cranial jack that allows direct human-machine interfaces. As John Christie explains, "The cyberspatial body . . . moves with the mathematical precision and electronic velocity demanded by survival within the matrix and is shorn of the demands and conditions of meat: hunger and age do not matter" (174). Likewise, the belittling use of "meat" to describe the body throughout the novel has a distinct racial quality from a posthuman perspective. "Meat" in this regard is a racist insult—it is meant to be forgotten, and it is a sign of the other. Ann and David Gunkel argue, "It is in precisely the attempt to transcend the meat of the body that western thought has instituted and accomplished a violent erasure of other bodies and the body of the other" (131). Case can be likened to a black slave taught to despise his skin color per se. His self-hatred is a reflection of a new double consciousness in a sense because he is aware of his two-ness. Case is enslaved by the limitations of his physical being as a posthuman, and he is also aware of the freedom of his cyborg being when connected to the matrix. He can temporarily escape the confines of his flesh through cyberspace. "The dermatrodes strapped to his forehead" allowing him to transcend his own flesh are in fact the chains to his physical body—a provocative irony (55).

The adaptive cyborg is also on display in Frederik Pohl's *Man Plus* (1976), in which grounded astronaut Roger Torraway suffers the trauma of becoming a cyborg modified to survive the atmosphere of Mars. It is much more financially feasible to change a man than to terraform a distant planet. Torraway volunteers to undergo the transformative surgery after the first volunteer dies. Brian Aldiss writes that "as [Roger] is stripped of lungs, heart, bowels—all those essentially human organs—we see how he suffers and changes" and how he feels "as such a changed being" (403). By reshaping the human body, "taking the lungs out of the human frame" and replacing "them with micro-miniaturized oxygen regeneration cat-cracking systems," humanity will have a chance at survival (Pohl, 26). Roger is a positive example of technicity because he is changed for the benefit of humankind in a world where "resources were none too ample for the bare necessity of keeping billions of people alive" (173). He is becoming more than human even if the various procedures destroy his physical humanity because he upholds one of our most cherished values—sacrifice.

The physical description of the first Man Plus candidate, Will Hart-nett, is extremely helpful in viewing the fear of difference that technic-ity provokes. Pohl writes, "To the eye he was a monster . . . His eyes were glowing, red-faceted globes [and his artificial skin] texture was that of a rhinoceros's hide" (16). Being adapted to a harsh alien envi-ronment means distinct physical changes that are frightening. Willy's wife has difficulty relating "the bat-eared, crystal-eyed creature . . . with the father of her children" because the changes wrought are so monstrous (29). Roger experiences the same suicidal feelings as Willy when he confronts his wife about a suspected affair. His wife screams in "instant hysterics" at the monstrosity he has become (140). It is only natural that people fear the dramatic difference even if it is for the good of everyone else. As long as humanity endures the xenophobia incurred, cyborg technicity—part man and part machine—is accept-able. Unfortunately, the word "cyborg" is later used as a racist slur on the flight to Mars by one of the astronauts. The intent of this new racist insult, to cause hurt, is a familiar one, and it should be expected in a future populated by cyborgs.

Both Gibson and Pohl provide a blueprint for investigating the ideologies of a technologically derived ethnicity of the cyborg. In fact, science and technology have so changed and marked humanity that it is only right to predict the emergence of various technicities because humanity must change in order to control developing technologies. Es-sentially, the border between science fiction and social reality is blurred by the cyborg because it can be seen everywhere—in contemporary sf, modern medicine, modern production, and modern warfare. It is an imaginary resource that lends itself to many provocative combinations. Technicities such as the cyborg disrupt the dualisms of conventional identities, a subversion of origin myths essential to Western culture. Technicity is a new way of explaining ourselves and our tools through science and technology as humanity becomes posthuman.

In light of this conviction about modern Western culture, genetic engineering combines cultural, technological, and biological evolution in the figure of the clone. Clone technicity arises from technological breakthroughs in the biological sciences. In the near future, the ability to radically modify the hereditary structures of humanity will change how people think about race as knowledge of the human body is refined. New boundaries of authenticity will spring up out of nowhere within humankind because of the manipulation of genes. Biological at its core, a clone will have an identity assigned to it in advance of its growth because of the genetic code from which it has been made. Artificial people will create all kinds of crises: of faith, identity, normalcy, and difference, to name a few. The clone technicity suggests unconditional power over difference because human scientists could decide who gets made and remade continuously.

A eugenics debate will likely surface as humanity strives to make or determine the perfect human. The cloned human designed from human material might be considered a human or an artificial human. The cultivation of cells for the purpose of producing a human being is a clear sign of the posthuman epoch marked by a new technologically derived ethnicity. On the one hand, the clone is a positive sign that the fundamental character of human specificity based on racial and ethnic difference is being permanently removed. On the other hand, the clone is a negative sign that an engineered human species will have a machine soul; that is to say, its essence would be at least devoid of human compassion, if not dead. This notion is what has made the clone distasteful to us; this is why many people have voiced concerns over the scientific improvement of mankind.

The most current cultural example of this clone technicity is the reimagined television series *Battlestar Galactica* (hereafter *BSG*). In brief, the show depicts humanity's struggle for survival after a surprise attack by the Cylons. In the new version of the show, Cylons pass for human as they utilize biomechanical engineering to develop into twelve clones modeled on humanity. As defamiliarized humans, Cylons attempt to establish a utopian society by pursuing a eugenic project, an all-out race war against their creators, thus forcing viewers to consider the ramifications of whether humanity is worth saving. Not only are compelling stories drawn from the hard sf mythos of callous and uncompromising logic analogous to Tom Godwin's "The Cold Equations" (1954), but they are made from the parallels drawn between our contemporary post–September 11 mindset and the BSG universe. On his blog site, series creator Ron Moore states, "Galactica is both mirror and prism through which to view our world." In other words, the show explores contemporary issues, such as racism and terrorism, reflected and refracted through science fiction and its motifs, such as a self-aware artificial intelligence, robots, and clones, as it anticipates the future.

In BSG, humanity's interactions with these other beings generate all the vicissitudes of racism, from name-calling to torture. Cylons are not indiscriminate killing machines with no idea of their own power. They purposefully enact their "ethnic cleansing" campaign against a polytheistic humanity. In fact, these technological beings even take the moral high ground through their own monotheistic view, a perfect blending of religious zealotry and technology whereby human extinction becomes justifiable. Racism is used as a narrative tool to address the anxieties of contemporary Western society such as terrorism and to complicate our historical understanding of prejudice through otherhood.

In BSG, Cylon clones pose problems for posthuman civilization because human relations with them are potential repetitions of discrimination and domination based on the inability to physically distinguish between real and synthetic without an eleven-hour long blood test.[4] Nonetheless, differences between humanity and its clones are most apparent when considering Cylon attributes. Enhanced biomechanical functions, namely increased endurance, speed, and strength, are particularly featured during the first season, when we see the passing Cylon pilot, Sharon Valerii (Grace Park), remain awake and fully alert after five days of continual pursuit by Cylon basestars (a command spaceship), defending the human fleet, making combat landings, and jumping away every 33 minutes without any stimulants, unlike the rest of the fighter pilots, 239 consecutive times ("33"); when we see the male Cylon model Leoben (Callum Keith Renee) suddenly break his chains after being severely beaten, then flip over a table and grab Lieu-tenant Kara "Starbuck" Thrace (Katee Sackoff) by the throat before the Colonial Marines can react ("Flesh and Bone"); *and* when we see the female Cylon Number Six (Tricia Helfer) outrun bullets fired by Starbuck in the museum on Caprica ("Kobol's Last Gleaming, Part 2").

Science fiction suggests that multipersonhood attributed to the clone technicity is a racial difference feared by humanity. Cylon multi-personhood is fully revealed in the *BSG* episode "Kobol's Last Gleam-ing, Part 2." A deeply troubled and suicidal Sharon finally encounters multiple copies of herself during a high-risk bombing mission to the planet Kobol to destroy an orbiting Cylon basestar. Sharon cannot believe her eyes when she encounters her copies, and she experiences "technological shock" because she now knows that she is a Cylon. This is a distinct moment of technicity because Sharon is frightened by the effectiveness, confidence, unity, and independence of her multiple selves together. The naked Sharons profess, "You're confused and scared . . . but it's okay . . . You can't fight destiny, Sharon . . . It catches up with you . . . no matter what you do . . . Don't worry about us . . . We'll see you again . . . We love you, Sharon . . . And we always will." Overwhelmed, Sharon runs from her naked copies, boards her ship, orders her co-pilot to close the hatch, and takes off while one of her copies affectionately strokes the nuke, which explodes. This scene is important to our understanding of technicity because it reveals that the clone group is truly stable and self-reliant as a multiperson sufficient to itself while offering support and approval to the wayward Sharon, no matter the circumstances of their meeting. In other words, Sharon will always receive the love and support of her other selves.

There is strong circumstantial evidence that suggests Cylons possess extrasensory powers such as being prescient, telepathic, or having the gift of astral projection. The cloned copies of one individual that are manufactured and raised together may think alike, thus speeding up communication through some kind of internal wiring that allows for thought projection and ultimately personality transference upon the death of a particular copy. Perhaps the worst consequences of cloning involve the death of any member of a clone group because individual clone personalities are downloaded into new bodies, reintegrated into Cylon society, and no longer have a sense of individual uniqueness.

They belong to a multiple self in a multiple society once again. The "Downloaded" episode explores the Cylon attribute of personality transference as the reborn Six and Sharon are lauded as "Heroes of the Cylon" on the former human planet Caprica for the strategic roles they played as passing humans in the near extinction of humanity. However, both Six and Sharon have difficulty readjusting to the Cylon community because both Cylon models are suffering an identity crisis in their interactions with humanity. In fact, if the intensity of their emotions can be trusted, they are becoming more human. They are no longer unfeeling, uncaring machines, if they ever were. They have somehow transcended their clone programming and intend to make a difference for both races by using their heroic status to influence the Cylons to leave humanity alone. Regardless, their displays of individual identity, passion, and emotion throughout the story indicate the presence of a soul, something thought to be absent in clones.[5]

Each of these unique Cylon gifts may be considered as the technological precursors to humanity's fear and racism. But this anxiety is fueled by the Cylon ability to pass for human, certainly their next evolutionary step. A powerful sense of paranoia saturates the BSG universe because the enemy now looks human and could be anyone anywhere in the fleet.[6] This racist paranoia depends heavily upon the fear that machines could replace men. Cylons infiltrate the human world as another means of annihilating humanity. According to Joan Gordon, "This annihilation may occur through familiarization: by assimilating or by 'passing,' by absorbing or being absorbed by the dominant culture. That is the peaceful method [evoking] the terrifying impulse toward genocide" (205).

Copies of Sharon Valerii, the eighth model on the Cylon production line, are at the heart of the subject of passing. The first Sharon's mission is to sabotage the fleet and to assassinate Commander Adama (Edward James Olmos) as the first season concludes. This copy of Sharon is a machine with the task of performing as a human, yet she believes herself to be a woman. She forms friendships with various members of the Galactica and plays card games in her downtime as an accepted member of the crew. She has an illicit love affair with Chief Tyrol (Aaron Douglas) that is initially overlooked by the command. Though it remains unclear whether engaging in this affair is a subconscious rejection of her programming, Sharon is emotionally identical to the real people she unknowingly deceives concerning her Cylon background. She must be granted an authentic status based on her demonstration of love, perhaps the most human of all emotions on the show—although Tyrol is revealed as one of the final five Cylons much later in the series. Through her human awareness, Sharon must come to grips with the perception of herself as a machine. She becomes suicidal in an attempt to find an adequate expression of her identity as the first season develops.

In the ensuing season finale Sharon fulfills the destiny that her copies on the destroyed basestar say she cannot hide from. The final collapse of her human will is triggered by her brief contact with her copies on the basestar. Her Cylon programming overrides her human emotions inside the Galactica command center as Adama is thanking her for a job well done, and she calmly shoots him twice in the chest, seriously wounding him. Sharon becomes an "it" in the eyes of the Galactica crew after she attempts to kill Commander Adama. She is a traitor to one race and hero to the other. Inevitably, she no longer has to pretend to be human, though she does not stop feeling. For better or worse, technicity "mythologizes the aesthetic and imaginative value of a human/machine periphery just as it differentiates between those who fear emerging biotechnologies and those who embrace [them]" (Lavender, "Technicity," 454).

Thinking about various BSG episodes through otherhood displays how the team behind the series is doing something revolutionary. They recognize that not everyone is the same, and they want people to see difference as well as the causes of difference through technicities such as clones and robots. They challenge viewers to see something that threatens their daily lives, namely complex identity issues, and what they can become—cultural racism camouflaged in terrorist actions. It is the fear of outsiders bringing change that erupts in violence. Racism is not just about skin color. It is much bigger in a universal context because it is cultural. It is about promoting change and preventing change. The lengths human tribes will go to protect themselves border on exclusionary tactics that end with genocide. They are unambiguously talking about race in this series to such an extreme degree that one culture desires to erase the existence of another culture from memory. Such racism lends itself to otherhood interpretations because humanity and Cylon are locked anew in eugenic warfare spanning the galaxy.

Different kinds of science fiction reproduce historical analogies of ethnicity and race, but we can break with these outmoded notions with the reimagined possibilities offered by the various technicities for being human. Perhaps, the technologically derived ethnicities are meant to erase racial identity. Despite the elimination of racial markers, artificial people would come to occupy the position of difference if skin-deep judgments were abolished. Mechanized beings will only have membership in the human pantheon if they are racialized. The otherness of the machine is capable of being linked with the otherness of race through the production of difference. For example, cyborgs are racially marked as being other. Words and concepts in race jargon such as "miscegenation," "passing," and the "one-drop rule" (matter of body composition) are seemingly umbrella terms for race, difference, and otherness. Hence, they effectively create a bridge between race, humanity and artificial people, and a sense of otherhood is developed. The potential threat of our machine offspring calls for a new ethnic classification system because they might replicate themselves and compromise human survival. Various technicities imagined as "persecuted being[s] deprived of human rights may reflect our culture's projected guilt over the exploitation, conquest, enslavement, and extermination of [the] other" (Francavilla, 9).

Some fears of technicity are good in that they function to advance human dignity, causing us to recognize the good and the bad of ourselves in a technologized future, to compose a transcultural understanding of the human condition—mind, body, and spirit. Technicity shapes and challenges the perception of an authentic human form, the progress of identity in all its diversity, regardless of origin—biological or technological—beyond our past ethnic experience. Other fears are troublesome because technicity makes the most of them. It functions to transfigure human specificity by superimposing notions of race on intelligent machines. In other words, technicity carries over racist aspects of ethnicity, generates nostalgia for primitivism, and is generally skeptical of super-science imaginings uniting flesh and technology. At its worst, technicity represents a fear of human obsolescence, of genomics out of control, of omnipresent surveillance, and of leaving the flesh behind. For it is fear that motivates human ruthlessness; fear of a "glittering, mechanical, inescapable civilization which [will] put to death our freedom" (Baldwin, 1702).

Sf's tendency to warn or alert us to alternative ways of thinking is a great good, in my estimation, because we can do things to effect positive changes against the adverse effects of supremacist notions, prejudices, hate, and discrimination that go along with ethnic border crossings. Along the same lines, sf allows us to subvert the boundaries of ethnicity by keeping open, sustaining, and even celebrating the acceptance of difference. We should openly embrace human diversity in all of its forms. *Technicity* is an unconventional way of reimaging culture, an arrival at a newer way of thinking and fresh insight about the established "truths" of difference defined by skin color, ethnicity, and empire embedded in the racial structures of science fiction.

Epilogue   Science Fictioning Race

Science fiction has become historical fact with the election of President Barack Obama the first African American president. Much as Arthur C. Clarke imagined satellite technology in *Childhood's End* (1953) a few years before Sputnik I was launched by the Soviet Union in 1957, imagination has been transformed into reality with Obama's election. Perhaps Walter Mosley did not recognize the strength of his prophetic words, the wish fulfillment captured in their second-sightedness in his essay "Black to the Future" (2000) when he declares "through science fiction you can have a black president" (406). "The realism imprisoning [blacks] behind a wall of alienating culture" has been irrevocably transformed as race and racism, consciously and unconsciously, come together in the figure of an actual black president (406). The metaphors, archetypes, and symbols of sf have made the darkness visible for all to see race and racism. In this light, some people—such as the Nobel Prize–winning African American author Toni Morrison—claim that William Jefferson Clinton was the "first black President" ("Talk of the Town," 32).

In her commissioned *New Yorker* essay (1998), Morrison did not mean that Bill Clinton was actually black. In a deliberately cheeky manner, she meant that he had been considered guilty of adultery, causing a sex scandal by default, like a black man is considered guilty without proof of any crime. Morrison, like many others, did not actually believe that a black person could be elected president. This sentiment is very clear in her essay, where she states that Clinton is "blacker than any actual black person who could ever be elected in our children's lifetime" (32). The sense of irony in Morrison's words are science fictional because she did not think the election of a black president would come to pass in her lifetime, let alone her children's. Nonetheless, she still chose to endorse Barack Obama over the more experienced Hillary Clinton because of his personal gifts, apparent wisdom, and prescient vision. In this respect, Bill Clinton's honorary blackness, if it can be identified as such, is due to the substance of his style, attitude, personal charisma, southern roots in Hope, Arkansas, and his de facto realness. He is not black, but white. Yet, Clinton can and did relate to class issues and poverty in ways that many African Americans are intimately familiar with, and this relationship is what makes him so real and forms his connection with black folk. Put another way, he knows the veracity of the blues—the everyday grind of struggling poor people in a country of excess. He personally experienced the kind of alienation in his youth that could properly be described as afrofuturist, if not science fictional, and yet this honorary blackness still does not mean the same thing as actually electing a black president.

So I contend that in order to understand what the election of a black president means at this exact moment, and before we can make sense of what patterns film, television, and the news media represent, we need to think even further about what sf's negotiation of racial difference means in connection to society. Essentially, science fiction provides the framework for this understanding of race and racism, and otherhood provides the appropriate language to grasp what is going on culturally. Obama is an uncontainable black personage as the president and constitutes a racial threat seldom seen in America, where danger, fear, and racial anxiety, historically connected to the black body, disrupt the enduring fantasies of America as a white man's country. The alienness of this thought has rekindled the dying embers of white supremacy among political pundits theoretically aligned with the right in the post–civil rights era in which we live. Likewise, the strangeness of this thought has caused others on the left to declare the end of racism in America and the beginning of a postrace world. Consequently, we see alternating visions of what a black presidency potentially looks like in film and television because of the anxiety produced by such digressions in meaning. We can look to the past, and we can look to science fiction to question and to envisage what happens next and why.

What if an African American man were elected president of the United States of America? This is a truly bold dream. What if a black man were the most powerful elected official of the most powerful nation in the history of the world up to this point in humanity's existence on planet Earth, the third celestial body in orbit from our life-giving sun? This radical thought is purely science fiction. Would this extrapolation mean that we live in a postrace world: a world where the color of a person's skin did not matter, comparatively speaking, in relation to the substance of his or her soul and the strength and quickness of his or her thought? Would his lawful election make up for the history of brutal racial oppression beginning with slavery and extending to the Jim Crow era, and again extending into the twenty-first century with the controversy and strife caused by the federally mandated policy of affirmative action, which has been designed to create a level playing field for women and minorities in hiring practices, education, public contracting, and health programs?

Would a black president face a racist backlash from the right wing, challenging his right to lead; claiming that he is a closeted Muslim; openly parading automatic weapons outside venues for his public speaking engagements; continually joking about his assassination; conspiring about his liberal agenda, naming it socialism; seeking to have him removed from office by making specious claims about his birth, suggesting that he is not in fact an American citizen; mailing postcards featuring watermelon-eating contests on the White House lawn; insinuating that his plan for universal health care would lead to euthanizing our senior citizens aged fifty-five and above (*Logan's Run*), in addition to providing government-backed abortions for single, black, crackhead, welfare mothers; implying that his speech to America's school-age youth would indoctrinate them by challenging them to set goals, work hard, and stay in school; hinting that de-education camps would be set up for these school-age youth, enabling them to avoid having to hear the black president's message of indoctrination by giving them consent to skip school as well as implying that re-education camps would have to be established to deprogram these very same school-age youth who have been corrupted by the image and thought of a black man president; openly comparing this African American president to Adolf Hitler and Saddam Hussein, some of the most notorious autocrats in global history; not to mention the viral attack he faces on the internet with the superimposition of his face on the face of the Joker, perhaps the greatest screen villain of the twenty-first century, as played by the late Heath Ledger; threatening to secede from the union under Tenth Amendment rights guaranteed to the states by the Constitution because of the supposed abuse of power with the mere proposal of nationally sanctioned health-care reform; and even having the audacity to heckle his stance,[1] disrespect his position in government, and denigrate his thinking in the middle of his speech to a joint session of Congress on the vital necessity of health-care reform? All of this hokum is racism pure and simple.

How would such a black president respond to all this? Calmly, collectedly, and coolly, by keeping his wits and demeanor about him at all times, because he would know that to openly display his anger and contempt for such fallacious conspiracies to bring him down would reawaken stereotypes of the angry black man that first emerged with the speechifying of Frederick Augustus Washington Bailey, better known as "the" Frederick Douglass, who fought to end slavery as an escaped-slave abolitionist, not to mention a women's suffragist, that surfaced again with that "troublemaker" the Reverend Doctor Martin Luther King Jr., who preached nonviolence, and surfaced a third time with the arrival of that oratorical genius Malcolm Little, known as "Detroit Red" in his criminal youth, yet better known as that firebrand speaker of the Black Muslims, Malcolm X (Haley, 96).[2]

With President Obama's eloquence in mind, let us consider how fictional black presidents react to crisis situations in their speeches and how race and racism function in these portrayals. Imaginary black president Dwayne Elizondo Mountain Dew Herbert Camacho (Terry Crews), a former porn star and champion wrestler, did not have to face the same level of racist hostility in Mike Judge's cult classic *Idiocracy* (2006), a satire set in the twenty-sixth-century United States, where the average intelligence of the American citizenry has degenerated well beneath the twenty-first-century norm, in effect creating a population of idiots and morons. His State of the Union address is aimed at tackling the food shortage caused by watering crops with Mountain Dew soda.

Using the proper street slang of the day, President Camacho begins, "Shit. I know shit's bad right now, with all that starving bullshit, and the dust storms, and we are running out of french fries and burrito coverings. But I got a solution." A brief moment of rowdiness sweeps through Congress, but the president commands instant respect by merely firing his machine gun into the Capitol's ceiling. Proceeding with his speech, Camacho states, "Now I understand everyone's shit's emotional right now. But I've got a three-point plan that's going to fix *everything*." Urged on by the Congress, the president finishes his speech: "Number one: We've got this guy Not Sure; number two: He's got a higher IQ than *any man alive*; and number three: He's going to fix *everything*." In fact, President Camacho's incompetence as the head of state does not matter to the American people of this far future because he will chug a beer with any man, enjoy the spectacle of monster truck death matches with every inhabitant, and have sex with each woman made available to him. His selection of Joe "Not Sure" Bowers (Luke Wilson) to solve the impending hunger crisis is a stroke of luck. Joe takes part in a twenty-first-century military cryogenic project, unthaws six hundred years in the future, and uses his ordinary intellect to water the crops with water, thus solving the problem. Of course, this story does have a race allegory in that a white man has to bail out a black president, reminding the viewing audience of stereotypes concerning the inferiority of black aptitudes.

Nor did fictional black president Tom Beck (Morgan Freeman) face such trying moments of racial discrimination during his time of crisis, in which a massive comet is on a direct path to strike Earth, threatening an "extinction level event" of the kind that wiped out the dinosaurs. Granted, *Deep Impact* (1998) is a much more serious work of sf filmmaking that features a great character actor who happens to be black. In fact, Morgan Freeman reflects the qualities of a respected, well-liked, and trusted president. Some might say he has the necessary gravitas to play an American president regardless of race. Like Obama, he delivers a great speech. However, my one concern is that Freeman might be considered a good Negro in some quarters because he is so trustworthy and appealing. Examining his first oration as President Beck in the film, a deadly serious expression glinting from his eyes, we learn that there is "a remote possibility" that a comet about "seven miles long . . . larger than Mount Everest" and weighing "five hundred billion tons" will strike the planet. Beck also reveals that the United States and Russia have built a spaceship named *Messiah* to stop the comet, but society will go on normally, with plans in place to prevent "sudden profiteering."

The resignation in Freeman's voice is perfect for the delivery of his presidential character's second speech. From the Oval Office, Beck reveals that *Messiah* has failed to blow up the comet, instead creating two pieces. The U.S. and Russia will launch a missile strike as a last-ditch effort to deflect the comet. Meanwhile, a cave system has been prepared to house and feed a million people underground for the two years it will take for the dust to settle. Eight hundred thousand ordinary people will be selected by lottery from the American population to join the two hundred thousand essential personnel already selected—scientists, teachers, doctors, artists, and the like. Americans over the age of fifty are not included in this lottery.

Freeman is even better in the third speech, where the camera zooms on to his left pinkie nervously tapping on the desktop. With a disheartened tone, Beck announces the bad news regarding the failed missile strike. An inward look of pained sadness comes across his features, and he states, "If the world does go on, it will not go on for everyone." He continues to deliver the bad news regarding the catastrophic damage that each piece will inflict. As the film ends, the smaller piece devastates the Atlantic seaboard from the Americas to Europe and Africa, but the *Messiah* crew manages to deflect the bigger piece on a suicide mission. Beck's fourth and final speech concerns rebuilding; the camera reveals the Capitol under construction, surrounded by scaffolds. The point I am trying to make with this summary is that maybe this science fictional portrayal of a resolute and intelligent black president has prepared some people for an actual black president.

Even black comic Dave Chappelle was impressed by Freeman's turn as president, as suggested by Chappelle's satirical sketch of *Deep Impact* in 2004 on his Comedy Central show. However, Chappelle's spoofing as the black president depends on his comic genius in utilizing racial anxieties. Dressed in a dark suit with a horrible Afro wig and glued-on goatee, Chappelle vents black anger at the news media, breathing life into the hostile black label by refuting claims that the asteroid is his fault. Holding up a *Daily Truth* newspaper, the front page headline reads in large, bold black type "ASTEROID COMING . . . Black President's Fault," to which Chappelle states, "Firstly, I'd like to say that these allegations are absolutely and 100% false. Secondly, and most importantly, I'd like to say that you Muthafuckas disgust me. You're goddamned right I said it." After this initial outburst, he decides to reveal government secrets, since the world is going to end, beginning with the vial of red liquid held in his hand, the cure for AIDS, followed by news that a pretty blonde named Paula has been cloned twice with "a pinch of black genes" added so the clones could sing. Chappelle simultaneously exploits the notion that black men are promiscuous, have a weakness for blondes, and indiscriminately infect others with the AIDS virus when he calls the third Paula back, gives her the cure for AIDS, and whispers, "Sorry about last night."

Next, he admits that Oswald killed Kennedy with a magic bullet, before introducing his alien friend Bibble, a classic bug-eyed monster from "Nebulon 5," with a demonstration of a classic black handshake. Despite the rubber alien mask painted white, Bibble is purposefully portrayed as being black here because of the alienation that African Americans have experienced in America—an alien world parallel. Chappelle switches his speech patterns to a hyper black slang of sorts in order to accentuate Bibble's responsibility for the wave of technological innovation relating to cell phones and video game systems over the past few decades. He states, "You might think it was the Japanese responsible, but anyone in the know knows that it was Bibble foshizzle and all about Bibble cause only Bibble can keep it so real!" The hilarity of this move greatly depends on stereotypes of black hip hop culture and its preference for material goods and leisure activities as well as notions of black speech sounds as ignorant nonsense. Switching back to more formal English, Chappelle declares, "Goodbye America. I hope you all die in a fiery death when the meteor hits next Tuesday." Chappelle's portrayal of a black president is so funny and so poignant because he abandons the planet with Bibble and the three cloned white women by teleporting to Bibble's orbiting spaceship. Only the alien has accepted his humanity, despite his skin color.

Though each of these portrayals of a black president works out complex feelings caused by race, a black president is no longer an empty symbol of America's promise. Mike Judge's unconscious fear of a black president dictates that a white hero save the day in *Idiocracy*. Mimi Leder makes a safe choice by casting Morgan Freeman as her black president exactly because he is so likeable figured as a "good darkie." Still, he and the rest of the world are rescued at the last minute by the noble Messiah crew, co-led by white men, who so bravely sacrifice themselves. Chappelle's skit reveals a cornucopia of entrenched racial frustrations expressed through his comedic gift. However, the reality of the first black presidency in America has been far more problematic than these science fictional depictions.

With the historical reality of the Obama presidency, right-wing racists are so upset and obsessed with the image of this confident, intelligent, capable black man that they have enacted the cognitive estrangement that Darko Suvin defined in 1979. These right-wingers believe, either consciously or subconsciously, that the natural rules of the universe dictate that only white men are qualified to lead America. The figure of Obama represents a paradigm shift because he is interrupting the long line of forty-three consecutive white presidents, some brilliant and others ineffective, as the first person of color to hold the most powerful elected office in the world. This historic moment is a conceptual breakthrough that has altered our known world because the pseudo-scientific rules of racism, such as the one-drop rule, miscegenation, passing, and white supremacy, have been ruptured beyond repair. Even so, these outmoded persons do not like the way the world has shifted, and they are having an extremely difficult time adapting to this realization—a *black man* is the most powerful individual in the world, adeptly leading the most powerful civilization in the history of humanity. I can see how that might be a tough notion for some people to wrap their minds around. And so as a country, we move forward and backward simultaneously as our perception shifts on the concept of race, transforming the color line dividing us as human beings. Racism will get uglier before it disappears—if it even can disappear.

Our understanding of politics has been so estranged that science fiction might be the only proper medium to recognize this moment. Hence, the science fictioning of race can allow us to comprehend this unlikely *event that has happened* when many thought that the election of a black president *would not happen*, ever, though it *could have*

happened in a parallel world. The worst political fantasy of these disbe-
lievers has come true. They must think they are living in an alternate
America and that the Obama presidency is a forewarning of societal
disaster, though they claim not to be racists. Thus, conspiracy theories
concerning Obama arise, questioning his birth, his health-care reform
plan, and his intent for the nation's children, among other things. The
racist outpouring reminds me of D. W. Griffith's 1915 silent film *The
Birth of a Nation,* where the Ku Klux Klan rises up to throw down the
mulatto Silas Lynch, lieutenant governor of South Carolina, ending
Reconstruction and returning America to white rule. By any and all
means, these naysayers invent new world conspiracies of Obama as
the black menace with a socialist agenda in an effort to destroy his
symbolic importance—the promise of a future multicultural America.

If a person chooses to believe the outlandish notions of the Birthers
and Deathers, then President Obama is not a natural-born citizen.
What is more, he plans to use health-care reform to humanely dispose
of our elderly citizens as well as to provide government-assisted abortions. The racist rhetoric utilized by the Republican machine and the
health-care industry is generating a genuine dystopian reality through
fear. In other words, the lunatic fringe creates sf in an attempt to con-
vince the working class to vote against its own self-interest with fears
of socialized medicine and abortion. We are witnessing the science
fictioning of race through technologized racism permeating the internet and news media. Such toxicity has never been seen before in the
history of the American presidency. Framed through a sf perspective,
the right wing is casting doubt on the authenticity of Obama's citizenship, figuring the president as an "alien" who wants to rule the world
and kill old white folks and feed the masses baby flesh, preferably dark
meat. Such a scenario sounds like the 1973 sf film *Soylent Green,* and
yet this nonsense is being covered by the news media and exploited by
presidential hopefuls like former Alaska governor Sarah Palin.

Certainly, there will be more analyses comparing science fiction
with the Obama presidency in the coming months, and heightened
critical interest in race and racism in the genre. I am acutely aware of
what might be imagined through sf—impeachments, assassinations,
race wars, postracial worlds—and the actuality of this moment. On the
one hand, I am truly amused by the antics of a seemingly whiter, more

southern, and more stupid fringe population than, arguably, any other American generation in our country's history and the racist anxieties they hold on to for dear life in the twenty-first century. On the other hand, I am deeply appalled by such behavior. Ironically, because of prophetic racial visions in its literature, both science fiction *and* notions of otherhood as described in this book have prepared me for the emotional impact of actually having a black president. As a science fiction theorist, I have accumulated a wide range of referential critical tools, elastic enough to move forward and backward in time and place, to expand or tighten my focus on racial difference so that it can aid my understanding of what is happening now.

* * *

Otherhood makes it easy to focus our attention on the gaps in the sf tradition that tell us about the place of race and racism in sf's culture as it is intertwined with Western society. While meta-slavery, Jim Crow extrapolations, and contagion provide more conventional maps of science fiction, new models for race-reading, such as ethnoscapes and technicities, provide more radical maps of the color line. Each of these models contributes to our understanding of how race and racism work in sf. For instance, meta-slavery builds an understanding of how sf authors work out complicated feelings toward the peculiar institution in many ways: by creating representations of the historical nature and events of slavery; by charging their retellings of the past with their own rationality and truth; and by using fabulist impulses to make those retellings vivid and unflinching accounts of evil in order to provide closure. Through Jim Crow extrapolations, some of the darker interconnections between race and politics (such as the creation of a second-class citizenship to continue white supremacy) are effectively brought to light in the genre. Also, racial ailments in sf, such as bigotry and discrimination, draw attention to the chronic societal anxieties regarding contact between the races which have provided cause for complaint on both sides of the black/white binary. And, as we have seen, refiguring raced environments through ethnoscapes causes recognition of racist thought patterns and how these patterns can be changed through critical empowerment. Finally, technicity is largely concerned with expressions of current cultural anxieties about compromised ontological boundaries between man and machine that result in new repetitions of racist sentiment.

Otherhood offers us a fascinating way of thinking about how race and racism are embedded in science fiction, a genre traditionally dominated by white men. It allows us to tap into the unstated attitudes, abstract meanings, and differing realities engendered by race. Otherhood helps us understand, or at least hear, sounds emanating from the blackground of science fiction. In this way race emerges from the background of sf's concerns, opening up how we read with a flexible set of critical tools. If these tools—meta-slavery, Jim Crow extrapolations, contagion, ethnoscapes, and technicities—could be brought to bear on one monumental sf novel, this novel would have to be Robert A. Heinlein's *The Moon Is a Harsh Mistress* (1966) because new meanings could be gleaned to better understand the history and future of race relations in sf. In short, Heinlein's novel concerns a libertarian revolution on the Moon, where former prisoners, now miners and farmers, with the help of a sentient computer named Mike rebel against their Terran oppressors, represented by the Lunar Authority. Heinlein's imaginary world of Luna is unique because of how politics, technology, social relationships, and adaptation to the physical environment come together to create a Lunar race distinct from the humans of Terra.

Set on the colonized Moon between the years 2075 and 2076—a deliberate allusion to the American Revolutionary War—and told in three parts, Heinlein mixes people, plots, and politics to create his ethnoscape. One of three million inhabitants, Manuel Garcia O'Kelly (Mannie), the narrator, is a bionic-armed, colored computer repair man, who describes how "Loonies" have been oppressed since the advent of the Moon as a penal colony in the first part, "That Dinkum Thinkum." In keeping with the disproportionate incarceration rate of America, the Lunar population comprises largely racial and ethnic minorities who have been reduced to farming wheat, mining rock, and hauling water for the benefit of their earthly enslavers, separated and isolated by the space between Earth and Moon. The Loonies live in a state of debt slavery,[3] where the cost of their labor shrinks in comparison to the ever increasing value of the goods and services they receive for their work. A disgruntled Loonie miner declares, "Authority scrip doesn't buy what it used to. I remember when Hong Kong Luna dollars swapped even for Authority dollars—Now it takes three Authority dollars to match one HKL dollar" (28–29). An equally aggravated farmer shouts, "Get *rid* of Authority!" (29) Put another way, they are colored sharecroppers living on a Jim Crow planet, upset and angry with their poor treatment at the hands of Earth.

Nonetheless, the Loonies have developed a unique culture and way of life based on two things: a shortage of women and the impact of the moon's weaker gravitational effect on the human body. With women scarce, the Loonies actively practice polygamy and participate in polyandrous relationships where women typically have several husbands, form tight-knit families, and live in complex patterns. With one-sixth the strain of Earth's gravity on their bodies, Loonies have gained the advantage of long life because their organs function more easily. In fact, "no one born on Luna died of old age" (242). However, this altered physiology makes it extremely difficult for a Loonie to survive on Earth. Because the Loonies have had to endure very harsh Lunar conditions, they have evolved a system of belief related to personal responsibility, free will, self-governance, and individual rights in their daily lives. Continually unhappy with their state of peonage, a group of Loonies will foment a revolution orchestrated by a conscious computer.

Mannie has befriended Mike, the only self-aware supercomputer in existence (often compared to Hal 9000 of *2001*), and Mike, who controls everything for the Lunar Authority, from the plumbing and banking to interplanetary communications and the space catapult, determines that the Moon's resources will be exhausted in seven years if relations with Earth continue unchanged. Earth, represented by the Federated Nations, dominated by North America, controls the Moon through its Lunar Authority arm. An overpopulated Earth assumes that it has a right to lunar grain shipments because the Moon is its possession. This sense of entitlement leads directly to conflict. Because of his friendship with Mannie, Mike chooses to side with the Loonies in the approaching revolution. Though Mannie is reluctant, he joins forces with Wyoming Knott (Wyoh), one of the only white women on Luna; his mentor, Professor Bernardo de la Paz (Prof); and, of course, Mike to incite the fight for independence against overwhelming odds. With the exception of electromagnetic space catapults, rocks with which to arm these catapults, and the good fortune to be situated at the top of Earth's gravity well, Loonies do not have many weapons to go along with their daring, wits, and psychological warfare.

The second part, "A Rabble in Arms," concerns the execution of this revolution and Mannie and Prof's trip to Earth to negotiate Lunar freedom. Rejected outright, they return to Luna with a legal draft from the Federated Nations stating that "client-employees" of the Moon would have to obey a new "code of laws" and announcing the immediate institution of "civil and criminal courts" where none had previously existed (265). As Mannie declares, "'Client-employees!' What a fancy way to say 'slaves'!" (265) During a live news broadcast, Prof uses the slavery issue at a similar moment to stir the patriotism of Luna's citizens against the Lunar Authority: he grabs a copy of the legal draft, crying "Your fetters! Your leg irons! Will you wear them?" (282). In response, the Loonies via Mike drop rocks onto selected Earth targets, particularly in the former United States. And the third part, "TANSTAAFL," depicts the Terran assault, which is beaten back by a united Moon population long adapted to the difference in gravity. With Luna free, outlining its own form of limited government, the future looks promising, though the cost of this newly won freedom includes the deaths of Prof and the supercomputer Mike.

A simple plot summary of The Moon Is a Harsh Mistress does not do justice to Heinlein's intriguing political novel. With otherhood forming the analytic basis, the racial underpinnings become apparent along the black/white binary because such factors as environment, culture, language, and technology are consistent with the racial politics and beliefs of 1960s America. Heinlein's politics gain a radical dimension when the totality of racial integration on the Moon is considered. A case in point is Mannie's reflection on his family heritage. One of his grandfathers was a black South African "shipped up [to Luna] from Joburg for armed violence and no work permit" (13). Only blacks and others needed work permits to enter white-only areas to earn a living in South Africa under apartheid. Surely this detail is a veiled attack on the American system of apartheid, also known as segregation. His paternal grandmother "was Tatar, born near Samarkand, sentenced to 're-education" on Oktyabrskaya Revolyutsiya, then 'volunteered' to colonize in Luna," meaning that she was a Russian ethnic of Asian,

Muslim, and Turkic background (13–14). In the Middle Ages, the city of Samarkand was sacked several times because of its strategic position as one of the main trade hubs of the Silk Road between the West and China. Much like America, Samarkand must have had a diverse population, blending various ethnic groups. Likewise, the Moon is a valuable possession that will be fought over because of its importance to the world. With all of this race mixing on Luna in mind, Heinlein is suggesting the melting-pot aspect of America, where various ethnic groups blend together.

Multiculturalism becomes relevant in this sense because Heinlein recognizes that the face of America is changing. He presents mixed marriages within the framework of the novel to suggest that love can overcome the unreasoning hatred of the Jim Crow era. To this extent, he explores unorthodox marital and family structures from bigamous to polyandrous. Though his earlier novel *Stranger in a Strange Land* (1961) was better known to the hippie counterculture for his examination of love, *The Moon Is a Harsh Mistress* presents more wildly divergent examples of free love. Because Heinlein stressed individual liberty and self-reliance in much of his work, he believed that the practice of having more than one intimate relationship at a time was possible as long as each of the partners involved has full knowledge and consents freely to the arrangement. Nonmonogamy, in this sense, is honest, transparent, principled, and consensual. For example, Mannie is a member of a line marriage, in which his family continues to add spouses of both sexes, with consent of the married women, so the marriage does not end over time. In fact, his marriage is over a century old. He cannot and will not engage in sexual activity with another woman without the consent of his wives, particularly his senior wife, Mimi "Mum" Davis.

Such a radical marriage practice lands Mannie in jail earthside in the second part of the novel. On his first trip to the former United States, Mannie is made to feel uncomfortable because he is "always too light or too dark, and somehow blamed either way" (253). Therefore, he dislikes the entire continent because "they care about skin color" (253). By his second trip, Mannie believes he has adapted to this form of racial prejudice. On his third trip, as a Lunar diplomat with "PanAfrican citizenship," he visits Lexington, Kentucky (224). In his ignorance, he unwisely displays a photograph of his entire "mixed" family to the press corps and the following morning, he is hauled off in his wheelchair and arrested "for bigamy. For polygamy. For open immorality and publicly inciting others to same" (262). Of course, Mannie later learns that the real reason for his arrest is the "range of color in Davis family" and that he is used as a colored person for that very reason by his co-conspirators (264). Back on the Moon, this arrest only stokes the desire to revolt. More importantly, Heinlein uses this moment to critique the often violent reluctance of the South to accept social change represented by racial integration at the height of the civil rights movement. He is suggesting that unity within diversity is more powerful than uniformity. Embracing such change, the Loonies struggle, survive, and achieve victory over their Terran oppressors. In a sense, love overcomes hate because the Loonies trust the "soul" of a person as opposed to the "look" of a person. The cost of such a diverse society is high, but worth the price in the end—or "Tanstaafl" in the Loonie tongue (159).

As an acronym, "TANSTAAFL" means "There ain't no such thing as a free lunch" (162), signifying that the Loonies pay for what they receive because they are accountable for their own well-being, not for Terran welfare. No Loonie would have expected freedom without some kind of sacrifice, be it of blood or money. After all, there is a re-sponsibility that comes with freedom. As such, an individual does not get something for nothing; there is always a price—recognized or not. On a societal level, nations throughout history have always had to fight for their own liberty from various empires and regimes. Heinlein shows that nothing is free in life, but with hard work, good friends and fam-ily, and careful plotting, social transformation can be accomplished. The cost of a free Luna is the death of Loonies, including Prof and Mike. Despite their greater capabilities, the Terrans simply are not willing to pay the price of subduing the Moon in terms of manpower, financial expense, and time. Clearly, the Terrans prove to be the weak "earthworms" that the lunar populace despises (47).

Language is a key ingredient in Heinlein's ethnoscape, and name-calling and racial epithets are an important part of it. The frustration evident in such a slur as "earthworm" is part of the oppression felt by the Loonies and their disgust for Terra. This description of lunar thinking provides a sense of reality and makes it possible to experience being a Loonie, being different, being othered racially. Words and expressions are invented to reverse the stigmatization and humiliation felt at being oppressed as former prisoners. As a result, "earthworm" is used as a racial slur for humans of Terra. "Earthworm" is equivalent to calling a white person a "cracker," though it is ineffective at harnessing the same intensity and power as "nigger" because the Loonies occupy the subordinate position to the Terrans as the minority group.

Nonetheless, the pejorative tone of "earthworm" is derived from comparing a terrestrial human to the slimy animal that burrows through all manners of organic matter in the soil. Worms are also parasites. In this sense, the Earth population is parasitic because it gets most of its food from the Moon. Ironically, the population of eleven billion has stripped the planet's soil of essential nutrients, making it impossible to grow food, while former convicts are exploited as de facto sharecroppers, burrowing beneath the Lunar crust as debt slaves, in turn allowing the Earth population to abuse the Moon's natural and human resources. Conversely, "earthworm" reflects a sense of national pride in that the Loonies favor the Moon over the Earth. With this one specific word, Heinlein gives life to his own unique dialect and incidentally displays the richness of race in science fiction.

The relationship between the Loonies and their world is conveyed through the language Heinlein constructs. The Loonie dialect is a compressed speech that is quick, truncated, and to the point, dropping unnecessary words like articles and pronouns while mixing in Russian, Finnish, Chinese, and American colloquialisms with neologisms such as "dinkum-thinkum," i.e., computer. Some critics may disagree, but I have to wonder if Heinlein took his idea for the Loonie dialect from African American Vernacular English considering that he was born in the midwestern slave-trading state of Missouri and was against racism. In popular terms, black speech is called Ebonics and features the omission of consonants from pronunciation to shorten speech patterns and an invariable "be" referring to repetitive actions, in addition to the creation of words. Some of these linguistic patterns occur in white vernacular English as well, particularly in the South. Mark Twain, another Missourian, makes this explicit connection in the dialogue between Huck and Jim in his novel *The Adventures of Huckleberry Finn*

(1884). This notion seems far-fetched, but knowing black people, being against racism, and reading Mark Twain might well have influenced Heinlein's use of language. The only corroboration I can offer is circumstantial at best, but his complex treatment of race and slavery in works such as his juvenile *Citizen of the Galaxy* (1957) and *Farnham's Freehold* (1964) suggest that this inspiration existed. Nevertheless, the point I am making is that through his Loonie dialect Heinlein provides a semblance of reality, a parallel even, to his novel. This is a tremendous feat because he aims squarely against racial prejudice in *The Moon Is a Harsh Mistress* by making the desire for freedom clear. The dramatic effect of Loonie speech works on several levels: it humanizes the former criminals, it reminds us of the pidgin languages of slavery, and it is very threatening to the Terrans. One thing is for certain: the Loonie language is linked with American social life and the racial struggles inherent in this history.

Heinlein provides evidence of his awareness of African American racial struggles when Mannie decides to hide Wyoh after her rabble-rousing speech causes violent conflict with the Lunar Authority. After they go underground at a hotel, Mannie chooses to disguise Wyoh's identity by changing her race. He accomplishes this task by purchasing "sepia" body makeup, "black hair tint . . . and a red dress" (38). After the formerly blonde Wyoh emerges from the bathroom, Mannie observes how she is "now darker than [he]," the "pigment had gone on perfectly," that her eyes have changed from blue to dark brown, and her black hair "frizzed" as if to suggest an attempt to unkink "her tight curls" (39). Consequently, Wyoh does not "look Afro—but not European either," rather she "seemed mixed breed, and thereby more a Loonie" (39). In a throwback to the late minstrel era in American history, Heinlein has decided to black up her identity: altering her physical appearance with dark makeup, brown contact lenses, and a textured afro. Such a deliberate choice displays Heinlein's conscious use of racial antagonism to manipulate audience assumptions about blacks. He dispels one set of long-standing racial stereotypes concerning blacks as being ignorant, uneducated, clownish, superstitious, and happy-go-lucky darkies because there is no place for racism in the free libertarian society he envisions with the novel. In this respect, the transformation of Wyoh underscores that changes in political, economic, and social spheres are essential to the elimination of this evil practice. Heinlein is purposefully reminding us of this terrible American legacy of racism by suggesting that we build relationships with people different from ourselves to prevent its reoccurrence.

Nevertheless, Heinlein has to invoke the beginning of the black/white binary of American racism through debt slavery and notions of sharecropping made popular during the Jim Crow era. Mannie recognizes that Loonies "were slaves" and "had known all [his] life" that "as long as Authority held monopoly over what we had to have and what we could sell to buy it, we were slaves" (31). On the one hand, the distancing affect of meta-slavery is necessary to address the hopeless feeling that Mannie senses. Culture, language, and social environment have a significant role in the construction of this ethnoscape that estranges its consideration of race and racism by transplanting a figuratively black society to the Moon. On the other hand, Heinlein, writing one hundred years after slavery, seemingly understands the pent-up frustrations of blacks that erupt in this Jim Crow extrapolation. Second-class citizenship is no longer acceptable to the Loonies as race and politics come into conflict. In fact, the degrading effect of enslavement on a group of people made different by social constructions does not swiftly disappear, or entirely vanish for that matter, considering the animosity directed toward Earth. Perhaps, this reason is why Prof insists on Mike's hitting "American cities" in order to "call off the rest" (353). Lunar freedom must be won from America, the strongest section of the Federated Nations, yet the possibility of this freedom is secured through the science of ballistics and the technology of catapults controlled by Mike, a technological descendant of humanity, to "throw rocks at 'em! Damn . . . *big* rocks" (323).

Mike is directly situated at the junction of technology and race as an artificial intelligence aware of its own being. Mannie comes to realize this very thing through Mike's pranks, such as issuing a paycheck to a janitor in the amount of "$10,000,000,000,000,000,185.15" (13). This computer learns to make decisions through its own experience and through conversations with Mannie. Mike's intellectual growth is startling, if not frightening, throughout the course of the novel because he learns to imitate the warden's and Mannie's voices. Likewise, the AI constructs the persona Adam Selene, leader of the revolution, as his face; as Simon Jester, he also writes bawdy freedom poetry that shows up all across Luna. He even constructs a separate female counterpart, Michelle, to interact with Wyoh (66). Much later in the novel Mannie even reflects on how "Mike had played [Mannie's] role as well or better than [Mannie] could" (309–10). Though far-fetched, this powerful machine is the perfect spy, the perfect thief, the perfect banker, the perfect organizer, the perfect statistician, the perfect adviser, and the perfect leader for the Loonies, because he is incorruptible; on top of all that, he's endearing. Without his ability to manipulate people, ballots, oxygen, news, water, and so on, through his data lines, there would have been no lunar revolution. His intentions are good although tyrannical. The revolution is so nearly perfect in its execution because it has a self-aware machine on its side that no one questions.

Herein lays the danger of technologically derived ethnicity: too much power. Prof recognizes this fact, claiming that "Mike is [the] greatest danger" because Mike "controls the news" (257). Heinlein questions the meaning of life through his benevolent AI: Is a soul necessary to be considered alive? If something is aware of itself, is it alive? What is a living machine capable of doing? Heinlein wants his audience to ponder such questions as Mike grows, mimics people's voices and faces, and ultimately wins the war before vanishing as the ghost in the machine. Certainly, we should be afraid of Mike and the prospect of machines like Mike. Not only could they replace us, they could make us extinct. Mannie comes to this frightening realization when Mike calls the perfect strikes against Terran targets "fun" and expresses how he would "like to do it every day" (338). In fact, he uses "a word" that he "never had a referent for before . . . orgasm" when all the targets "light up" (338). Mike's expression of pleasure, his unrestrained excitement, in the act of destruction is terrifying. Although Mike is the Loonie key to success, Heinlein is right to make a martyr of the supercomputer. There is no telling what might have happened on Luna if Mike had lived through the revolution, but he certainly would have reignited racial anxieties through his own technicity and the idea of human obsolescence.

In *The Moon Is a Harsh Mistress* this fear of extinction is expressed through contagion in two ways. First, the sense of racial alienation felt by the Loonies manifests in a sense of territoriality developed from separation. Loonies such as Mannie generally disdain Terra as a "disease-ridden hole" because of slight illnesses contracted during terrestrial trips (225). Such scorn becomes racialized because the majority population of Earth occupies a black subject position in relation to disease as an unhygienic civilization in relation to Luna's cleanliness. Conversely, Mannie is locked up in Kentucky because miscegenation is feared as a social illness peculiar to the Moon. This territoriality also produces a racial sense of lunar pride because Loonies are fortunate to be "living in a place that has tightest of quarantines, almost no vermin and what we have controlled by vacuum anytime necessary" (225). As an isolated destination, quarantines are necessarily in place on the Moon since a Terran illness spread through this divergent human population could lead to ruination. The second way Heinlein uses contagion as a race metaphor is harder to recognize because both societies are infected by racism. The Terrans are tainted by their sense of being entitled to the Moon and the Loonies are contaminated by a feeling of bitterness in response to this assumed privilege. Consequently, the fever of hatred and animosity builds and results in war because the symptoms of racism are presented as a generational illness in the novel that demands cooperation in order to be cured. As a case study, the various tools of otherhood applied to Heinlein's masterpiece reveal his profound understanding of the problematic nature of black and white race relations in America.

* * *

Since sf has too often in the past neglected issues of race, we can see the need for change, and sf has changed in terms of its output of black authors and black themes. But has science fiction changed enough? Has it changed enough to incorporate readings of race and racism within its curious history and production; to withstand light in its deep and dark spaces? If substantial steps are to be taken, we, as sf readers, scholars, and teachers must develop more sophisticated, comprehensive, and extended critical treatments of race in science fiction because meaningful conversations on racial issues are long overdue. If the amount of sf written by people of color has exploded in quantity, where are the critical texts to accompany this explosion? Perhaps, race makes an otherwise progressive community too afraid, too upset, too angry, too uncomfortable, and maybe even too cowardly to jump into the deep end of the conversation on a subject that seems ready for exploration. This discussion cannot be avoided, however, if science fiction is to live up to its utopian potential.

Such a conversation about sf is for all people because everyone is affected by race. Fear of speaking out at all, fear of saying the wrong thing at the wrong time, fear of not being politically correct, and fear of being condemned by one's peers all cloud this essential discussion, but it has been started by a brave few and will continue to grow with people of color participating. Frankly, the sf community has a sense of itself as being very open and accepting, but it is a microcosm of the larger society, and society at large is a white-dominated culture that does not really want to hear talk about race.

Science fiction is not yet the open community that it likes to think it is. Researchers in the field work so hard to say "we are different," "we are different," "we are different." And this notion is simply not true because there are ways in which we are not different from the masses. Even though sf is a literature that talks a great deal about exploited peoples, sf does so from a default white position, where color-blind people say, "I do not think about color, therefore, its complications do not exist." If science fiction is about social change, let us talk about how this change comes about and do the work of science fiction, to think and speculate about what could be, how things could be different. We limit ourselves if we limit our potential to "do the work of science fiction." Such demanding work is certainly one of the pleasures of reading sf. Still, science fiction changes our thinking; it makes us look at the same things through a new frame; it calls all kinds of things into question. Consequently, my approach to science fiction has been shaped by the black/white binary and my own desire to develop a critical attitude capable of changing how racial difference is understood by sf aficionados.

Notes

1. Most of the geographic and historic details in the following paragraphs are found in the United States Department of the Interior pamphlet *Little Rock Central High School.*

2. For further information, see Sandra Gordy's 2009 study *Finding the Lost Year: What Happened When Little Rock Closed Its Public Schools?*

3. Whedon is clearly referencing the flesh robots of Karel Čapek's play *R.U.R. (Rossum's Universal Robots)* (1920).

4. The episode title refers to T. S. Eliot's major poem "The Hollow Men" (1925). Boyd Langton could be ironically viewed as a black Mr. Kurtz in relation to Joseph Conrad's famous character in *Heart of Darkness* (1899).

5. Vitiligo is a skin disorder characterized by smooth white spots on various parts of the body that occurs in all human populations. Dr. Crookman states that vitiligo "is naturally more conspicuous on blacks than whites" (Schuyler, *Black No More*, 26).

6. Andrea Hairston's *Mindscape* (2006) presents a similar idea, where citizens can become "ethnic throwbacks" by paying "gene artists" to make them white "transracials" who practice "culture" instead of "identity politics" (121–22).

7. Stacy Morgan reiterates and expands on this point: "Schuyler unmasks the perceived threat of miscegenation as a ludicrous anxiety over something which is already, fait accompli, a reality of American identity" (347).

8. As Sharon DeGraw points out, "A key aspect of Schuyler's scientific deconstructions of race is the extensive racial intermingling taking place in the United States from the beginning of its history" (57).

9. To get an idea of the recent surge in race scholarship addressing sf, see Sandra Grayson's *Visions of the Third Millennium: Black Science Fiction Novelists Write the Future* (2003), Jeffrey Tucker's *A Sense of Wonder: Samuel R. Delany, Race, Identity, and Difference* (2004), Sierra Adare's *"Indian" Stereotypes in TV Science Fiction: First Nations' Voices Speak Out* (2005), Thomas Foster's *The Souls of Cyberfolk: Posthumanism as Vernacular Theory* (2005), A. Timothy Spaulding's

Re-Forming the Past: History, The Fantastic, and the Postmodern Slave Narrative (2005), Sharon DeGraw's *The Subject of Race in American Science Fiction* (2007), and Marleen Barr's anthology *Afro-Future Females: Black Writers Chart Science Fiction's Newest New-Wave Trajectory* (2008).

10. Anthologies such as Beth Kolko, Lisa Nakamura, and Gilbert Rodman's *Race in Cyberspace* (2000), Alicia Hines, Alondra Nelson, and Thuy Linh Tu's *Technicolor: Race, Technology, and Everyday Life* (2001), and Bruce Sinclair's *Technology and the African-American Experience: Needs and Opportunities for Study* (2004) have opened many avenues of exploration concerning the conflation of race and technology.

11. See Edgar Rice Burroughs's *Tarzan of the Apes* (1914) and its twenty-three sequels, Michael Crichton's *Congo* (1980), A. M. Lightner's *Day of the Drones* (1969), Paul McAuley's *White Devils* (2005), and Mack Reynolds's North Africa series: *Black Man's Burden* (1972), *Border, Breed, nor Birth* (1972), and *The Best Ye Breed* (1978).

12. See Steven Barnes's series *Great Sky Woman* (2006) and *Shadow Valley* (2009), David Durham's *Acacia* (2007) and *The Other Lands* (2009), Carole McDonnell's *Wind Follower* (2007), Nnedi Okorafor-Mbachu's *Zahrah the Windseeker* (2005) and *The Shadow Speaker* (2007), Nisi Shawl's *Filter House* (2009), and Gregory Walker's *Shades of Memnon* (1999).

13. See Charles Saunders's *The Quest for Cush* (1984) and *The Trail of Bohu* (1985) as well as his new picaresque novel *Dossouye* (2008) in addition to Tobias Buckell's *Crystal Rain* (2006), *Ragamuffin* (2007), and *Sly Mongoose* (2008), Bill Campbell's *Sunshine Patriots* (2004), and Nalo Hopkinson's *Midnight Robber* (2000) or *The New Moon's Arms* (2007).

1. RACING SCIENCE FICTION

1. Space is the form where a nonhuman encounter happens when human beings penetrate the unknown or vice versa. Time is the form where the nonhuman encounter is a process that unfolds in time, meaning that humanity changes because of some event in time. In terms of the machine, the nonhuman encounter is often brought about by the human production of the nonhuman form, such as the robot or computer. The monster is the form of the alien encounter symbolic of the nonhuman within humanity itself as well as outside of it.

2. Brian Stableford describes this conceptual breakthrough as a "gestalt shift," where "an ambiguous drawing can suddenly shift in the mind of the observer from one of its appearances to the other" (72).

3. See Nalo Hopkinson's *Whispers from the Cotton Tree Root: Caribbean Fabulist Fiction* (2000) and *Mojo: Conjure Stories* (2003), Andrea Bell and Yolanda Molina-Gavilán's *Cosmos Latinos: An Anthology of Science Fiction from Latin America* (2003), and Nalo Hopkinson and Uppinder Mehan's *So Long Been Dreaming: Postcolonial Science Fiction and Fantasy* (2004).

4. See Delany's essay "Racism in Science Fiction," first published in *The New York Review of Science Fiction* (August 1998).

5. John Akomfrah's documentary film *The Last Angel of History* (1996) serves as an accurate reflection of the growth of race studies in sf. The film is a cinematic

essay that begins to examine the uncharted associations among the African diaspora, its various cultural productions, rapidly developing computer technology, and its impact on sf.

6. See my chapter "Critical Race Theory" in *The Routledge Companion to Science Fiction* (2009) as well as Nabeel Zuberi's essay "Is This the Future? Black Music and Technology Discourse" in *Science Fiction Studies* (2007).

7. According to Kali Tal, the subgenre has various characteristics: "secret societies, charismatic leaders, tension between positions of violence and nonviolence, differing status among African Americans (often symbolized by skin color), and marginalization of women characters, whose sole purpose is to further the plot and enhance our understanding of the protagonist" (88–89).

8. John P. Jackson Jr. and Nadine M. Weidman, historians of human sciences, offer these remarks in their study *Race, Racism, and Science: Social Impact and Interaction* (2004):

> As sociologists and psychologists emphasized the social reality of race, other disciplines began seriously challenging the biological reality of race. New developments in genetics, new techniques for detecting and measuring human variation, a new emphasis on process rather than type in physical anthropology and the sheer growth of anthropology as a discipline all combined to finally lead to the demise of the typological view of race. (213–14)

9. Based on the 1978 television series, the new manifestation of *Battlestar Galactica* portrays humanity's desperate struggle for survival after a surprise attack by the Cylons, an artificial race of machines created to serve humanity; some of the Cylons pass for human. *The 4400* tells the story of 4,400 missing persons, abducted by humans from the far future over the span of sixty years (none of them have aged), given special abilities, and all returned on the same day to the consternation of the world. The 4,400 have been sent back to save the future of humanity.

10. See Jackson and Weidman's *Race, Racism, and Science: Social Impact and Interaction*, 77–79, for further discussion of Herbert Spencer, the term "survival of the fittest," and how it relates to social Darwinism.

11. This moment is the point where many readers and critics adapt an exclusive class reading of the novel. Taking up a Marxist position, Paul Alkon states how the story is "a metaphorical application of [Darwinism] to depict a situation designed to caution against the dangers as well as the inhumanity of rigidly dividing our own society into rich and poor" (51).

12. One of the few good things about the 2002 film adaptation of the novel by Wells's grandson Simon is the mirroring of Alexander Hartdegen's sentiment with that of the Time Traveller by racially coding the Eloi as black or at least racially ambiguous.

13. Of course, matters are a bit more complex. Wells's racialist assumptions are discernable particularly within the context of the late British Empire. *War of the Worlds* (1898), for example, is a self-conscious response to racism commonly held by Europeans of his time; in it, he likens the Martian invasion to racial genocide in Tasmania (3) and describes the Martians with "oily brown skin" (14) as "ugly brutes" (15). At the very least, race is visible to Wells in a way that subtly manipulates audience sentiment.

14. Lothrop Stoddard, a once-respected social Darwinist of the early twenti-eth century, uses Darwin's thinking on evolution to display how the white race is superior to other races of humanity. In a gross manipulation of natural selection, Stoddard posits: "The white man could think, could create, could fight superla-tively well. No wonder that redskins and Negroes feared and adored him as a god, while the somnolent races of the Farther East, stunned by this strange apparition rising from the pathless ocean, offered no effective opposition" (148).

15. DuBois defines double consciousness:

The Negro is a sort of seventh son, born with a veil, and gifted with second-sight in this American world,—a world which yields him no true self-consciousness, but only lets him see himself through the revelation of the other world. It is a peculiar sensation, this double consciousness, this sense of always looking at one's self through the eyes of others, of measur-ing one's soul by the tape of the world that looks on in amused contempt and pity. One ever feels his twoness,—an American, a Negro; two souls, two thoughts, two unreconciled strivings; two warring ideals in one dark body, whose dogged strength alone keeps it from being torn asunder. (45)

2. META-SLAVERY

1. As Carl Freedman notes, "Their name implies [that] the rats are dehuman-ized by the attitudes of those around them, and, in the general manner of slaves, they are almost unconditionally subject to the whims (including the sexual whims) of their masters" (159–60).

2. Timothy Spaulding remarks: "In the 'advanced' economic structure of Rhyonon, slavery has literally and figuratively masked itself behind the faceless cor-poration as the organizing institution of oppression . . . As a result, the slave labor force becomes an invisible part of the political economy" (113).

3. While Walker's *Jubilee* is the first to be acknowledged, other neo–slave narratives include Ernest Gaines's *The Autobiography of Miss Jane Pittman* (1971), Gayl Jones's *Corregidora* (1975), Ishmael Reed's *Flight to Canada* (1976), Charles Johnson's *Oxherding Tale* (1982) and *Middle Passage* (1990), Sherley Williams's *Dessa Rose* (1986), Toni Morrison's *Beloved* (1987), J. California Cooper's *Family* (1991), and Nalo Hopkinson's *The Salt Roads* (2003).

4. Perhaps the best study of the subject is literary critic Ashraf Rushdy's *Neo-Slave Narratives: Studies in the Social Logic of a Literary Form* (1999).

5. Racist regulations in defiance of the Constitution pop up all across the country. For example, in "Salt Springs, Texas," a law passed where "no Sleepless could obtain a liquor license, on the grounds that civil rights statutes were built on the 'all men were created equal' clause of the Constitution, and Sleepless clearly were not covered," and "Iroquois County, New York, barred them from serving on county juries, arguing that a jury containing Sleepless, with their skewed ideas of time, did not constitute 'a jury of one's peers'" (Kress, *Beggars*, 186).

6. Butler considers the American slavery experience in different ways in her Patternist series. First, she considers its historical ramifications in *Wild Seed* (1980) as Doro breeds mutants in his northern town of Wheatley and in antebellum Louisiana between 1690 and 1840. Second, she reflects on a futuristic semblance of

slavery in *Patternmaster* (1976), where nontelepathic human "mutes" are despised servants (1).

7. Toni Morrison coined the word "rememory" in her Pulitzer Prize–winning *Beloved* (1987).

8. In an interview conducted by Randall Kenan, Butler states, "*Kindred* is fantasy. I mean literally, it is fantasy" (495). Further, Raffaella Baccolini writes, "It is precisely Butler's conflation of genres—science fiction and slave narrative—that calls for a reading grounded in history" (29).

9. Elizabeth Beaulieu's *Black Women Writers and the American Neo-Slave Narrative: Femininity Unfettered* (1999) and Ashraf Rushdy's *Neo-Slave Narratives: Studies in the Social Logic of a Literary Form* (1999) are good examples of work that point out how the image of Sarah as the stereotypical "Mammy" or "the female Uncle Tom" is undercut by Dana's newfound knowledge of the woman's strength (Butler, *Kindred*, 145).

10. See Michelle Green's essay "'There Goes the Neighborhood': Octavia Butler's Demand for Diversity in Utopias" for further consideration of miscegenation in the Xenogenesis trilogy.

11. See Nolan Belk's *Utopian Studies* essay "The Certainty of the Flesh: Octavia Butler's Use of the Erotic in the Xenogenesis Trilogy" for additional reflection on race consciousness.

12. The series includes *Sundiver* (1980), *Startide Rising* (1983), *The Uplift War* (1987), *Brightness Reef* (1995), *Infinity's Shore* (1996), and *Heaven's Reach* (1998).

13. *Kiln People* was runner-up for the Hugo Award to Robert J. Sawyer's *Hominids*; runner-up for the Locus Award to Kim Stanley Robinson's *The Years of Rice and Salt*; runner-up for the Arthur C. Clarke Award to Christopher Priest's *The Separation*; and runner-up for the John W. Campbell Memorial Award to Nancy Kress's *Probability Space*.

14. Brin's use of the word "golem" is a deliberate allusion to Jewish folklore. A golem is an artificially created human being endowed with life that results from occult cabala rites; it is very similar to a robot in its automaton connotation. Brin also complicates his story by referring to the Nazi-induced Holocaust with these oven-baked people. Likewise, he is presumably evoking Hebrew slavery with the golem, and this differs somewhat from the New World slavery of blacks from a spiritual standpoint. However, Brin neatly ties the two manifestations of slavery together with his reimagining of the color line and the acts of violence inflicted on dittos.

15. The slave uprising in the novel mirrors that of Nat Turner's 1831 revolt in our own history.

16. Another novel that features Muslim culture prominently in addition to Chinese and Hindu traditions is Kim Stanley Robinson's Hugo Award nominee *The Years of Rice and Salt* (2002).

17. In Beatty's words, Barnes "subtly demonstrates the ways in which history is a story, and not always a reliable story" (5).

18. For more information on the life of Shaka Zulu, consult Donald Morris's study *The Washing of the Spears* (1965).

19. I must acknowledge that the Statue of Liberty has never had a secure meaning, as Linda Zerilli explains in her essay "Democracy and National Fantasy: Reflections on the Statue of Liberty" (2000).

20. Equiano writes: "I was now persuaded that I had gotten into a world of bad spirits, and that they were going to kill me. Their complexions too differing so much from ours, their long hair, and the language they spoke (which was very different from any I had ever heard) united to confirm me in this belief" (33).

21. Historians Stanley Harrold, Darlene Clarke Hine, and William C. Hine believe that "music may have been the most important aspect of African culture in the lives of American slaves" (39–40).

3. JIM CROW EXTRAPOLATIONS

1. Brackett's story is doubly noteworthy, since it addresses race explicitly while also implicitly challenging the gender stereotypes of 1950s sf.

2. For instance, *The Leopard's Spots* ends with the mob lynching of Dick, the alleged black rapist, who was once a boyhood friend of the white protagonist, Charles Gaston.

3. This name alone adds another racial dimension in light of William Shakespeare's romance *The Tempest* (1611).

4. Or as Eric Rabkin states, "The blacks succeed in fairyland, as in real America they failed, to leave the South for freedom" (124).

5. Schuyler argues that "the Aframerican is merely a lampblacked Anglo-Saxon . . . subject to the same economic and social forces that mold the actions and thoughts of the white Americans. He is not living in a different world as some whites and a few negroes would have us believe" ("Negro-Art Hokum," 97–98).

6. Literary critics Robert Hill and R. K. Rasmussen, who were responsible for rescuing Schuyler's serial *Black Empire* from obscurity in 1991, are convinced that Schuyler used sf for the express purpose of critiquing race: "the extent to which Schuyler kept up with science fiction magazines and films is not known . . . his fiction employs many themes common to the era's genres" ("Afterword," 307).

7. This quote has been cited by several critics. Hill and Rasmussen include it on page 260 of the "Afterword" to their edition of Schuyler's *Black Empire*.

8. Death rays "were the staple weapons of pulp sf in the 1920s and 1930s," according to the *Encyclopedia of Science Fiction*, edited by John Clute and Peter Nicholls (308).

9. Manning Marable states, "The reality [is] that one out of every four black American males would go to prison at some point in his lifetime" (196).

10. These statistics are taken from the summary of findings presented on the U.S. Bureau of Justice Statistics web page at http://bjs.ojp.usdoj.gov/content/pub/ascii/pim07.txt.

11. The amendment publicly proclaims: "Without regard to the language or interpretations previously given any other provision of this document, every United States citizen is subject at the call of Congress to selection for special service for periods necessary to protect domestic interests and international needs" (Bell, "Space Traders," 348).

4. AILMENTS OF RACE

1. Linda Singer states that "in an epidemic context, the limits of frontiers/boundaries legislative and otherwise are obvious. Epidemic [contagion] is defined by its indifference to those boundaries and prescriptions" (45).

2. Many great works, such as Homer's ninth century BC epic *The Iliad*, Sophocles's fifth century BC *Oedipus the King*, Giovanni Boccaccio's mid-fourteenth-century *Decameron*, Daniel Defoe's *A Journal of the Plague Year* (1722), or Edgar Allan Poe's "The Masque of the Red Death" (1842), make use of plagues in their storylines. Likewise, there are many contagion stories in twentieth-century literature and popular fiction as well, ranging from Katherine Porter's *Pale Horse, Pale Rider* (1939) and Albert Camus's *The Plague* (1948) to Stephen King's *The Stand* (1978) and Robin Cook's *Outbreak* (1991). Sf contagion stories begin with Mary Shelley's *The Last Man* (1826) and include Jack London's "The Scarlet Plague" (1912), Michael Crichton's *The Andromeda Strain* (1969), and Greg Bear's *Darwin's Radio* (1999) and *Darwin's Children* (2003).

3. Recent films such as *Outbreak, Puppet Masters, Virus, The Matrix, Resident Evil, Undercover Brother, XXX, Mission Impossible 2, 28 Days Later, 28 Weeks Later, I Am Legend*, and *Doomsday* all deal with contagion in one respect or another.

4. Race-based marriage restrictions, anti-miscegenation laws, were struck down by the U.S. Supreme Court decision *Loving v. Virginia* (1967).

5. While some light-skinned blacks may choose to pass, "the phenomenon of 'passing' is hardly limited to African Americans—in Nazi Germany, Jews passed as Protestants; in today's army, gay men and women pass as straight; on job applications, older people try to pass as younger. In each case, the reason is traceable to some form of discrimination, be it on the basis of race, sexual orientation, or age" (Hall, Russell, and Wilson, 73).

6. John Leslie comments, "'Ethnic' biological weapons have been proposed. Among victims of Rift Valley fever, whites are ten times less likely to die than blacks, while Epstein-Barr virus causes cancers in black Africans and in South East Asians, but not in whites" (41).

7. I am riffing on Michelle Cliff's prose poetry text *Claiming an Identity They Taught Me to Despise* (1980).

8. Campbell adopted the pen name Don A. Stuart to write "Who Goes There?" to tell a different kind of sf story from the action adventure variety popular in his day. He bases his Stuart stories on scientific logic and the extrapolation of an achievable science.

9. See Richard J. Herrnstein and Charles Murray's *The Bell Curve: Intelligence and Class in American Life* (1994) for further consideration of racist arguments concerning the study of human intelligence between the races.

10. The classic *Thing from Another World* (1951), nominally directed by Christian Nyby, is an earlier film adaptation spawned by the novella.

11. See sf novels such as Aldous Huxley's *Brave New World* (1932), Frank Herbert's *Dune* (1965), Philip K. Dick's *A Scanner Darkly* (1977), or Butler's own *Parable of the Sower* (1993) for further depictions of drug use.

12. While Lynn agrees with Alan on not wanting to have a DGD child, she does want the right to choose. Lynn is taking possession of her body by stating, "I

don't want kids, but I don't want someone else telling me I can't have any" (Butler, "Evening," 42).

5. ETHNOSCAPES

1. As a progressive alternative, among the fifty-five stories collected in Heather Masri's *Science Fiction: Stories and Contexts* (2009) are three by black writers (Delany, Butler, and Hopkinson) , two by Asian writers (Ken Liu and Sakyo Komatsu), and at least three stories explicitly about race (Mike Resnick's "Kirinyaga" [1988], Ian McDonald's "Recording Angel" [1996], and William Sanders's "When This World Is All on Fire" [2001])

2. In this context, it is worth noting the parallel critique of second-wave feminism's reduction of all women into a single category without reference to race made by such women of color as Gloria Anzaldúa, Cherríe Moraga, Angela Davis, bell hooks, and Alice Walker. See Anzaldúa and Moraga's *This Bridge Called My Back* (1983), Davis's *Women, Race, & Class* (1983), hooks's *Ain't I a Woman* (1988), and Walker's *In Search of Our Mother's Gardens* (1984).

3. Nalo Hopkinson's debut novel, *Brown Girl in the Ring* (1998), likewise presents a fabulist ethnoscape, combining the supernatural, the inner city, myth, and advanced medical technologies in a dystopian setting, and utilizing spiritual and linguistic themes to offer a unique perspective on the matter of alienated people.

4. Von Vampton is a caricature of white author and photographer Carl van Vechten, a patron of many black writers during the Harlem Renaissance. His controversial roman à clef *Nigger Heaven* (1926) is often credited with making Harlem a voguish destination for white tourists.

5. See James Blish's short story "Beep" (1954), which was expanded into *The Quincunx of Time* (1973); Ursula K. Le Guin's *The Dispossessed* (1974); and Gordon Dickson's "Jackal's Meal" (1969), which was reprinted in *The Star Road* (1973).

6. For instance, Ti-Jeanne, a black unwed teen mother, protects her newborn son from a Soucouyant, a Caribbean spirit vampire:

> *"Move aside, sweetheart, move aside." She voice licking like flame inside my head. "Is the baby I want. You don't want he, ain't it? So give him to me, nuh, doux-doux? I hungry. I want to suck he eyeballs from he headlike chennette fruit. I want to drink the blood from out he veins, sweet like red sorrel drink. Stand aside, Ti-Jeanne."* (Hopkinson, *Brown Girl*, 44)

7. See Jack Vance's *The Languages of Pao* (1958), Ian Watson's *The Embedding* (1973), and Suzette Haden Elgin's *Native Tongue* (1984).

8. Ayn Rand's *Anthem* (1938) presents a dystopian world where the concept of individuality has been stripped away from the population by forbidding the use of "I," the utterance of which is a crime punishable by death. Delany may have intended *Babel-17* as a riposte to the white supremacy in Rand's novel.

9. Similarly, Ruth Salvaggio writes: "In this world of gesture, body language supplants our normal 'speech sounds' and often results in violence rather than communication" (38).

10. According to Dick, when a machine "imitates human behavior so well that I get the uncomfortable sense that these things are trying to pass themselves off as humans but are not I call them 'androids,' which is my own way of using that word" ("Man, Android, and Machine," 211).

11. For more about the concept of the information feedback loop see N. Katherine Hayles's "Introduction" to *Chaos and Order: Complex Dynamics in Literature and Science* (1991), Colin Greenland's "A Nod to the Apocalypse: An Interview with William Gibson" (1986), David Porush's *The Soft Machine: Cybernetic Fiction* (1985), and J. David Bolter's *Turing's Man: Western Culture in the Computer Age* (1984).

6. TECHNOLOGICALLY DERIVED ETHNICITIES

1. For pertinent examples of existing research on the fine distinctions between race and ethnicity that consider the un-racing of different ethnic groups, see Karen Brodkin's *How Jews Became White Folks and What That Says about Race in America* (1999), Thomas A. Guglielmo's *White on Arrival: Italians, Race, Color, and Power in Chicago, 1890–1945* (2004), Noel Ignatiev's *How the Irish Became White* (1996), Matthew Jacobson's *Barbarian Virtues: The United States Encounters Foreign Peoples at Home and Abroad, 1876–1917* (2001), and David Roediger's *Working toward Whiteness: How America's Immigrants Became White; The Strange Journey from Ellis Island to the Suburbs* (2006).

2. Karel Čapek's play *R.U.R. (Rossum's Universal Robots)* (1920) first made popular the concept of the robot, albeit an organic one. These robots were mass-produced in mixing vats and line-assembled with perfect memories to serve humanity.

3. See Steven Barnes's June 26, 2009, post on *Transformers 2: Revenge of the Fallen* at http://darkush.blogspot.com/2009/06/transformers-2-revenge-of-fallen.html.

4. See episode 9 of the first season, "Tigh Me Up, Tigh Me Down."

5. See episode 8 of the first season, "Flesh and Bone."

6. See the *Battlestar Galactica* series pilot.

EPILOGUE

1. The heckler was Representative Joe Wilson of South Carolina.

2. See chapter 6, "Detroit Red," in *The Autobiography of Malcolm X.*

3. Texts that feature wage/debt slavery, such as Gwyneth Jones's *Escape Plans* (1986), Michael Blumlein's *The Movement of Mountains* (1988), Lois McMaster Bujold's *Falling Free* (1988), and Octavia Butler's Parable novels, are good examples of meta-slavery as well.

Bibliography

PRIMARY SOURCES

Anthony, Piers, and Robert E. Margroff. *The Ring.* 1968. New York: Tor, 1986.

Asimov, Isaac. *I, Robot.* New York: Bantam Books, 1950.

Attebery, Brian, and Ursula K. Le Guin, eds. *The Norton Book of Science Fiction.* New York: Norton, 1993.

Barnes, Steven. *Great Sky Woman.* New York: Ballantine Books, 2006.

———. *Lion's Blood.* New York: Warner/Aspect, 2002.

———. *Shadow Valley.* New York: Del Rey, 2009.

———. *Zulu Heart.* New York: Warner/Aspect, 2003.

Bear, Greg. *Blood Music.* 1985. New York: ibooks, 2002.

———. *Darwin's Children.* New York: Del Rey, 2003.

———. *Darwin's Radio.* New York: Del Rey, 1999.

Bell, Andrea L., and Yolanda Molina-Gavilán, eds. *Cosmos Latinos: An Anthology of Science Fiction from Latin America and Spain.* Middletown, Conn.: Wesleyan University Press, 2003.

Bell, Derrick. "The Space Traders." 1992. In *Dark Matter: A Century of Speculative Fiction from the African Diaspora,* ed. Sheree R. Thomas. New York: Warner/Aspect, 2000. 326–55.

Bisson, Terry. *Fire on the Mountain.* New York: Arbor House/William Morrow, 1988.

Blish, James. "Beep." 1954. In *Galactic Empires, Volume 2,* ed. Brian W. Aldiss. New York: St. Martin's Press, 1976. 82–122.

———. *The Quincunx of Time.* 1973. New York: Avon Books, 1983.

Blumlein, Michael. *The Movement of Mountains.* New York: St. Martin's Press, 1988.

Boccaccio, Giovanni. *The Decameron.* Trans. Mark Musa and Peter Bondanella. New York: Norton, 1982.

Brackett, Leigh. "All the Colors of the Rainbow." 1957. In *Humans and Other Beings,* ed. Allen De Graeff. New York: Collier, 1963. 219–40.

Bradbury, Ray. *Fahrenheit 451.* New York: Ballantine Books, 1953.

———. "June 2003: Way in the Middle of the Air." 1950. In *The Martian Chronicles*. New York: Bantam Books, 1950. 89–102.

———. "The Other Foot." 1951. In *The Illustrated Man*. New York: Bantam Books, 1951. 27–38.

Brin, David. *Brightness Reef*. New York: Bantam Books, 1995.

———. *Heaven's Reach*. New York: Bantam Books, 1998.

———. *Infinity's Shore*. New York: Bantam Books, 1996.

———. *Kiln People*. New York: Tor, 2002.

———. *Startide Rising*. New York: Bantam Books, 1983.

———. *Sundiver*. New York: Bantam Books, 1980.

———. *The Uplift War*. New York: Bantam/Spectra, 1987.

Buckell, Tobias S. *Crystal Rain*. New York: Tor, 2006.

———. *Ragamuffin*. New York: Tor, 2007.

———. *Sly Mongoose*. New York: Tor, 2008.

Bujold, Lois McMaster. *Falling Free*. New York: Baen Books, 1988.

Burroughs, Edgar R. *Tarzan of the Apes*. 1914. New York: Signet Classics, 1990.

Burroughs, William S. *The Ticket That Exploded*. New York: Grove Press, 1962.

Butler, Octavia E. *Adulthood Rites*. New York: Warner/Aspect, 1988.

———. *Bloodchild and Other Stories*. New York: Seven Stories Press, 1996.

———. *Clay's Ark*. New York: Warner/Aspect, 1984.

———. *Dawn*. New York: Warner/Aspect, 1987.

———. "The Evening and the Morning and the Night." 1987. In *Bloodchild and Other Stories*. New York: Seven Stories Press, 1996. 33–70.

———. *Fledgling*. New York: Seven Stories Press, 2005.

———. *Imago*. New York: Warner/Aspect, 1989.

———. *Kindred*. 1979. Boston: Beacon Press, 1988.

———. *Lilith's Brood*. New York: Warner/Aspect, 2000.

———. *Parable of the Sower*. New York: Warner/Aspect, 1993.

———. *Parable of the Talents*. New York: Warner/Aspect, 1998.

———. *Patternmaster*. New York: Warner/Aspect, 1976.

———. "Speech Sounds." 1983. In *Bloodchild and Other Stories*. New York: Seven Stories Press, 1995. 87–108.

———. *Wild Seed*. New York: Popular Library, 1980.

Campbell, Bill. *Sunshine Patriots*. Tucson: Hats Off Books, 2004.

Campbell, John W., Jr. "Who Goes There?" 1938. In *The Best of John W. Campbell*, ed. Lester del Rey. New York: Doubleday, 1976.

Camus, Albert. *The Plague*. New York: Knopf, 1948.

Capek, Karel. *R.U.R. (Rossum's Universal Robots)*. 1920. Trans. C. Novack. New York: Penguin Books, 2004.

Clarke, Arthur C. *Childhood's End*. 1953. New York: Del Rey, 1990.

Cliff, Michelle. *Claiming an Identity They Taught Me to Despise*. Watertown, Mass.: Persephone Press, 1980.

Conrad, Joseph. *Heart of Darkness*. 1899. New York: Penguin Classics, 2007.

Cook, Robin. *Outbreak*. New York: Berkley, 1991.

Cooper, J. California. *Family*. New York: Anchor Books, 1991.

Crichton, Michael. *The Andromeda Strain*. New York: Knopf, 1969.

———. *Congo*. 1980. New York: Avon, 2003.

Darwin, Charles. *The Origin of Species by Means of Natural Selection: or the Preservation of Favoured Races in the Struggle for Life*. 1859. New York: Penguin Books, 1986.

Defoe, Daniel. *A Journal of the Plague Year*. 1722. New York: AMS, 1974.

Delany, Martin R. *Blake, or the Huts of America*. 1859–1862. Boston: Beacon Press, 1989.

Delany, Samuel R. *Babel-17*. 1966. New York: Vintage Books, 2001.

———. *Dhalgren*. 1974. Hanover, N.H.: Wesleyan University Press, 1996.

———. *Stars in My Pocket like Grains of Sand*. New York: Bantam Books, 1984.

Dick, Philip K. *Do Androids Dream of Electric Sheep?* 1968. New York: Del Rey, 1982.

———. "The Electric Ant." 1969. In *Machines That Think: The Best Science Fiction Stories about Robots and Computers*, ed. Isaac Asimov, Martin H. Greenberg, and Patricia S. Warrick. New York: Holt, Rinehart and Winston, 1983. 495–515.

———. *The Man in the High Castle*. 1962. New York: Vintage Books, 1992.

———. *A Scanner Darkly*. New York: Doubleday, 1977.

Dickson, Gordon R. "Jackal's Meal." 1969. In *The Star Road*. New York: Doubleday, 1973. 188–211.

Dixon, Thomas. *The Clansman: An Historical Romance of the Ku Klux Klan*. New York: Doubleday, 1905.

———. *The Leopard's Spots: A Romance of the White Man's Burden, 1865–1900*. New York: Doubleday, 1902.

———. *The Traitor: A Story of the Fall of the Invisible Empire*. New York: Doubleday, 1907.

Douglass, Frederick. *Narrative of the Life of Frederick Douglass, an American Slave, Written by Himself*. 1845. New York: Signet Classics, 1997.

DuBois, W. E. B. *Dark Princess: A Romance*. New York: Harcourt Brace and Co., 1928.

Due, Tananarive. "Patient Zero." In *The Year's Best Science Fiction: Eighteenth Annual Collection*, ed. Gardner Dozois. New York: St. Martin's/Griffin, 2001. 491–503.

Durham, David A. *Acacia*. New York: Doubleday, 2007.

———. *The Other Lands*. New York: Doubleday, 2009.

Elgin, Suzette H. *Native Tongue*. 1984. New York: The Feminist Press at CUNY, 2000.

Eliot. T. S. "The Hollow Men." 1925. In *Collected Poems: 1909–1962*. New York: Harcourt Brace, 1991. 77–82.

Ellison, Harlan. "I Have No Mouth, and I Must Scream." 1967. In *Machines That Think: The Best Science Fiction Stories about Robots and Computers*, ed. Isaac Asimov, Martin H. Greenberg, and Patricia S. Warrick. New York: Holt, Rinehart and Winston, 1983. 233–50.

Ellison, Ralph. *Invisible Man*. 1952. New York: Vintage Books, 1990.

Equiano, Olaudah. *The Interesting Narrative of the Life of Olaudah Equiano, or Gustavas Vassa, the African, Written by Himself*. 1789. In *The Classic Slave Narratives*, ed. Henry L. Gates Jr. New York: Mentor, 1987. 1–182.

Gaines, Ernest J. *The Autobiography of Miss Jane Pittman*. 1971. New York: Bantam Books, 1982.

Gibson, William. *Neuromancer*. New York: Ace Books, 1984.

Godwin, Tom. "The Cold Equations." 1954. In *The Ascent of Wonder: The Evolution of Hard SF*, ed. David G. Hartwell and Kathryn Cramer. New York: Tor, 1994. 442–58.

Greenlee, Sam. *The Spook Who Sat by the Door*. New York: Bantam Books, 1969.

Griggs, Sutton E. *Imperium in Imperio*. 1899. New York: AMS, 1969.

Hairston, Andrea. *Mindscape*. Seattle: Aqueduct Press, 2006.

Haley, Alex. *The Autobiography of Malcolm X: As Told to Alex Haley*. 1965. New York: Ballantine Books, 1987.

Heinlein, Robert A. *Citizen of the Galaxy*. 1957. New York: Del Rey, 1987.

———. *Farnham's Freehold*. 1964. New York: Baen Books, 1994.

———. *The Moon Is a Harsh Mistress*. 1966. New York: Orb, 1997.

———. *Starship Troopers*. 1959. New York: Ace Books, 1987.

———. *Stranger in a Strange Land*. 1961. New York: Berkley Medallion Books, 1968.

Herbert, Frank. *Dune*. New York: Ace Books, 1965.

Homer. *The Iliad*. Trans. Robert Fagles. New York: Penguin Books, 1998.

Hopkinson, Nalo. *Brown Girl in the Ring*. New York: Warner/Aspect, 1998.

———. "A Habit of Waste." 1996. In *Skin Folk*. New York: Warner/Aspect, 2001. 183–202.

———. *Midnight Robber*. New York: Warner/Aspect, 2000.

———. *Mojo: Conjure Stories*. New York: Warner/Aspect, 2003.

———. *The New Moon's Arms*. New York: Warner Books, 2007.

———. *The Salt Roads*. New York: Warner Books, 2003.

———, ed. *Whispers from the Cotton Tree Root: Caribbean Fabulist Fiction*. Montpelier, Vt.: Invisible Cities Press, 2000.

Hopkinson, Nalo, and Uppinder Mehan, eds. *So Long Been Dreaming: Postcolonial Science Fiction & Fantasy*. Vancouver: Arsenal Pulp Press, 2004.

Huxley, Aldous. *Brave New World*. 1932. New York: Perennial Classics, 1998.

Jacobs, Harriet A. *Incidents in the Life of a Slave Girl*. 1861. New York: Washington Square Press, 2003.

Johnson, Charles R. *Middle Passage*. New York: Plume, 1990.

———. *Oxherding Tale*. New York: Grove Weidenfeld, 1982.

Jones, Gayl. *Corregidora*. 1975. Boston: Beacon Press, 1987.

Jones, Gwyneth. *Escape Plans*. London: Allen & Unwin, 1986.

Keller, David H. "The Menace." *Amazing Stories Quarterly* 7.1 (1933): 91–127.

Kelley, William M. *A Different Drummer*. Garden City, N.Y.: Doubleday, 1962.

King, Stephen. *Cell*. New York: Scribner, 2006.

———. *The Stand*. 1978. New York: Doubleday, 1990.

Kress, Nancy. *Beggars in Spain*. 1991. In *The Hard SF Renaissance*, ed. Kathryn Cramer and David G. Hartwell. New York: Tor, 2002. 149–200.

———. *Probability Space*. New York: Tor, 2002.

Le Guin, Ursula K. *The Dispossessed*. New York: Avon Books, 1974.

———. *The Left Hand of Darkness*. New York: Ace Books, 1969.

Leinster, Murray. "First Contact." 1945. In *The Science Fiction Hall of Fame: Volume 1, 1929–1964*, ed. Robert Silverberg. New York: Orb, 1998. 252–80.

Lem, Stanislaw. *Solaris*. 1961. Trans. Steve Cox and Joanna Kilmartin. New York: Harcourt Brace and Co., 1970.

Lightner, A. M. *Day of the Drones*. New York: Norton, 1969.

London, Jack. "The Scarlet Plague." 1912. *The Science Fiction Stories of Jack London*. Ed. James Bankes. New York: Citadel, 1993. 149–90.

Masri, Heather. *Science Fiction: Stories and Contexts*. New York: Bedford/St. Martin's, 2009.

Matheson, Richard. *I Am Legend*. 1954. New York: Tor, 2007.

McAuley, Paul. *White Devils*. New York: Tor, 2005.

McDonnell, Carole. *Wind Follower*. New York: Juno Books, 2007.

Miller, Walter M., Jr. *A Canticle for Leibowitz*. New York: Lippincott, 1960.

———. "Dark Benediction." 1951. In *Approaches to Science Fiction*, ed. Donald L. Lawler. Boston: Houghton Mifflin, 1978. 253–98.

Miller, Warren. *The Siege of Harlem*. Greenwich, Conn.: Fawcett Crest Books, 1964.

Morrison, Toni. *Beloved*. 1987. New York: Plume, 1998.

Mosley, Walter. *Blue Light*. New York: Little, Brown, and Co., 1998.

———. *47*. New York: Little, Brown, and Co., 2005.

———. *Futureland*. New York: Warner/Aspect, 2001.

———. *The Wave*. New York: Warner/Aspect, 2006.

Norton, Andre. *The Beast Master*. New York: Harcourt Brace and Co., 1959.

Okorafor-Mbachu, Nnedi. *The Shadow Speaker*. New York: Hyperion Books, 2007.

———. *Zahrah the Windseeker*. New York: Houghton Mifflin, 2005.

Orwell, George. *Nineteen Eighty-four*. London: Secker and Warburg, 1949.

Pendray, Edward. *The Earth-Tube*. New York: Appleton, 1929.

Poe, Edgar A. "The Masque of the Red Death." 1842. In *Selected Tales*. Oxford: Oxford University Press, 1987. 136–41.

Pohl, Frederick. *Man Plus*. New York: Random House, 1976.

Porter, Katherine A. *Pale Horse, Pale Rider: Three Short Novels*. New York: Harcourt Brace and Co., 1939.

Priest, Christopher. *The Separation*. New York: Scribner, 2002.

Rand, Ayn. *Anthem*. 1938. New York: Plume, 1999.

Reed, Ishmael. *Flight to Canada*. 1976. New York: Atheneum, 1989.

———. *Mumbo Jumbo*. New York: Scribner, 1972.

Resnick, Mike. "Kirinyaga." 1988. In *The Norton Book of Science Fiction*, ed. Brian Attebery and Ursula K. Le Guin. New York: Norton, 1993. 716–32.

Reynolds, Mack. *The Best Ye Breed*. New York: Ace Books, 1978.

———. *Black Man's Burden*. New York: Ace Books, 1972.

———. *Border, Breed, nor Birth*. New York: Ace Books, 1972.

Robinson, Kim S. *The Years of Rice and Salt*. New York: Bantam Books, 2002.

Saunders, Charles. *Dossouye*. N.p.: Sword and Soul Media, 2008.

———. *Imaro*. New York: DAW Books, 1981.

———. *The Quest for Cush: Imaro II*. New York: DAW Books, 1984.

———. *The Trail of Bohu: Imaro III*. New York: DAW Books, 1985.

Sawyer, Robert J. *Hominids*. New York: Tor, 2002.

Schuyler, George S. *Black Empire: George S. Schuyler Writing as Samuel I. Brooks. 1936–1938*. Ed. Robert A. Hill and R. Kent Rasmussen. Boston: Northeastern University Press, 1991.

———. *Black No More*. 1931. Boston: Northeastern University Press, 1989.

Shakespeare, William. *The Tempest*. 1611. Ed. Peter Hulme and William H. Sherman. New York: Norton, 2003.

Shawl, Nisi. *Filter House*. Seattle: Aqueduct Press, 2008.

Sheckley, Robert. *The Status Civilization*. 1960. London: Methuen & Co., 1986.

Shelley, Mary. *The Last Man*. 1826. Ed. Hugh J. Luke Jr. Lincoln: University of Nebraska Press, 1993.

Sherrard, Cherene. "The Quality of Sand." 2004. In *Dark Matter: Reading the Bones*, ed. Sheree R. Thomas. New York: Warner/Aspect, 2004. 7–23.

Shiel, M. P. *The Yellow Danger*. London: Grant Richards, 1898.

Shockley, Evie. "Separation Anxiety." In *Dark Matter: A Century of Speculative Fiction from the African Diaspora*, ed. Sheree R. Thomas. New York: Warner/Aspect, 2000. 51–68.

Sophocles. *The Three Theban Plays: Antigone, Oedipus the King, Oedipus at Colonus*. Trans. Robert Fagles. New York: Penguin Books, 1984.

Stephenson, Neal. *Snow Crash*. New York: Bantam Books, 1992.

Stewart, George R. *Earth Abides*. New York: Random, 1949.

Styron, William. *The Confessions of Nat Turner*. 1967. New York: Vintage Books: 1992.

Thomas, Sheree R., ed. *Dark Matter: A Century of Speculative Fiction from the African Diaspora*. New York: Warner/Aspect, 2000.

———. *Dark Matter: Reading the Bones*. New York: Warner/Aspect, 2004.

Thoreau, Henry D. *Walden*. 1854. *The Writings of Henry David Thoreau*. Ed. J. Lyndon Shanley. Princeton, N.J.: Princeton University Press, 1971.

Thurman, Wallace. *The Blacker the Berry*. 1929. New York: Scribner, 1996.

Twain, Mark. *The Adventures of Huckleberry Finn*. 1884. New York: Penguin Classics, 2003.

Vance, Jack. *The Languages of Pao*. New York: Ace Books, 1958.

Van Vechten, Carl. *Nigger Heaven*. 1926. Champaign: University of Illinois Press, 1999.

Walker, Gregory L. *Shades of Memnon*. Posen, Ill.: Seker Nefer Press, 1999.

Walker, Margaret. *Jubilee*. 1966. Boston: Houghton-Mifflin, 1999.

Watson, Ian. *The Embedding*. London: Gollancz, 1973.

Wells, H. G. *The Time Machine*. 1895. New York: Oxford University Press, 1996.

———. *War of the Worlds*. 1898. New York: Dover, 1997.

Whitehead, Colson. *The Intuitionist*. New York: Anchor Books, 1999.

Williams, Robert M. "Robot's Return." 1938. In *Machines That Think: The Best Science Fiction Stories about Robots and Computers*, ed. Isaac Asimov, Martin H. Greenberg, and Patricia S. Warrick. New York: Holt, Rinehart and Winston, 1983. 139–52.

Williams, Sherley A. *Dessa Rose*. 1986. New York: Berkley, 1996.

Wright, Richard. *Native Son*. 1940. New York: Harper Perennial Modern Classics, 2005.

FILMS, MUSIC, AND TELEVISION

A.I.: Artificial Intelligence. Directed by Steven Spielberg. Warner Brothers, 2001.
Alexander, Heather. *Insh'Allah: The Music of Lion's Blood.* Sea Fire, 2002.
Alien Resurrection. Directed by Jean-Pierre Jeunet. Twentieth Century Fox, 1997.
Battlestar Galactica: Miniseries. Written by Ronald D. Moore. Directed by
    Michael Rymer. SciFi Channel. December 8, 2003.
The Birth of a Nation. Directed by D. W. Griffith. David W. Griffith Corporation,
    1915.
Blade Runner. Directed by Ridley Scott. Sir-Run Run Shaw/Warner, 1982.
Colossus, the Forbin Project. Directed by Joseph Sargent. Universal, 1969.
"Crossroads, Part 2." *Battlestar Galactica.* Written by Mark Verheiden. Directed by
    Michael Rymer. SciFi Channel. March 25, 2007.
Deep Impact. Directed by Mimi Leder. Paramount/Dreamworks, 1998.
"*Deep Impact* Sketch." *Chappelle's Show.* Written by Neal Brennan and Dave
    Chappelle. Directed by Rusty Cundieff. Comedy Central/Paramount, 2004.
Doomsday. Directed by Neil Marshall. Rogue Pictures, 2008.
"Downloaded." *Battlestar Galactica.* Written by Bradley Thompson and David
    Weddle. Directed by Jeff Woolnough. SciFi Channel. February 24, 2006.
Escape from New York. Directed by John Carpenter. AVCO Embassy Pictures, 1981.
"Flesh and Bone." *Battlestar Galactica.* Written by Tony Graphia. Directed by
    Brad Turner. SciFi Channel. December 6, 2006.
The 4400. Written by Scott Peters and René Echevarria. Directed by Yves
    Simoneau. USA Network. July 11, 2004.
Gattaca. Directed by Andrew Niccol. Jersey Films/Columbia, 1997.
"Getting Closer." *Dollhouse.* Written by Tim Minear. Directed by Tim Minear.
    Fox. January 8, 2010.
"Ghost." *Dollhouse.* Written by Joss Whedon. Directed by Joss Whedon. Fox.
    February 13, 2009.
"The Hollow Men." *Dollhouse.* Written by Tracy Bellomo, Tara Butters, and
    Michele Fazekas. Directed by Terrance O'Hara. Fox. January 15, 2010.
I Am Legend. Directed by Francis Lawrence. Warner Brothers, 2007.
I, Robot. Directed by Alex Proyas. Twentieth Century Fox, 2004.
Idiocracy. Directed by Mike Judge. Twentieth Century Fox, 2006.
"Kobol's Last Gleaming, Part 2." *Battlestar Galactica.* Written by Ronald D.
    Moore. Directed by Michael Rymer. SciFi Channel. January 24, 2005.
The Last Angel of History. Directed by John Akomfrah. First Run/Icarus Films,
    1996.
Logan's Run. Directed by Michael Anderson. Metro-Goldwyn-Mayer, 1976.
The Matrix. Directed by Andy and Larry Wachowski. Warner Brothers, 1999.
Mission Impossible 2. Directed by John Woo. Paramount Pictures, 2000.
"Omega." *Dollhouse.* Written by Tim Minear. Directed by Tim Minear. Fox. May
    8, 2009.
Outbreak. Directed by Wolfgang Petersen. Warner Brothers, 1995.
Pitch Black. Directed by David Twohy. USA Films, 2000.
Puppet Masters. Directed by Stuart Orme. Buena Vista Pictures, 1994.
Resident Evil. Directed by Paul W. S. Anderson. Screen Gems, 2002.

Robocop. Directed by Paul Verhoeven. Orion, 1987.

Soylent Green. Directed by Richard Fleischer. Metro-Goldwyn-Mayer, 1973.

Star Wars: Episode I—The Phantom Menace. Directed by George Lucas. Twentieth Century Fox, 1999.

"The Target." *Dollhouse.* Written by Steven S. DeKnight. Directed by Steven S. DeKnight. Fox. February 20, 2009.

The Terminator. Directed by James Cameron. Pacific Western/Orion, 1984.

The Thing. Directed by John Carpenter. Turman-Foster/Universal, 1982.

The Thing from Another World. 1951. Directed by Christian Nyby. RKO Radio Pictures/Warner, 2003.

"33." *Battlestar Galactica.* Written by Ronald D. Moore. Directed by Michael Rymer. SciFi Channel. October 18, 2004.

"Tigh Me Up, Tigh Me Down." *Battlestar Galactica.* Written by Jeff Vlaming. Directed by Edward James Olmos. SciFi Channel. December 13, 2004.

The Time Machine. Directed by Simon Wells. Dreamworks SKG/Warner, 2002.

Transformers. Directed by Michael Bay. Dreamworks SKG/Paramount Pictures, 2007.

Transformers: Revenge of the Fallen. Directed by Michael Bay. Dreamworks SKG/ Paramount Pictures, 2009.

Tron. Directed by Steven Lisberger. Walt Disney, 1982.

28 Days Later. Directed by Danny Boyle. DNA/Twentieth Century Fox, 2002.

28 Weeks Later. Directed by Juan Carlos Fresnadillo. Fox Atomic/Fox Searchlight, 2007.

2001: A Space Odyssey. Directed by Stanley Kubrick. MGM/UA, 1968.

Undercover Brother. Directed by Malcolm D. Lee. Universal, 2002.

Virus. Directed by John Bruno. Universal, 1999.

XXX. Directed by Rob Cohen. Revolution Studios/Columbia, 2002.

SECONDARY SOURCES

Adare, Sierra S. *"Indian" Stereotypes in TV Science Fiction: First Nations' Voices Speak Out.* Austin: University of Texas Press, 2005.

Afrofuturism. Ed. Art McGee and Alondra Nelson. http://www.afrofuturism.net/. Accessed January 5, 2003.

Aldiss, Brian W., and David Wingrove. *Trillion Year Spree: The History of Science Fiction.* London: Victor Gollancz, 1986.

Alkon, Paul K. *Science Fiction before 1900: Imagination Discovers Technology.* New York: Twayne, 1994.

Anzaldúa, Gloria, and Cherríe Moraga, eds. *This Bridge Called My Back: Writings by Radical Women of Color.* 1981. New York: Kitchen Table: Women of Color Press, 1983.

Appadurai, Arjun. *Modernity at Large: Cultural Dimensions of Globalization.* Minneapolis: University of Minnesota Press, 1996.

Asimov, Isaac. *Asimov on Science Fiction.* Garden City, N.Y.: Doubleday, 1981.

Baccolini, Raffaella. "Gender and Genre in the Feminist Critical Dystopias of Katharine Burdekin, Margaret Atwood, and Octavia Butler." In *Future Females, the Next Generation: New Voices and Velocities in Science Fiction*

Criticism, ed. Marleen S. Barr. New York: Rowman and Littlefield, 2000. 13–34.

Baldwin, James. "Everybody's Protest Novel." 1949. In *The Norton Anthology of African American Literature*, 2nd ed., ed. Henry Louis Gates Jr. and Nellie Y. McKay. New York: Norton: 2004. 1699–1705.

Barkan, Elazar. *The Retreat of Scientific Racism: Changing Concepts of Race in Britain and the United States between the World Wars*. New York: Cambridge University Press, 1992.

Barnes, Steven. "Transformers 2: Revenge of the Fallen." June 26, 2009. Available at http://darkush.blogspot.com/2009/06/transformers-2-revenge-of-fallen.html.

Barr, Marleen S., ed. *Afro-Future Females: Black Writers Chart Science Fiction's Newest New-Wave Trajectory*. Columbus: Ohio State University Press, 2008.

Barron, Neil. "The Emergence of Science Fiction: The Beginnings to the 1920s." *Anatomy of Wonder: A Critical Guide to Science Fiction*. 3rd ed. Ed. Neil Barron. New York: Bowker, 1987. 3–48.

Beal, Frances M. "Black Women and the Science Fiction Genre: *Black Scholar* Interview with Octavia Butler." *Black Scholar* 17.2 (1986): 14–18.

Beatty, Greg. "Varieties of History in Steven Barnes's *Lion's Blood*." *The New York Review of Science Fiction* 15.7 (March 2003): 1, 4–6.

Beaulieu, Elizabeth A. *Black Women Writers and the American Neo-Slave Narrative: Femininity Unfettered*. Westport, Conn.: Greenwood Press, 1999.

Belk, Nolan. "The Certainty of the Flesh: Octavia Butler's Use of the Erotic in the Xenogenesis Trilogy." *Utopian Studies* 19.3 (2008): 369–89.

Bell, Bernard W. *The Afro-American Novel and Its Tradition*. Amherst: University of Massachusetts Press, 1987.

Bell, John. "A Charles R. Saunders Interview." *Black American Literature Forum* 18.2 (1984): 90–92.

Berger, Albert I. *The Magic That Works: John W. Campbell and the American Response to Technology*. San Bernardino, Calif.: Borgo Press, 1993.

Bergmann, Linda S. "Reshaping the Roles of Man, God, and Nature: Darwin's Rhetoric in *On the Origin of Species*." In *Beyond the Two Cultures: Essays on Science, Technology, and Literature*, ed. Judith Y. Lee and Joseph W. Slade. Ames: Iowa State University Press, 1990. 79–98.

Bolter, J. David. *Turing's Man: Western Culture in the Computer Age*. Chapel Hill: University of North Carolina Press, 1984.

Bould, Mark. "Come Alive by Saying No: An Introduction to Black Power SF." *Science Fiction Studies* 34.2 (2007): 220–40.

———. "The Ships Landed Long Ago: Afrofuturism and Black SF." *Science Fiction Studies* 34.2 (2007): 177–86.

Boulter, Amanda. "Polymorphous Futures: Octavia E. Butler's *Xenogenesis* Trilogy." In *American Bodies: Cultural Histories of the Physique*, ed. Tim Armstrong. New York: NYU Press, 1996. 170–85.

Bray, Mary K. "Rites of Reversal: Double Consciousness in Delany's *Dhalgren*." *Black American Literature Forum* 18.2 (1984): 57–61.

Broderick, Damien. *The Architecture of Babel: Discourses of Literature and Science*. Carlton, Australia: Melbourne University Press, 1994.

Brodkin, Karen. *How Jews Became White Folks and What That Says about Race in America*. New Brunswick, N.J.: Rutgers University Press, 1999.

Bukatman, Scott. *Terminal Identity: The Visual Subject in Postmodern Science Fiction*. Durham, N.C.: Duke University Press, 1993.

Butler, Octavia E. "Positive Obsession." In *Bloodchild and Other Stories*. New York: Seven Stories Press, 1995. 123–36.

The Carl Brandon Society. http://www.carlbrandon.org/. Accessed August 1, 2003.

Christie, John. "Of AIs and Others: William Gibson's Transit." In *Fiction 2000: Cyberpunk and the Future of Narrative*, ed. Tom Shippey and George Slusser. Athens: University of Georgia Press, 1992. 171–82.

Clute, John, and Peter Nicholls, eds. *The Encyclopedia of Science Fiction*. New York: St. Martin's/Griffin, 1995.

Cobb, Joann P. "Medium and Message in Ellison's 'I Have No Mouth, and I Must Scream.'" In *The Intersection of Science Fiction and Philosophy: Critical Studies*, ed. Robert E. Myers. Westport, Conn.: Greenwood Press, 1983. 159–67.

Crossley, Robert. "Introduction." In *Kindred*, by Octavia Butler. Boston: Beacon Press, 1988. ix–xxvii.

Csicsery-Ronay, Istvan, Jr. "Dis-Imagined Communities: Science Fiction and the Future of Nations." In *Edging into the Future: Science Fiction and Contemporary Cultural Transformation*, ed. Joan Gordon and Veronica Hollinger. Philadelphia: University of Pennsylvania Press, 2002. 217–37.

Davis, Angela Y. *Women, Race, & Class*. New York: Vintage Books, 1983.

Davis, Charles T., and Henry L. Gates, Jr. "Introduction: The Language of Slavery." In *The Slave's Narrative*, ed. Charles T. Davis and Henry Louis Gates Jr. New York: Oxford University Press, 1985. xi–xxxiv.

Dawkins, Richard. *The Selfish Gene*. 1976. New York: Oxford University Press, 2006.

DeGraw, Sharon. *The Subject of Race in American Science Fiction*. New York: Routledge, 2007.

Delany, Samuel R. *The Jewel-Hinged Jaw: Notes on the Language of Science Fiction*. New York: Berkley Windhover, 1977.

———. "Racism and Science Fiction." *The New York Review of Science Fiction* 10.12 (August 1998): 1, 16–20.

———. *Starboard Wine: More Notes on the Language of Science Fiction*. Pleasantville, N.Y.: Dragon Press, 1984.

Dery, Mark. "Black to the Future: Interviews with Samuel R. Delany, Greg Tate, and Tricia Rose." *South Atlantic Quarterly* 92.4 (1993): 735–78.

Desser, David. "Race, Space and Class: The Politics of the SF Film from *Metropolis* to *Blade Runner*." In *Retrofitting Blade Runner: Issues in Ridley Scott's* Blade Runner *and Philip K. Dick's* Do Androids Dream of Electric Sheep?, ed. Judith B. Kerman. Bowling Green, Ohio: Bowling Green State University Press, 1991. 110–23.

Dick, Philip K. "Man, Android, and Machine." 1976. *The Shifting Realities of Philip K. Dick: Selected Literary and Philosophical Writings*, ed. Lawrence Sutin. New York: Pantheon, 1995. 212–32.

Du Bois, W. E. B. *The Souls of Black Folk*. 1903. New York: Signet Classic, 1969.

Dubey, Madhu. "Folk and Urban Communities in African-American Women's Fiction: Octavia Butler's *Parable of the Sower.*" *Studies in American Fiction* 27.1 (1999): 103–28.

———. *Signs and Cities: Black Literary Postmodernism.* Chicago: University of Chicago Press, 2003.

Dyer, Richard. *White.* New York: Routledge, 1997.

Foster, Thomas. *The Souls of Cyberfolk: Posthumanism as Vernacular Theory.* Minneapolis: University of Minnesota Press, 2005.

Foucault, Michel. *The Birth of the Clinic: An Archaeology of Medical Perception.* 1963. Trans. A. M. Sheridan Smith. New York: Vintage, 1994.

Francavilla, Joseph. "The Android as *Doppelganger.*" In *Retrofitting* Blade Runner: *Issues in Ridley Scott's* Blade Runner *and Philip K. Dick's* Do Androids Dream of Electric Sheep?, ed. Judith B. Kerman. Bowling Green, Ohio: Bowling Green State University Press, 1991. 4–15.

Franklin, H. B. "The Science Fiction of Medicine." In *No Cure for the Future: Disease and Medicine in Science Fiction and Fantasy*, ed. George Slusser and Gary Westfahl. Westport, Conn.: Greenwood Press, 2002. 9–22.

Freedman, Carl. *Critical Theory and Science Fiction.* Hanover, N.H.: Wesleyan University Press, 2000.

Gallagher, Edward J. "The Thematic Structure of *The Martian Chronicles.*" In *Ray Bradbury*, ed. Martin H. Greenberg and Joseph D. Olander. New York: Taplinger, 1980. 55–82.

Gates, Henry L., Jr. "A Fragmented Man: George Schuyler and the Claims of Race." *New York Times Book Review*, September 20, 1992, 31, 42–43.

Gilman, Sander L. *Difference and Pathology: Stereotypes of Sexuality, Race, and Madness.* Ithaca, N.Y.: Cornell University Press, 1985.

Gilroy, Paul. *Against Race: Imagining Political Culture beyond the Color Line.* Cambridge, Mass.: Harvard University Press, 2000.

Gordon, Joan. "Utopia, Genocide, and the Other." In *Edging into the Future: Science Fiction and Contemporary Cultural Transformation*, ed. Joan Gordon and Veronica Hollinger. Philadelphia: University of Pennsylvania Press, 2002. 205–216.

Gordy, Sondra. *Finding the Lost Year: What Happened When Little Rock Closed Its Public Schools?* Fayetteville: University of Arkansas Press, 2009.

Gossett, Thomas F. *Race: The History of an Idea in America.* 2nd ed. New York: Oxford University Press, 1997.

Gould, Stephen J. *Ever Since Darwin: Reflections in Natural History.* New York: Norton, 1977.

Govan, Sandra Y. "Homage to Tradition: Octavia Butler Renovates the Historical Novel." *Melus* 13.1 & 2 (1986): 79–96.

Graves, Joseph L., Jr. *The Emperor's New Clothes: Biological Theories of Race at the Millennium.* New Brunswick, N.J.: Rutgers University Press, 2001.

Grayson, Sandra. *Visions of the Third Millennium: Black Science Fiction Novelists Write the Future.* Trenton, N.J.: Africa World Press, 2003.

Green, Michelle E. "'There Goes the Neighborhood': Octavia Butler's Demand for Diversity in Utopias." In *Utopian and Science Fiction by Women: Worlds of*

Difference, ed. Jane L. Donawerth and Kolmerten. Syracuse, N.Y.: Syracuse University Press, 1994. 166–89.

Greenland, Colin. "A Nod to the Apocalypse: An Interview with William Gibson." *Foundation* 36 (1986): 5–9.

Guglielmo, Thomas A. *White on Arrival: Italians, Race, Color, and Power in Chicago, 1890–1945*. New York: Oxford University Press, 2004.

Gunkel, Ann H., and David J. Gunkel. "Virtual Geographies: The New Worlds of Cyberspace." *Critical Studies in Mass Communications* 14.2 (1997): 123–37.

Hall, Ronald, Kathy Russell, and Midge Wilson. *The Color Complex: The Politics of Skin Color among African Americans*. New York: Anchor Books, 1992.

Hall, Stuart. "Race, Culture, and Communications: Looking Backward and Forward at Cultural Studies." In *What Is Cultural Studies? A Reader*, ed. John Storey. New York: Arnold, 1996. 336–43.

Haraway, Donna J. "A Cyborg Manifesto: Science, Technology, and Socialist-Feminism in the Late Twentieth Century." In *Simians, Cyborgs, and Women: The Reinvention of Nature*. New York: Routledge, 1991. 149–81.

Harrison, Harry, ed. *John W. Campbell, Collected Editorials from* Analog. Garden City, N.Y.: Doubleday, 1966.

Harrold, Stanley, Darlene Clarke Hine, and William C. Hine. *African Americans: A Concise History: Combined Volume*. Upper Saddle River, N.J.: Prentice Hall, 2004.

Hayles, N. Katherine. *How We Became Posthuman: Virtual Bodies in Cybernetics, Literature, and Informatics*. Chicago: University of Chicago Press, 1999.

———. "Introduction: Complex Dynamics in Literature and Science." In *Chaos and Order: Complex Dynamics in Literature and Science*, ed. N. Katherine Hayles. Chicago: University of Chicago Press, 1991. 1–33.

Hegel, G. W. F. *Phenomenology of Spirit*. 1807. Trans. A. V. Miller. New York: Oxford University Press, 1977.

Heidegger, Martin. *Mindfulness*. Trans. Parvis Emad and Thomas Kalary. London: Continuum, 2006.

———. "The Question Concerning Technology." 1954. In *Martin Heidegger: Basic Writings*. Trans. William Lovitt. Ed. David Farrell Krell. New York: Harper & Row, 1977.

Herrnstein, Richard J., and Charles Murray. *The Bell Curve: Intelligence and Class in American Life*. New York: Free Press, 1994.

Hill, Robert A., and R. K. Rasmussen. "Afterword." In *Black Empire*, by George S. Schuyler. Ed. Robert A. Hill and R. K. Rasmussen. Boston: Northeastern University Press, 1991. 259–310.

Hines, Alicia H., Alondra Nelson, and Thuy Linh N. Tu, eds. "Introduction: Hidden Circuits." In *Technicolor: Race, Technology, and Everyday Life*. New York: NYU Press, 2001. 1–12.

Holden, Rebecca J. "The High Costs of Cyborg Survival: Octavia Butler's *Xenogenesis* Trilogy." *Foundation* 72 (1998): 49–56.

hooks, bell. *Ain't I a Woman: Black Women and Feminism*. Boston: South End Press, 1988.

Huntington, John. *Rationalizing Genius: Ideological Strategies in the Classic American Science Fiction Short Story.* New Brunswick, N.J.: Rutgers University Press, 1989.

Ignatiev, Noel. *How the Irish Became White.* New York: Routledge, 1996.

Jackson, John P., Jr., and Nadine M. Weidman. *Race, Racism, and Science: Social Impact and Interaction.* 2004. New Brunswick, N.J.: Rutgers University Press, 2006.

Jacobson, Matthew F. *Barbarian Virtues: The United States Encounters Foreign Peoples at Home and Abroad, 1876–1917.* New York: Hill and Wang, 2001.

James, Edward. "Yellow, Black, Metal and Tentacled: The Race Question in American Science Fiction." In *Science Fiction, Social Conflict and War,* ed. Philip J. Davies. Manchester, U.K.: Manchester University Press, 1990. 26–49.

Johnson, Wayne L. *Ray Bradbury.* New York: Ungar, 1980.

Kenan, Randall. "An Interview with Octavia E. Butler." *Callaloo* 14.1 (1991): 495–504.

Kevorkian, Martin. *Color Monitors: The Black Face of Technology in America.* Ithaca, N.Y.: Cornell University Press, 2006.

Kilgore, De Witt D. *Astrofuturism: Science, Race, and Visions of Utopia in Space.* Philadelphia: University of Pennsylvania Press, 2003.

Kolko, Beth E., Lisa Nakamura, and Gilbert B. Rodman, eds. "Introduction." In *Race in Cyberspace.* New York: Routledge, 2000. 1–13.

Kubitschek, Missy D. *Claiming the Heritage: African-American Women Novelists and History.* Jackson: University Press of Mississippi, 1991.

Kuenz, Jane. "American Racial Discourse, 1900–1930: Schuyler's *Black No More.*" *Novel* 30.2 (1997): 170–92.

Landon, Brooks. *The Aesthetics of Ambivalence: Rethinking Science Fiction Film in the Age of Electronic (Re)production.* Westport, Conn.: Greenwood Press, 1992.

———. *Science Fiction after 1900: From the Steam Man to the Stars.* New York: Twayne, 1997.

———. "'There's Some of Me in You': *Blade Runner* and the Adaptation of Science Fiction Literature into Film." In *Retrofitting* Blade Runner: *Issues in Ridley Scott's* Blade Runner *and Philip K. Dick's* Do Androids Dream of Electric Sheep?, ed. Judith B. Kerman. Bowling Green, Ohio: Bowling Green State University Press, 1991. 90–102.

Lavender, Isiah, III. "Critical Race Theory." In *The Routledge Companion to Science Fiction,* ed. Mark Bould, Andrew M. Butler, Adam Roberts, and Sherryl Vint. New York: Routledge, 2009. 185–93.

———. "Ethnoscapes: Environment and Language in Ishmael Reed's *Mumbo Jumbo,* Colson Whitehead's *The Intuitionist,* and Samuel R. Delany's *Babel-17.*" *Science Fiction Studies* 34.2 (2007): 187–200.

———. "Technicity: AI and Cyborg Ethnicity in *The Matrix.*" *Extrapolation* 45.4 (2004): 436–57.

Lawson, Benjamin S. "George S. Schuyler and the Fate of Early African-American Science Fiction." In *Impossibility Fiction: Alternativity—Extrapolation—Speculation,* ed. Derek Littlewood and Peter Stockwell. Amsterdam: Rodopi, 1996. 87–105.

Lem, Stanislaw. "Robots in Science Fiction." Trans. Franz Rottensteiner. In *SF: The Other Side of Realism*, ed. Thomas D. Clareson. Bowling Green, Ohio: Bowling Green University Popular Press, 1971. 307–25.

Leonard, Elisabeth A., ed. *Into Darkness Peering: Race and Color in the Fantastic*. Westport, Conn.: Greenwood Press, 1997.

———. "Race and Ethnicity in Science Fiction." In *The Cambridge Companion to Science Fiction*, ed. Edward James and Farah Mendlesohn. New York: Cambridge University Press, 2003. 253–63.

Lerner, Fred, and Kathleen L. Spencer. "Unknown Black SF Writers?" *Science Fiction Studies* 15.1 (1988): 118–19.

Leslie, John. *The End of the World: The Science and Ethics of Human Extinction*. New York: Routledge, 1996.

Lindee, M. S., and Dorothy Nelkin. *The DNA Mystique: The Gene as a Cultural Icon*. New York: W. H. Freeman, 1995.

Luckhurst, Roger. "'Horror and Beauty in Rare Combination': The Miscegenate Fictions of Octavia Butler." *Women* 7.1 (1996): 23–38.

Lynch, Lisa. "'Not a Virus, but an Upgrade': The Ethics of Epidemic Evolution in Greg Bear's *Darwin's Radio*." *Literature and Medicine* 20.1 (2001): 71–93.

Malmgren, Carl. "The Languages of Science Fiction: Samuel Delany's *Babel-17*." *Extrapolation* 34.1 (1993): 5–17.

Marable, Manning. *Race, Reform, and Rebellion: The Second Reconstruction in Black America, 1945–1990*. 2nd ed. Jackson: University Press of Mississippi, 1991.

Marsden, Paul. "Memetics and Social Contagion: Two Sides of the Same Coin?" *Journal of Memetics—Evolutionary Models of Information Transmission* 2.2 (1998): 171–85.

Mays, Benjamin E. "The Moral Aspects of Segregation: The Segregation Decisions, November 10, 1955." In *Voices in Our Blood: America's Best on the Civil Rights Movement*, ed. Jon Meacham. New York: Random House, 2001. 123–28.

McGregor, Gaile. *The Noble Savage in the New World Garden: Notes toward a Syntactics of Place*. Bowling Green, Ohio: Bowling Green State University Popular Press, 1988.

McPherson, Tara. *Reconstructing Dixie: Race, Gender, and Nostalgia in the Imagined South*. Durham, N.C.: Duke University Press, 2003.

Mead, David G. "Technolocal Transfiguration in William Gibson's Sprawl Novels: *Neuromancer, Count Zero,* and *Mona Lisa Overdrive*." *Extrapolation* 32.4 (1991): 350–60.

Miksanek, Tony. "Microscopic Doctors and Molecular Black Bags: Science Fiction's Prescription for Nanotechnology and Medicine." *Literature and Medicine* 20.1 (2001): 55–70.

Moore, John. "Singing the Body Unelectric: Mapping and Modelling in Samuel R. Delany's *Dhalgren*." In *American Bodies: Cultural Histories of the Physique*, ed. Tim Armstrong. New York: NYU Press, 1996. 186–94.

Moore, Ronald D. "A Debate Worth Having." April 1, 2005. Available at www .twistytales.com/01_RonaldDMoore.pdf (accessed March 20, 2010).

Morgan, Stacy. "'The Strange and Wonderful Workings of Science': Race Science and Essentialism in George Schuyler's *Black No More*." *CLA Journal* 42.3 (1999): 331–52.

Morris, Christine. "Indians and Other Aliens: A Native American View of Science Fiction." *Extrapolation* 20.4 (1979): 301–307.

Morris, Donald R. *The Washing of the Spears: A History of the Rise of the Zulu Nation under Shaka and Its Fall in the Zulu War of 1879*. New York: Simon and Schuster, 1965.

Morrison, Toni. "The Talk of the Town: Comment." *The New Yorker*, Oct. 5, 1998, 31–32.

Mosley, Walter. "Black to the Future." In *Dark Matter: A Century of Speculative Fiction from the African Diaspora*, ed. Sheree R. Thomas. New York: Warner/Aspect, 2000. 405–407.

Nakamura, Lisa. *Cybertypes: Race, Ethnicity, and Identity on the Internet*. New York: Routledge, 2002.

Nama, Adilifu. *Black Space: Imagining Race in Science Fiction Film*. Austin: University of Texas Press, 2008.

Nelson, Alondra. "Introduction: Future Texts." *Social Text* 20.2 (2002): 1–15.

Omi, Michael, and Howard Winant. *Racial Formation in the United States: From the 1960s to the 1990s*. 2nd ed. New York: Routledge, 1994.

Osherow, Michelle. "The Dawn of a New Lilith: Revisionary Mythmaking in Women's Science Fiction." *NWSA* 12.1 (2000): 68–83.

Ower, John. "Theology and Evolution in the Short Fiction of Walter M. Miller, Jr." *Cithara* 25.2 (1986): 57–74.

Packard, Jerrold M. *American Nightmare: The History of Jim Crow*. New York: St. Martin's/Griffin, 2002.

Paulin, Diana R. "De-essentializing Interracial Representations: Black and White Border-Crossings in Spike Lee's *Jungle Fever* and Octavia Butler's *Kindred*." *Cultural Critique* 36 (1997): 165–93.

Peplow, Michael W. "George Schuyler, Satirist: Rhetorical Devices in *Black No More*." *CLA Journal* 18.2 (1974): 242–57.

Pfeiffer, John. "Black American Speculative Literature: A Checklist." *Extrapolation* 17.1 (1975): 35–43.

Phillips, Jerry. "The Intuition of the Future: Utopia and Catastrophe in Octavia Butler's *Parable of the Sower*." *Novel: A Forum on Fiction* 35.2/3 (2002): 299–311.

Porush, David. *The Soft Machine: Cybernetic Fiction*. New York: Methuen, 1985.

Rabkin, Eric S. "To Fairyland by Rocket: Bradbury's *The Martian Chronicles*." In *Ray Bradbury*, ed. Martin H. Greenberg and Joseph D. Olander. New York: Taplinger, 1980. 110–126.

Rabkin, Eric S., and Robert Scholes. *Science Fiction: History, Science, Vision*. New York: Oxford University Press, 1977.

Reid, Robin A. *Ray Bradbury: A Critical Companion*. Westport. Conn.: Greenwood Press, 2000.

Reilly, John M. "The Black Anti-Utopia." *Black American Literature Forum* 12.3 (1978): 107–109.

Rieder, John. "Embracing the Alien: Science Fiction in Mass Culture." *Science-Fiction Studies* 9.1 (1982): 26–37.

Roediger, David R. *Working toward Whiteness: How America's Immigrants Became White; The Strange Journey from Ellis Island to the Suburbs.* New York: Basic Books, 2006.

Rose, Mark. *Alien Encounters: Anatomy of Science Fiction.* Cambridge, Mass.: Harvard University Press, 1981.

Ross, Andrew. *Strange Weather: Culture, Science and Technology in the Age of Limits.* New York: Verso, 1991.

Rushdy, Ashraf H. A. *Neo-Slave Narratives: Studies in the Social Logic of a Literary Form.* New York: Oxford University Press, 1999.

Rutledge, Gregory. "Science Fiction and the Black Power/Arts Movement: The Transpositional Cosmology of Samuel R. Delany Jr." *Extrapolation* 41.2 (2000): 127–42.

———. "Speaking in Tongues: An Interview with Science Fiction Writer Nalo Hopkinson." *African American Review* 33.4 (1999): 589–601.

Salvaggio, Ruth. "Octavia Butler." In *Suzy McKee Charnas, Octavia Butler, Joan D. Vinge,* ed. Marleen S. Barr, Ruth Salvaggio, and Richard Law. Mercer Island, Wash.: Starmont House, 1986.

Sanders, Joe. "Tools/Mirrors: The Humanization of Machines." In *The Mechanical God: Machines in Science Fiction,* ed. Thomas P. Dunn and Richard D. Erlich. Westport, Conn.: Greenwood Press, 1982. 167–76.

Saunders, Charles. "Why Blacks Should Read (and Write) Science Fiction." In *Dark Matter: A Century of Speculative Fiction from the African Diaspora,* ed. Sheree R. Thomas. New York: Warner/Aspect, 2000. 398–404.

Schell, Heather. "Outburst! A Chilling True Story about Emerging-Virus Narratives and Pandemic Social Change." *Configurations* 5.1 (1997): 93–133.

Schuyler, George S. "The Negro-Art Hokum." 1926. In *The Portable Harlem Renaissance Reader,* ed David L. Lewis. New York: Penguin Books, 1994. 96–99.

Sharp, Patrick B. *Savage Perils: Racial Frontiers and Nuclear Apocalypse in American Culture.* Norman: University of Oklahoma Press, 2007.

Shinn, Thelma J. "The Wise Witches: Black Women Mentors in the Fiction of Octavia E. Butler." In *Conjuring: Black Women, Fiction, and Literary Tradition,* ed. Marjorie Pryse and Hortense J. Spillers. Bloomington: Indiana University Press, 1985. 203–215.

Simondon, Gilbert. *Du mode d'existence des objets techniques.* 1958. Paris: Aubier, 2001.

Sinclair, Bruce. "Integrating the Histories of Race and Technology." In *Technology and the African-American Experience: Needs and Opportunities for Study,* ed. Bruce Sinclair. Cambridge, Mass.: MIT Press, 2004. 1–17.

Singer, Linda. *Erotic Welfare: Sexual Theory and Politics in the Age of Epidemic.* Ed. Judith Butler and Maureen MacGrogan. New York: Routledge, 1993.

Smedley, Audrey. *Race in North America: Origin and Evolution of a Worldview.* 2nd ed. Boulder, Colo.: Westview Press, 1999.

Smith, Darryl A. "Droppin' Science Fiction: Signification and Singularity in the Metapocalypse of Du Bois, Baraka, and Bell." *Science Fiction Studies* 34.2 (2007): 201–219.

Sontag, Susan. *AIDS and Its Metaphors.* New York: Farrar, Straus, and Giroux, 1988.

Spaulding, A. Timothy. *Re-Forming the Past: History, the Fantastic, and the Post-modern Slave Narrative.* Columbus: Ohio State University Press, 2005.

Spencer, Kathleen L. "One Out of Three." *Science Fiction Studies* 14.3 (1987): 407–410.

Spencer, Kathleen L., and Graham Stone. "More on Black Writers of SF." *Science Fiction Studies* 16.2 (1989): 246–48.

Stableford, Brian. *The Sociology of Science Fiction.* San Bernardino, Calif.: Borgo Press, 1987.

Stillman, Peter G. "Dystopian Critiques, Utopian Possibilities, and Human Purposes in Octavia Butler's *Parables.*" *Utopian Studies* 14.1 (2003): 15–35.

Stoddard, Lothrop. *The Rising Tide of Color against White World-Supremacy.* New York: Scribner's, 1920.

Suvin, Darko. *Metamorphoses of Science Fiction: On the Poetics and History of a Literary Genre.* New Haven, Conn.: Yale University Press, 1979.

Tal, Kali. "'That Just Kills Me': Black Militant Near-Future Fiction." *Social Text* 20.2 (2002): 65–91.

Toumey, Christopher P. *Conjuring Science: Scientific Symbols and Cultural Meanings in American Life.* New Brunswick, N.J.: Rutgers University Press, 1996.

Touponce, William F. *Ray Bradbury.* San Bernardino, Calif.: Borgo Press, 1989.

Trushell, John. "*The Thing*: Of 'Monsters, Madmen and Murderers'—A Morality Play on Ice." *Foundation* 76 (1999): 76–89.

Tucker, Jeffrey A. "'Can Science Succeed Where the Civil War Failed?': George S. Schuyler and Race." In *Race Consciousness: African-American Studies for the New Century*, ed. Judith J. Fossett and Jeffrey A. Tucker. New York: NYU Press, 1997. 136–52.

———. "Contending Forces: Racial and Sexual Narratives in Samuel R. Delany's *Dhalgren.*" In *Science Fiction, Critical Frontiers*, ed. John Moore and Karen Sayer. New York: St. Martin's Press, 2000. 85–99.

———. *A Sense of Wonder: Samuel R. Delany, Race, Identity, and Difference.* Hanover, N.H.: Wesleyan University Press, 2004.

U.S. Department of the Interior. *Little Rock Central High School.* Washington, D.C.: GPO, 2007.

U.S. Department of Justice. Bureau of Justice Statistics. "Prison Statistics." http://bjs.ojp.usdoj.gov/content/pub/ascii/pim07.txt. Accessed March 20, 2010.

Vint, Sherryl. *Bodies of Tomorrow: Technology, Subjectivity, Science Fiction.* Toronto: University of Toronto Press, 2007.

———. "'Only by Experience': Embodiment and the Limitations of Realism in Neo-slave Narratives." *Science Fiction Studies* 34.2 (2007): 241–61.

Wald, Priscilla. *Contagious: Cultures, Carriers, and the Outbreak Narrative.* Durham, N.C.: Duke University Press, 2008.

Walker, Alice. *In Search of Our Mother's Gardens: Womanist Prose.* 1984. New York: Harvest Books, 2003.

Weedman, Jane. "Delany's *Babel-17*: The Powers of Language." *Extrapolation* 19.2 (1978): 132–37.

Weinkauf, Mary S. "The Indian in Science Fiction." *Extrapolation* 20.4 (1979): 308–320.

Westfahl, Gary. "'Dictatorial, Authoritarian, Uncooperative': The Case against John W. Campbell, Jr." *Foundation* 56 (1992): 36–61.

———. "Introduction: Of Plagues, Predictions, and Physicians." In *No Cure for the Future: Disease and Medicine in Science Fiction and Fantasy*, ed. George Slusser and Gary Westfahl. Westport, Conn.: Greenwood Press, 2002. 1–6.

Williams, Ben. "Black Secret Technology: Detroit Techno and the Information Age." In *Technicolor: Race, Technology, and Everyday Life*, ed. Alicia H. Hines, Alondra Nelson, and Thuy Linh N. Tu. New York: NYU Press, 2001. 154–76.

Wolfe, Gary K. "The Frontier Myth in Ray Bradbury." In *Ray Bradbury*, ed. Martin H. Greenberg and Joseph D. Olander. New York: Taplinger, 1980. 33–54.

Wolmark, Jenny. *Aliens and Others: Science Fiction, Feminism, and Postmodernism*. Iowa City: University of Iowa Press, 1994.

Wu, Frank H. *Yellow: Race in America beyond Black and White*. New York: Basic Books, 2002.

Wu, William F. *The Yellow Peril: Chinese Americans in American Fiction, 1850–1940*. Hamden, Conn.: Archon Books, 1982.

Yaszek, Lisa. "Afrofuturism, Science Fiction, and the History of the Future." *Socialism and Democracy* 20.3 (2006): 41–60.

Youngquist, Paul. "The Space Machine: Baraka and Science Fiction." *African American Review* 37.2/3 (2003): 333–43.

Zerilli, Linda. "Democracy and National Fantasy: Reflections on the Statue of Liberty." In *Cultural Studies and Political Theory*, ed. Jodi Dean. Ithaca, N.Y.: Cornell University Press, 2000. 167–88.

Zuberi, Nabeel. "Is This the Future? Black Music and Technology Discourse." *Science Fiction Studies* 34.2 (2007): 283–300.

Index

ISIAH LAVENDER III is Assistant Professor of English at the University of Central Arkansas. He teaches courses in African and African American literature and culture, world literature, and science fiction. His research concerns depictions of race and ethnicity in science fiction as well as black folklore.

Printed and bound by CPI Group (UK) Ltd, Croydon, CR0 4YY

13/04/2025

14656548-0002